MARXIAN ECONOMICS

MARXIAN ECONOMICS

Meghnad Desai

Basil Blackwell · Oxford

© Meghnad Desai 1979

First published in Great Britain by
Basil Blackwell Publisher
5 Alfred St., Oxford, England

ISBN 0 631 19070 8

0 631 19080 5

Typeset by Preface Ltd., Salisbury, Wilts.
Printed in Great Britain by
Billing and Sons Ltd.
London, Guildford and Worcester

To the memory of my Grandfather Jayakarbhai
who was my first teacher

CONTENTS

viii

LIST OF ALGEBRAIC SYMBOLS

M_i Money capital advanced as inputs by the ith capital, measured in money units.

M'_i Money capital received by the ith capital upon selling output, measured in money units.

$m_i = (M'_i - M_i)$

C_i Commodity, usually commodity capital bought as inputs by i^{th} capital measured in labour hours.

C'_i Commodity capital, measure of output of the ith capital, measured in labour hours.

$c_i = (C'_i - C_i)$

L   Labour, also labour power, measured in labour hours.

MP   Materials of production measured in physical units.

C   Constant capital ⎫

V   Variable Capital ⎬ measured in labour hours*

S   Surplus value ⎭

$r = S/V$ Rate of surplus value

$g = C/(C + V)$ Organic composition of capital

$\bar{\pi}$ (Value) rate of profit

π Rate of profit (ambiguous as to money or value)

ρ (Money) rate of profit

Y_i Value of output produced by the ith Department in labour units

Q_i Quantity of output produced by the ith Department in physical units

P_i Price per unit of labour value embodied in the ith commodity of the commodity produced by the ith Department. (M'_i/Y_i)

*In places where C occurs as both commodity capital and constant capital, the latter category has been symbolized in italics (C_i, V_i, S_i) to avoid confusion.

q_i Price per physical unit of ith commodity or the commodity produced by the ith Department (M'_i/Q_i)

R_i Profit of the ith Department

W   money wage rate

w   Value wage rate

l_i Units of labour hours embodied in the ith commodity $= Y_i/Q_i$.

{ }   Indicates number of quotation from Marx, listed in Appendix.

PREFACE

It is five years since *Marxian Economic Theory* was published. It attempted to look at the area both by way of a survey and to indicate some unresolved problems in it. The book however bore tell-tale signs of a hurried birth in its makeshift form. Despite this, it proved useful and it became clear by the summer of 1977 that a revised edition would be needed.

But if in 1974 the subject was just re-emerging into academic economic discourse, there has been a veritable explosion since. Books by and about Marx, old and newly discovered, have continued to appear. There are now specialist journals in Marxian/Socialist/Radical economics/political economy, and mainstream academic journals increasingly publish contributions in Marxian economics. This meant that there was much to catch up with. In the meantime, my own ideas have crystallized somewhat; puzzles which seemed easy to tackle then have continued to evade solution. It was clear that merely 'local' revisions would not do.

The result is this book which is only distantly related to the earlier work. It is not a textbook in the sense that it purveys what is agreed among all the students of the subject; such a thing is at this stage inconceivable. Marxian economics is a controversial subject and likely to remain so, for its concerns, even when couched in driest of mathematical formulae, imply political consequences. One cannot therefore write a textbook on such a subject. I have tried to cover the main themes as thoroughly as possible but the choice of themes and many interpretations are admittedly personal. I have also taken the opportunity to report on some work on expanded reproduction which is as yet incomplete in the hope that it will encourage others to improve upon it.

Marx's economics was an integral part (but only a part) of his total system, which sought to grasp the nature, of capitalism in order to be able to change it. The ambitious nature of this research programme and the incomplete state in which he left it mean that in places there are mistakes and loose ends and enough ambiguity to sanction many orthodoxies. I have tried neither to defend nor to reject Marx. My hope is to be able to advance a sympathetic but critical understanding of Marx's economics.

Many people have enriched my understanding of Marxian economics, among whom I must mention Makoto Itoh of the University of Tokyo. Bob Rowthorn, Anwar Shaikh, Mario Cogoy and Peter Skot also have clarified many things to me. Gail Wilson, Mark Blaug, Peter Skot and Paul Auerbach read chapters of earlier drafts and corrected many errors. The remaining ones are mine to acknowledge.

Meghnad Desai

I

INTRODUCTION

A book on Marxian economics at this time needs less explanation than at many other times. In the confident Fifties and Sixties, full employment and steady economic growth seemed to be the rule of the day in all developed capitalist economies. International monetary stability and steady expansion of international trade and capital movements had become part of the settled picture of economic life. Even regarding the problems of poverty within the rich countries and the prospect of poor countries, there was optimism.

At such times, economics comes into its own. The neoclassical synthesis – Keynesian macroeconomic policy and Walrasian microeconomic theory – had become the established teaching discipline in economics. Armed with the new capabilities of quantitative techniques and electronic instruments, economists thought all economic problems could be overcome. Voices of dissent – 'underground economics' – were few and far between. Some thought that Keynes had been emasculated in the translation to the textbooks and the treasuries. Others thought that neoclassical synthesis compromised the libertarian promise of free market capitalism. There was the perennial obstinate minority who still thought Marx's economics had something to offer in its analysis of capitalism.

Marxists were, as always, divided into sects and they spoke with many voices, but agreed, if at all, on one thing – it could not last forever. Sooner or later they said the boom must come to an end. True, there was more prophecy than prediction in what they said. They had not much to offer by way of a new analysis of modern capitalism. For most it was enough to repeat that Marx had said it all before. There was in these halcyon days no group of people seriously studying and advancing Marx's economic theory.

There was in those days one book that students could read if they wanted to acquaint themselves with Marx's thought. *The Theory of Capitalist Development*, when all is said and done, still remains a classic introduction to Marxian economics. It is of course much more than a textbook, as anyone will realize on reading its concluding chapters. It was a definitive statement of a certain period about how Marx and his system were a key to the understanding of capitalism. While the book comes in for much casual criticism today, Paul Sweezy can be credited for having kept the eventual prospect of a revival of Marxian economics alive.

Students in those days had not much besides Sweezy. The names of Maurice Dobb and Ronald Meek, of Joseph Steindl and Joseph Gillman, practically exhausted the available library of Marxian economics in English. Even Marx's own works were not available in English to any great extent except for *Capital* and *A Contribution to the Critique of Political Economy*.

Much has changed in the last ten years. Vietnam, Czechoslovakia, the transformations in Cuba and China began to alter the climate. The Seventies saw the old certainties collapse. Far from having been made obsolete, the business cycle has returned. For the last five years, high unemployment, inflation and economic stagnation have prevailed in the developed capitalist countries. International payments are in some disarray and the search for a new economic order still continues. There is a constant fear that protectionism may break out as it did in the Thirties.

Faced with stagflation and international economic disorder, the economists have lost their previous cohesion. The neoclassical synthesis is in ruins. Many contending economic schools have flowered in the field of macroeconomic policy at any rate. Economists are re-examining Keynes as well as the classics. The desirability and the possibility of government control of economic activity are being challenged. Economists are looking again at the foundations of economic theory.

The same period has seen a revival of interest in Marx and his economics. The initial push came from the student upheavals of the Sixties. The demand that Marxian economics be taught was contained by a variety of responses of outrage, boredom or concession in the hope of exorcising the old devil. To begin with, students could do little but work over the old ground, hurry into challenges more with the zeal of the converted than with the sureness of the expert. They also had to sustain on a thin diet of available material.

The first writings of radical economists could be easily dismissed by the mainstream economists. (See Solow (1971).) But in the meantime a beachhead had been established. Marx and Marxian economics were once again a subject of learning, debate and controversy, something which had not happened since the Twenties. The mainstream economists turned to scrutinize Marx, and their students were able to look again at the foundations of Marxian economic theory.

There has been a tremendous growth in the Seventies. The publication of many of Marx's manuscripts, such as the *Grundrisse*, has no doubt helped. But there is also now an interplay between the varieties of economic theory. Economics, while it may flounder at policy prescription, can still claim as its core the Walrasian general equilibrium model, which is a finely honed logical structure, demanding both as a learning device and as a challenge for rival models. Modern economists who study Marx bring to the subject inquiring and disciplined minds trained in general equilibrium theory and they are no longer happy with old dogmatic repetitions.

The student today is therefore in a happy position concerning materials for study but also faces the continual challenge of re-examining Marxian theory critically and using it as a tool to understand the working of modern capitalism. As the evaluation of Marx by economists changes, the opportunity for studying him becomes greater. As the bibliography will show, much of the material covered here in the form of books and journal articles dates from the Seventies.

This change is taking place at an accelerated pace. *Marxian Economic Theory*, the previous incarnation of this book, was written during 1973 and published in 1974. It was already obvious then that the time between writing and publication had brought important material, such as the publication of the *Grundrisse* in English (1973), or the excellent article by Wolfstetter (1973) on value theory. The four years since then have seen much work. To mention but a few names, Baumol, Morishima, Steedman, Shaikh, Okishio, Rowthorn, Wolfstetter and Samuelson have all published on the subject in the last four years.

It is hardly yet time for writing a 'textbook' on Marxian

economics. One can but report on an area where much progress is being made, but at the same time where there are still many unsettled issues. Such a book can offer only one interpretation of the subject. This is especially so when some of the work reported here is the author's own research. But books on Marxian economics will always have that tentative air, as they will also have an implicit or explicit political perspective. Briefly summarized, the view taken here is that Marx's theory is different from classical (Ricardian) economics as well as from neoclassical economics; that while it is an engine for understanding capitalism, much work remains to be done to realize its full potential. To understand this let us consider Marx and his place in current economics briefly.

The 'Whig' view of the history of economic thought would claim that what we teach today incorporates the best of the past, discarding erroneous views and fallacies, correcting and sharpening previous formulations of problems with our newer and better techniques. Since the late 1960s and early 1970s, this view has tried to absorb Marx in the fold of economics, cured of course of his errors and ideology. Of course, the 'push' provided by the changing political circumstances is seldom acknowledged in the new evaluations of Marx. The evaluation of Marx by economists in the 1950s was very different from that of the 1970s.

There is another view of economics that marks a sharp break in the tradition of economic thought and distinguishes between the classical school and neoclassical school. In this view, the revival of interest in Ricardian and Marxian economics is as much due to the analytical shortcomings of neoclassical economics as to the superior ability of classical economics to shed light on economic problems when conflict rather than consensus is the order of the day. Thus the political economy of inflation has attracted the attention of statesmen and economists to the classical view in terms of the division of national income between classes.[1]

In this view, economic theory does not proceed so much in a smooth evolutionary progress as in a cyclical fashion and we know today little more (except in being equipped with more mathematics) than the early nineteenth century economists. This view, however, though similar to a Marxian view, is not the same. The Marxian view has often crudely tried to characterize the transition from classical to vulgar economics and then to neoclassical economics in terms of the motivations of the economists or in terms of a synthetic history of capitalism in the UK and USA. It places the beginning of a deterioration in post-Ricardian economics in 1830 and tries to build up some explanation in political terms of the rise of marginalism. The crudeness of the sociology of knowledge adopted in such explanations is obvious.

We do not, however, need to face the sociology of knowledge question here. The important problem for us is to place Marx in the context of the classical tradition. Marx, in the view taken here, derived from, but also broke away from, the classical tradition. He does not, therefore, belong in the harmonious Whig tradition of economics, nor is he just a classical economist. There have been many recent debates among 'Neo-Ricardians' and 'Marxists,' especially in the UK. We shall survey these debates at least in as much as they throw light on analytical issues. We shall not evade the problem of confronting Marx's ideas with modern economic theory or with the classical tradition. Many analytical techniques developed in recent years are powerful logical aids. But in treating Marx on his own grounds, one is saved the error of confusing his concerns with those of Ricardo. One is also saved the temptation of rewriting Marx in marginalist terms or of reducing his work to a fundamental theorem or two. Here again, in the 1950s when the neoclassical tradition was most powerful, there were attempts to 'marginalize' Marx by sympathetic economists. In the 1960s and 1970s, these have been replaced with attempts to 'linearize' Marx. Interesting as such attempts are, they often succeed only by emasculating Marx's system. I have tried to resist rewriting Marx in such a fashion.[2]

The principle thesis of this book is that Marx's value theory is different from Ricardo's as well as from the Neoclassical theory. The role of value theory in Marx's work is to bring out the influence of the class struggle in capitalism on the economic relationships of exchange. Thus it is a necessary feature of the Marxian model that we have value equations and price equations as two separate systems. What is visible at the surface is the system of exchange relationships, and price equations describe this system. Underlying the exchange relationships are relations of production where the class division becomes manifest. Value equations describe these relations. A transformation from values to prices and vice versa is essential for understanding the reality of class division beneath the phenomenon of equality and of free exchange under law. If this concern is ignored, then Marx's system becomes a variant of Ricardo's system, and so suffers from the same analytical problems as the latter.

This view also makes it clear that the labour theory of value in Marx is not a theory of relative prices or a theory of resource allocation. Value is a social relationship, and not just an old-fashioned name for (production) price. This does not mean, however, that Marx is treated uncritically in these pages. His failure to adhere to the value price distinction rigorously is seen as the source of his mistakes in solving the transformation problem. His failure to relate his arithmetical examples of extended reproduction to his theory of uneven development and crises elsewhere in his works was pointed out by Rosa Luxemburg. We extend that discussion further and relate it to the value-price distinction.

A problem one faces when discussing Marx is that our minds are made up regarding his work before we ever read a word written by him. Some of us know that his prophecies have been proved wrong, that revolutions have not taken place in the developed capitalist countries, that workers have not been impoverished and that prosperity rather than crisis prevails. Others are equally convinced that he and he alone told the truth and that doom is around the corner. Few of us read Marx. We read about him. But when he is read it is in the form of isolated quotations. Reading this book is therefore no substitute for reading *Capital* in all its three volumes. But in order that readers may look at Marx's words without interpolation by me, all quotations from Capital have been grouped together at the end (see Appendix, p. 215). It is sincerely hoped that readers will read these quotations in conjunction with the text.

PART ONE

Basic Concepts

II

THE ROLE OF VALUE THEORY IN CLASSICAL, NEOCLASSICAL AND MARXIAN ECONOMICS

A theory of value is at the heart of every major school of economic thought. The notion of value is in itself philosophical, but a logically satisfactory value theory is crucial not only for tackling theoretical problems but for answering practical and operational questions as well. We begin with an attempt to understand the difference in the role value theory plays in Marxian as against neoclassical and classical economics. By classical economics we mean the tradition of Adam Smith, David Ricardo and John Stuart Mill. Neoclassical economics is the dominant tradition today, pioneered by William Stanley Jevons, Carl Menger and Leon Walras in the 1870s.

In modern (neoclassical) economic theory, the role of value theory is to provide a theory of relative prices. The simultaneous determination of relative prices of all goods (except the numeraire) and of the quantities produced and exchanged is the central problem of the existence of general equilibrium. A major achievement of recent developments in mathematical economics has been the fashioning of an apparatus which with minimal assumptions about the nature of consumer preferences and technology can prove the existence of an equilibrium set of prices and quantities.[1]

In classical economics, by contrast, value theory had a different role. Its first task was to counter the Mercantilist fallacy of regarding only precious metals (treasure) as valuable by showing that wealth consisted of useful goods. But not all goods that had use value commanded exchange value. Exchange values were determined not so much by the ratio of a commodity to precious metals (its money price) as by the relative difficulty of producing that commodity. To simplify matters appropriately for an era before the advent of large scale factory production, the labour expended seemed to be the best determinant of relative values. Wealth consisted of valuable goods, goods that could be made by labour available in conjunction with other goods (machinery) which were also products of current or previous labour.

The rate of accumulation of wealth, then, depended on whether the recipients of income spent their wealth on producing more goods or on other and therefore non-productive uses. The final task of value theory was to tie together the questions of who received income and how they were likely to spend it to bring out the interdependent nature of value, accumulation and distribution.[2] In the classical labour theory of value, prices of all goods are sought to be derived from the current labour input and the labour input embodied in materials of production. There was in the classical tradition always some ambiguity as to whether labour was being used solely as a *measure* of value of whether it was being asserted that labour alone was the *cause*, the source of value. Much depended on which of these two possibilities was being asserted, since from the view that labour is the sole source of value, a view adopted by many English radicals in the 1820s and 1830s, profits could be thought of as an unjust deduction from value created by labour alone. But even taking labour as a measure of value, many logical difficulties remain with the classical labour theory of value.

A major problem is that the measure of value is not invariant with respect to the structure of production and the distribution of income. As an economy grows, changes in technology, in the amounts and varieties of goods produced and in the pattern of consumption, whether due to the growth of income or to changes in tastes, alter the value of a unit of labour. In order to avoid this problem one has to assume a rigidly fixed subsistence wage and an unchanged technology. If allowance is to be made for growth and technical change, these have to be specified as occurring in such a way that the value of labour remains unchanged. The exercise at this stage becomes unrealistic and tautological.[3]

Recent developments in mathematical economics and, in particular, the work of Leontieff, von Neumann and Sraffa have clarified many of the issues regarding the classical labour theory of value.[4] The first issue is whether relative prices are proportional to the ratio of labour content alone. We now know that in as much as direct as well as indirect labour is used in the production of any commodity, indirect labour being embodied in the commodity inputs, we have to weight the indirect inputs by the rate of profit. Thus, we need information on the technology of labour and commodity inputs as well as the rate of profit prevailing in the economy, in order to derive relative prices. If in addition durable capital goods are used in the production process, the calculus of labour theory is further complicated. But all these problems can now be analytically solved and and equilibrium vector of prices and quantities can be derived given the technical coefficients and the rate of profit. The Classical labour theory of value as reformulated in modern mathematical economics gives many insights into certain problems of economic theory such as valuation of capital and brings out the dependence of prices on the distribution of income.

The role of value theory in Classical and Neoclassical economics is to provide an explanation of the structure of observed prices and quantities. The differences in the approaches concern their emphasis on the static resource allocation problem as against a growth theoretic orientation. They are, however, confined to studying strictly economic relationships and aim to explain observed economic facts concerning quantities of different commodities, including labour produced and consumed, prices charged for them, the rate of accumulation and of technical change, and so on.

MARXIAN VALUE THEORY

For Marx, value theory was a key to explaining the nature of capitalist society. The notion of value for him was central to an explanation of the prevailing social and economic conditions – of growing productive powers and wealth accumulation, of a class division of society into those who had to work for a living and those for whom they worked, of the contrast of poverty and riches. But value calculus for Marx was specific to a capitalist society. Unlike Neoclassical economic theory, which extends its model to cover all possible societies through time and space, Marxian theory emphasizes the historical relativity of economic categories. Thus for Marx value relationships are not valid for feudal or communist societies, only for a capitalist society. It is absolutely essential that Marx's notion of value be understood and contrasted with the similar-looking Classical theory of value. Extreme confusion and much futile debate has resulted from a failure to do so.

Value for Marx is a social relationship. The best way to understand this notion of value is to see how Marx deals with the problem of exploitation. A premise of the French Revolution and other parallel liberal democratic revolutions is the end of feudal privilege and of serfdom, the establishment of equality, freedom of contract and the ownership of private property without arbitrary hindrance. In a society where everybody is equal in the eyes of the law, and people freely enter into contract without coercion of compulsion, how can there be exploitation? It is this question that for Marx value theory sets out to answer first.

The first idea to get out of the way here is the notion of exploitation based on ignorance on the part of the exploited or due to imperfection in competitive structure. Following Joan Robinson, exploitation is defined in modern economics as the gap between wage and the marginal product of labour due to monopoly elements. The notion of exploitation in Marx does not depend on such imperfections. The important task is to explain exploitation in a world free of such imperfections, however real they may be.[5]

Exchange is mutually beneficial in a world where exchange is based on freedom of contract {11}. In capitalist societies, labourers are free to hire themselves out to the highest paying employer and employers are similarly free. These conditions are not universal in time and space, but arise as specific historical condition under capitalism. In a feudal society, a serf is not free to enter into contract with his lord nor with anyone else. At the level of free exchange and mutually beneficial trade, one cannot explain exploitation. If we confine ourselves to studying exchange relationships – at the level of economic forms as Marx would say – it is impossible to observe and/or explain exploitation {21}. To do this, we must go to production relationships or, as Marx would put it, to the realities behind the forms. For Marx, the bourgeois political economy of his days was at fault because it studied economic problems only at the formal level of market exchange.

RELATIONS OF PRODUCTION

What are the relationships of production? As with all concepts and categories in Marx, these arise historically and are specific to certain societies or modes of production. One is now speaking of relationships of production specific to capitalism and the capitalist mode of production (and, one may add, a nineteenth century capitalism as Marx saw it). How, for example, are the relationships of production different in capitalist as against feudal society or in a subsistence economy? Let us begin with capitalism, referring to other modes only as background.

In capitalism, first we have the category of free labour {16}. This free labour is free in two senses. It is free from feudal ties and any extra-economic compulsion: it is free to enter into contract. It is also free in another sense. It has been divested of its means of production. Unlike a farmer tilling his (owned or rented) land or a weaver with his loom working either for himself or in a putting out system, the free labourer has no means of production, no tools of trade to work with. This severing of means of production from labour is the outcome of a long historical process which renders peasants into unskilled industrial labour and breaks up guilds and ruins cottage industries {17}. Capitalism sees the emergence of free labour that has no other way of sustaining itself except to find some machinery to work with, machinery owned by the capitalist. In a model of pure capitalism, you have only free labour and capitalists. In the real world, there are intermediate categories of self-employed, professional, owner-cultivators, etc. The bulk of the population falls, however, into the free labour category.

The emergence of free labour may take different historical forms in different societies. In the United States, for example, except for the slavery in the southern states, much of the country had no feudal institutions and plenty of available land on which the individual farmer-cultivator could settle. The availability of uncultivated land provided an alternative outlet for the large waves of immigrants from Europe who formed the labour force in the industrial areas. These immigrants had often left a near-feudal peasant status and taken up the status of free labour in the US. The degree of exploitation in such a situation would be mediated by the availability of land on which a person could produce for himself.[6] By contrast, the emergence of free labour in many other countries takes the form of dispossessing of peasants or of share croppers by some form of land reform legislation, by processes now known as detribalization-urbanization, by migration to foreign plantations, etc.[7]

In the UK the classic pattern was the Enclosure Movement and the breakdown of cottage industries which dispossessed farmers and craftsmen and created over a period of two or three hundred years an industrial proletariat.[8] In many countries where the introduction of capitalism has not immediately led to industrialization, we may have pools of landless labourers in a relation of feudal dependence on, or in permanent employment of, the local landlord only slowly emerging as casual labour being paid money wages and free of the dependent status. One often encounters nostalgia for the days of 'benevolent landlords' who took paternal care of their labourers who upon migration are worse off. The attainment of the status of free labour is a progressive step in terms of the elimination of social coercion but often it may lead to a worsening economic position. It is important when analysing the economic situation in any particular country or age to know the historical form taken by the emergence of free labour or the proletariat.[9]

On the obverse side of the emergence of free labour is the consolidation of the class monopoly of the means of production in the hands of the capitalist. This is once again a historical phenomenon, taking different particular forms in different societies but also revealing uniformities. First, it is a *class* monopoly, not an individual monopoly. A class monopoly of the means of production is consistent with, and indeed appears as, competition among individual entrepreneurs. The class in whose hands the means of production concentrate is frequently called the bourgeoisie, but as this word may also denote other elements – professionals, upper echelons of state bureaucracy, higher clergy – we shall therefore refer to the monopoly class as the class of capitalists.[10]

The consolidation of the means of production in the hands of the capitalists takes place at the expense of the feudal class on the one hand and of many self-employed artisans and craftsmen on the other. A struggle between the feudal and capitalist elements is a major feature of the seventeenth, eighteenth and nineteenth century history of many European countries, and while the outcome was in favour of the capitalists, it took different forms. The agitation regarding the abolition of Corn Laws and in favour of Free Trade was the classical platform for the struggle between feudal landlords and industrial capital in England (and like all such classical events is partly mythological). In other countries, the feudal landlords transformed themselves into industrial capitalists often with state aid (as in Japan after the Meiji Restoration) and even in England the feudal elements are not entirely absent from the capitalist class to this day. The American Civil War is another example (once again rather simplified) of a confrontation between the industrial capitalism of the North and the feudalism of the South. Another element is the transformation of commercial and merchant capitalists into industrial capitalists. This transformation is facilitated by a variety of institutional and legal forms; for example, financial institutions such as Land Banks or State Industrial Banks, or reforms involving confiscation of foreign capital or land-holdings. In different countries, particular events have dictated the combination of these various forms which have led to the concentration of the means of production in the hands of the capitalists.[11]

It needs to be kept in mind constantly that while a model of capitalism with two antagonistic classes is at the heart of Marxian economics, in any particular historical (concrete) situation, one has to take into account many classes.[12]

EXPLOITATION AND THE RELATIONS OF PRODUCTION

The task of value theory is to explain why and how these relations of production lead to exploitation. Here we have a contradiction in the Hegelian sense between the emergence of free labour and its exploitation, between the breakdown of all artificial barriers to competition and the emergence of a class monopoly of the means of production. The importance of value theory for Marx is that it makes the exploitation behind exchange visible; while price theory or value theory in neoclassical economics analyses exchange, and relationships defined by exchange, the task of a value theory for Marx was to unmask exploitation. The visible relationship between the employer and the worker is a commodity relationship {59}. We have, in the sense of neoclassical economic theory, commodity markers everywhere, and the labour market is only a particular example of a commodity market. The price of labour power (the commodity that the labourer sells) is determined by supply and demand like the price of any other commodity. But unlike other commodities used during the production process, in which the buyer as well as the seller is a capitalist, in the exchange of labour power (L) for money (M), we have a transaction taking place between two people belonging to two classes of society – the class of labourers dispossessed of the means of production and the class of capitalists, who own the means {60}. This class relation is hidden by the commodity relationship which takes place on an apparent basis of equality. The labourers appear as the commodity labour power, and in selling labour power they seek to gain access to another commodity – a sum of money advanced – which in its turn takes the form of capital as a supplier of which the capitalist appears in the market. In each case, men come into relationship with each other through the commodities they represent. This transformation of a social relationship, a class relationship into a commodity relationship, a relationship of exchange, is what Marx calls commodity fetishism. Commodity fetishism is peculiar to capitalism {3} {4}.

To understand this, let us look at feudalism. The relationship of the serf to the master is an openly exploitative social relationship {7}. The serf has to spend some part of his working days or some days in the week working for the lord. The lord thus directly appropriates a portion of the serf's labour for his own output. The serf's unfree position makes his exploitation directly visible. Not only free labourers but also a form of specialization are characteristic of capitalism. In earlier societies, people produced partly for their own consumption and partly for exchange in the market to buy other commodities. The producer appears on the market with the fruits of his labour. In capitalism, production is not for use but for exchange. The worker does not bring his product on to the market for exchange. He brings his labour power; he exchanges it for a sum of money, but this is independent of whichever commodity he is engaged in producing. He is not directly involved with the end product of his work and in this sense he is 'alienated' from his productive activity. But the only way he can live is by working (since he has no means of production at his disposal) and thus his 'free' status leads to his being transformed from a producer of use-values to a seller of the commodity labour power – his capacity for work {15}. His productive activity, essential for his existence, is alienated from its end product. Labour power is purchased and transformed into a final product, which is exchanged against other final products, which are also transformed versions of labour power of other workers. Thus workers relate to each other and to the capitalist mainly through the mediation of commodities.

The productivity of labour power keeps the labourer alive and perpetuates his 'free' status {44}. Similarly, the productivity of machinery legitimizes the surplus the capitalist appropriates. The productivity of the thing perpetuates the status of the human beings corresponding to the thing. The capitalist gets the surplus because of the historically given social relationship of private property and the circumstances of the class monopoly of means of production. At the level of exchange, the productivity of capital, for example machinery or buildings, appears as the productivity of usefulness of the capitalist. (In other modes of production – in socialism in particular – machines can be productive but the surplus need not go to a capitalist class since such a class may not exist.) Since social relationships appear as commodity relationships we have commodity fetishism {4}. Commodity relationships tend to be seen as ahistorical and timeless. One is led to regard exchange relationships as timeless and the calculus of economic theory as being applicable to all states of society. You can visualize the feudal lords as 'optimizing' in the same sense as an economic firm or entrepreneur. At the level of exchange this appears to be so and is legitimate, but the nature of exploitative relationships is different for feudal and capitalist systems.

The contradiction between the juridically free status of the labourer and his exploitation is the original contradiction of capitalism. It is original since it appears at the origin of capitalism.[13] In no other society does exploitation take the value form, since in no society does it have to be masked from visible relationships. The commodity form of labour power confronting the commodity form of capital is a peculiarly capitalist event. In some societies (for example, in the USSR), the legal form of property ownership may change and take such forms as state ownership of all or some means of production, but the original contradiction remains in as much as the labourer has to sell himself for living, as he is alienated from his production process, and as he confronts a ruling class in a commodity form.[14]

III

VALUE AND SURPLUS VALUE

We have been using the words 'product' and 'commodity' interchangeably, but for Marx there is an important distinction between the two. All economies produce products; only in capitalism do products take the form of commodities {2}. Commodities are produced mainly, if not entirely, for exchange. Products as well as commodities have use value, but commodities need exchange value. In a subsistence economy, producers produce for their own consumption. In capitalism, all production is for exchange.

USE VALUE / EXCHANGE VALUE: SPECIFIC
LABOUR / ABSTRACT LABOUR

This is a very important distinction – the dual value form, as Marx called it {5}. It is hardly novel, as economists before Marx and since have known of the distinction between use value and exchange value (though they did not draw the distinction between products and commodities). For Marx, the commodity mode of production and the dual value form became determining social categories in the following sense. Products embody different kinds of labour, the specific labour of a tailor or a carpenter or a joiner. When they are exchanged as commodities, relative value ratios are established which make these separate products freely transformable into one another. A coat becomes a table which becomes a machine, since they all exchange at determinate ratios. The specific labour (and workmanship) of a joiner or a tailor is stripped away, and ratios are determined in relation to abstract of undifferentiated labour {3}. [See Itoh (1976) for a deeper discussion of value concepts.]

At one stage this is a formula – the basic formula of the labour theory of value. What determines the ratio is the amount of socially necessary labour time required to produce one commodity relative to another {1}. This is quite a standard definition in classical labour theory. For Marx, what is important is that this reduction of all products to a general value formula hides behind it a specific historical process. Specific labour can be reduced at a common measure – to abstract labour more efficiently under capitalism – under the commodity mode of production rather than under any previous mode because of the simultaneous disappearances of skilled specialized labour. The historical process is that which converts craftsmen into the proletariat divorced from their means of production, free of guild regulations. The process of division of labour reduces a particular man to a particular operation. The element of skill is reduced to common, homogeneous, undifferentiated labour. This is a long historical process and never fully achieved. There are hand-made goods by skilled craftsmen in developed economies today but the overwhelming bulk of commodities can be exchanged against each other without reference to the specific labour they embody.

The labour value ratio is therefore simultaneously a formula and a historical process. This is why the category of abstract, undifferentiated labour is not an abstraction but a historical tendency. Upon reduction to undifferentiated labour, the only thing that commonly characterizes specific types of labour is that it is human labour. There is no other distinction, whether of skill, location, caste or tribe. The general exchange formula – by virtue of the fact that all products exchange on the market – bares the common element in different working situations and thus combines the individual workers into a class of proletariat [I/1/Sections 1 and 4].

The special feature of capitalism – of the commodity mode of production – is not so much that production is for exchange, since in many pre-capitalist economies extensive internal as well as external trade often existed. The emergence of a commodity market in labour is for Marx the special feature distinguishing capitalism from previous modes of production. The market for labour is different from all other commodity markets, and this difference has to be understood if we are to distinguish Marx from, say, Ricardo. Marx introduces the distinction between labour and labour power {14}. The agreement to sell labour is a recurring agreement, daily, weekly or annually re-entered into. In order to be free to re-contract at the end of the day, the labourer must preserve his freedom. He cannot make a life-long contract – that is akin to slavery. What, in fact, the labourer sells everyday is, according to Marx, labour power – the potential capacity to work for a given length of working day {15}. In order that he can do this again and again, he must be able to reproduce himself – not reproduction in the sense of population growth but in the sense of keeping alive and preserving his capacity for work. The value of labour power – the commodity the labourer sells – is determined, like the value of any other commodity, by the social labour necessary for its reproduction – the subsistence basket taking into account historical as well as moral considerations {19}. The value of labour power is the same for all labourers, since all labours are interchangeable and have been reduced to abstract, undifferentiated labour by the historical process referred to above. The value of labour power according to Marx is decided *independently of and prior to* the specific job that the labourer might be engaged upon. Once he has sold labour power (L) in exchange for a sum of money (M) to obtain a certain basket of goods, the labourer's time for the length of the working day is at the disposal of the capitalist. The gap between exchange value of labour and its use value now becomes important. What the labourer expends during the working day is no longer labour power – no longer the potential capacity but actual labour. The use value of labour when employed by the capitalist along with the materials of production (MP) is the value added by the worker {20}. This use value of labour is in excess of the exchange value of labour power. This gap is the surplus value, and the capitalist seeks to buy labour because he expects to reap surplus value {22}.

The three elements crucial to Marxian Labour theory are: (1) the gap between the exchange value and use value of labour; (2) the notion that under capitalism what the labourer sells is labour power; and (3) the determination of the exchange value of labour power independent of the specific job the labourer engages in. In each case we must bear in mind that for Marx the class relation is crucial in the labour market; indeed it is unique to it, since other commodities are exchanged by buyers and sellers who are formally as well as actually on an equal footing. The exchange relationship and the form that the transaction – the sale of labour power – takes is embodied in the wage form. Neither the worker nor the capitalist directly perceives the division between the value of labour power and surplus labour. The worker sees himself being paid for the full day's work, though only a part of that day is equivalent to the value of the labour power he sells.

Marx clearly is concerned here with unskilled labour or labour of that level of skill that can form a common denominator, and interchangeable mass. But it is very important not to interpret the Marxian model mechanically. Thus many critics and defenders of Marx have equated the value of labour power with the wage rate and insisted that a rigid subsistence real wage rate is an essential element of Marx's model. Marx himself mentions in one instance that the value of labour power forms a floor below which the wage does not fall {35}. Indeed the determination of the wage rate or of the gap between the real wage and the value of labour power is a relatively unexplored area in Marxian economics. The partisans of Marx insisted on the tendency towards a subsistence wage as an indictment of capitalism, whereas for Marx's critics a subsistence wage represented an assumption at the same time necessary for the model and obviously falsified by empirical trends. We must, however, bear in mind that for Marx class relations are crucial to the course of the labour market and the dynamics of class relations must be recognized as an important factor in the Marxian model {48}. What is important to bear in mind is that the true course of real wages, whether upward or downward, is not automatic, nor does it depend mechanically on rising productivity of labour. It is the workers' struggle as a class against the capitalists as a class – a struggle that witnesses growth of unions, strikes, lockouts, legislation, political action, and so on – which is the important moving force in determining the course of real wages. The importance of the class struggle is specifically mentioned by Marx in the context of forces determining the length of the working day {25}{27}. His rejection of any mechanical rule such as a wage fund doctrine, and his emphasis on worker's struggle is brought out in his occasional writings, for example, *Wages, Price and Profit*.

THE CALCULUS OF SURPLUS VALUE

We have already quoted Marx as saying that exchange cannot create surplus value nor can one observe exploitation at the level of exchange. It is essential for our purposes to understand the process of the creation of surplus value, for this is the explanation and measure of exploitation. Since exchange cannot create surplus value, it cannot be through an analysis of exchange value that we can explain exploitation. Thus, given the dual value form, it must be use-value. We seek an explanation of exploitation in use-value.

In modes of production previous to the commodity mode, products are exchanged for money and then money is converted back into products. Indeed, the only role of money in this situation is to facilitate and generalize the two-person form of barter. If this happened in a commodity mode, we could describe this exchange cycle as Commodity-Money-Commodity or $C - M - C$. The commodity mode is, however, distinguishable by the fact that production is for exchange and not for use. The capitalist appears on the market with money (M), buys raw materials, rents machines and buys labour power (C) and sells the final product at a profit (M'). M' is larger than M. Indeed, there would be no sense in having a commodity form if at the end of the production process profit was not made by the capitalists. We have then the cycle $M - C - M'$. How is it that $M' > M$; what explains the money profit made by the capitalist?

The clue for Marx is in the initial stage where the capitalists buy commodities, that is factors of production, with money. There are three components here – raw materials, labour power and machinery. Since raw materials are bought from other capitalists (excluding for the time being such circumstances as a peasant sector or a colony from which these may be bought), except for incidental swindling and cheating, the full value must be paid. This is uncontroversial and is indeed the definition of value added. It is more important to understand why Marx says that machines do not create surplus value. Marx does not deny that machines are productive, that is, that they have value. The value produced by a machine during the production process is equated to the rental paid by the capitalist for the use of the machine. Whether the capitalist owns the machine or rents it is irrelevant here for the economic calculation. The point is that the value produced by the machine – the value transferred from the machine to the final product, as Marx would put it – is exactly matched by the flow price of the machine. This means that the cost of the machine and the cost of the raw materials are already included in the initial sum of money advanced, M. It is the third element purchased with M –

labour power, which is then left as the only possible source of surplus value – value over and above that incorporated in the purchase price {13}.

Labour creates surplus value by virtue of the fact that the unequal relation operating in the market for labour creates a gap between its use value and exchange value {22}. Of the three factors of production, machines and raw materials are bought and sold by capitalists and hence there is no possibility of surplus value being extracted. Such incidental cheating or underpricing that may occur affects only the distribution of surplus value within the class of capitalists. Labour is the one commodity that is sold by the worker and bought by the capitalist {60}. It is the productivity of labour – that labour produces value and surplus value – that creates the demand for labour on the part of the capitalist {20}.

We have come to the significant divide between Marxian economic theory and all other schools of economics – Classical, Neoclassical and Keynesian. The frequent misunderstanding concerning Marxian theory and especially the confusion between Marxian and Ricardian theory stems from the seemingly identical labour theory of value used by both Marx and Ricardo. Ricardo begins by taking as given the existence of three classes of income receivers and his concern is with the effect of accumulation on the shares received by the three classes. The Ricardian theory is thus also a theory of distribution in a growing economy. As a part of this theory, prices are reduced to present and past labour inputs. It has now been shown conclusively by many people that if fixed capital is used in the production process, a rate of profit must be included in a price calculation. Marx's concern is not so much with the determination of prices. He is perfectly aware that from the viewpoint of the capitalist (and of political economy) one can have a cost of production theory of prices {80} {81}. In this case, profits are a difference between price and unit costs; various explanations – abstinence, entrepreneurship, risk bearing and so on – can be advanced for this difference. Marx is interested in the relation between prices and values, since this alone can explain profits as being generated by surplus value. Only value theory shows for Marx that cost-based prices are disguising the social relations of value.

For Marxian theory it is surplus value that is created by labour. All commodities have value. Machines are productive and so is labour. In the case of labour alone, due to the unequal nature of social relations, there is a gap between the use-value and the exchange value of labour power. At the end of each productive process the labourer reproduces himself and the capitalist accumulates wealth {44}. This asymmetry of result is due to the asymmetry of class relation. Under conditions of exchange, such an asymmetry cannot be derived directly from the initial conditions of equality. Divorced from this class context, Marxian theory is indistinguishable from Ricardian theory. The difference is not in the characterization of the production process, similar for all schools of economics, but in the process of buying and selling labour power, which lies at the beginning of the productive process and leads to the appropriation of surplus value by one class. Throughout, all the participants perceive only legitimate exchange relations and not the unequal relations of class and exploitation.

Given any theory of price formation that is consistent and satisfies the usual requirement of equality of rate of profits in different industries, our task is to link value relations (also consistent within themselves) to price relations. We need to make value relationships explicit and outline their logical structure. Then we go on to discuss the translation – the transformation – of value relations into price relations.

IV

THE CREATION OF SURPLUS VALUE

We now look at the creation of surplus value as a social process. Marx analyses in some detail the labour process – the process whereby labour faced with conditions of production (raw materials, means of production) bought by the capitalist creates value and surplus value. It is important here to distinguish between the physical process of production and the value process of production as earlier we distinguished between exchange process and production process. This distinction also relates to the dual value form.

The physical process of production combines the services of the machine, the raw materials, the forces of nature and the specific skills of labour to produce output {63}. This is in general the process by which Labour appropriates Nature. In all models of production, the physical process of production – the production function – can be described in similar terms, though the level of technical knowledge may differ. This process is concerned with creation of *use values* and is not therefore specific to capitalism. Thus in Marxian theory, the contribution of nature (land and natural resources) is acknowledged in the process of production of *use values*.

This point is worth noting in some detail, as it is frequently thought that land has no role to play in Marx's theory. In his discussion of the Physiocrats in *Theories of Surplus Value*, Part I, Chapter II, Marx refers to nature as the 'fundamental condition of labour'. Again in explaining Physiocratic view of surplus value as a material thing (as *produit net*) he says, 'Here, in agriculture, from the very beginning there is a large measure of co-operation of the forces of nature – the increase of human labour-power through the use and exploitation of the forces of nature working automatically'. But land and forces of nature are important not only in agriculture. Marx chides Adam Smith for saying that nature plays no role in manufacturing. This, he says, reflects the 'pre-history of large-scale industry'. Ricardo, on the other hand, in Marx's view rightly appreciates the role of forces of nature, especially the 'common property resources' such as wind and water in industrial production process. (*TSV*, Part I, Chapter 2, pp. 49, 51, 60–61. Also 1/7.)

In capitalism, however, it is the creation of exchange values, and especially of surplus value in the form of exchange values rather than use values, which is the driving force of the system. The value process starts with the availability of labour power as a commodity and thus with the existence of markets for materials of production as well as for labour power and the realization of values and surplus values by the selling of commodity output.

Buyers of a commodity buy it – exchange it for the money equivalent of exchange value – because they want to avail themselves of the use value of the commodity. The notion of the utility of goods (their use value) as influencing demand is perfectly well known among classical economists. This does not, of course, mean that utility theory – especially the notion of marginal utility – can be attributed to them or to Marx.

This notion of commodity and of exchange-value is a central philosophical concept in Marx. The word commodity is used in modern economics as synonymous with product or good. For Marx, products and goods are use values. But a product acquires 'the form of a commodity' when it embodies a social relation – the social relation of value. Thus Marx would say that the product, which is a material thing, acquires the form of commodity, which is an abstraction, an imaginary form, since in capitalism the social relation of capital is embodied in a material thing. Social relations taking the form of things is again commodity fetishism. {85}

Philosophy is not a strong point for economists and they feign boredom when faced with such abstract notions. But this is an important point to grasp, so we look again at it, this time in terms of the notion of productive and unproductive labour. For Marx, the notion of productive labour has nothing to do with the material thing or service that the labourer produces. Thus he does not agree with Adam Smith's notion that productive labour is that which produces 'material *vendible* commodities', things which survive the process of their creation and not services which leave no solid trace behind. The specific skills of labour, the usefulness or noxiousness of its product, its durability or otherwise are for Marx irrelevant. According to Marx, productive labour is that which is bought with the money capital – *'exchanged against capital'* and which therefore enters the capitalist production process. It is then a crucial part of the definition of productive labour that such labour not only reproduces the value which it is advanced in form of wages but that over and above that it produces a surplus value. The capitalist, when he hires wage labour, does so in order to make a profit. Whether the end product is socially useful, whether it is a luxury or a necessity, sword or ploughshare, is of no relevance in defining productive labour. Labour that is hired for personal service as an item of consumption is unproductive labour. Unproductive labour is *exchanged against revenue* and does not produce surplus value.[1] Thus the same labour in one case takes the form of commodity and in the other of a product.

The role of money is different in these two instances. In the case of productive labour, money functions as money capital and in the case of unproductive labour merely as a medium of exchange. It is on the role of money in hiring productive labour that we can now concentrate. In the creation of surplus value, unproductive labour is by definition unimportant. The capitalist (Mr. Moneybags) comes on the market with a sum of money (M) but it is only when he *advances* it by buying means of production and raw materials (MP) as well as labour power (L) that the sum of money function as (takes the form of) *capital*. Labour power potentially available for sale will be a product if bought as unproductive labour but will take the form of a commodity when the labourer sells it for hire to a capitalist. The capitalist buys labour power not for direct use but for indirect use as producer of values. While the capitalist holds labour power, for raw materials and machines, these commodities take the form of *commodity capital*. In buying these various inputs, therefore, the capitalists convert *money capital* into commodity capital (C). When these inputs have been put into the production process, they take the form of productive capital (P). Here we have, then, half a cycle:

$$M \rightarrow C \Big<{\begin{matrix} L \\ \\ MP \end{matrix}} \Bigg\} = P$$

We have to be careful from now on and denote the units in which various of these things are measured. The sum of money, whether as a hoard or when advanced, is, of course, denoted in the numeraire (Gold in Marx's day but fiat money in our days – pounds, francs, dollars, yen). L and MP are, in their physical form, labour power as so many persons with their capacity for work hired to work a certain length of working day (12 hours in Marx's days, eight hours in developed countries in most industries today). MP – the materials for production – is a heterogeneous collection of things, raw materials, power, machinery, building. These heterogeneous things are then translated in terms of their labour content into C. Thus C is a homogeneous labour value aggregate of heterogeneous physical things. As P again these heterogeneous things will function in their separate roles. Heterogeneity of capital, which has been at the centre of controversy in recent debates in modern economics, is present in P and initially in the exchange process. Its conversion into a value aggregate C or its equivalent money form M gets over the heterogeneity problem. Marx maintains a clear distinction between these various forms that capital takes. We shall have to return to these distinctions many times in what follows.

The production process then converts the inputs P into another product – its output. The output, whatever its physical form, can be measured in terms of labour content. While it is held by the capitalist who produced it, the output takes the form of commodity capital C'. The transformation of inputs P (L and MP) into an output (call it Q) is the production function – the production of use values.[2] Output and inputs are physically heterogeneous. They can be made commensurable in two ways. The first is to measure both in terms of labour content – hence the measures C and C'. Equally, one can measure the money equivalent of inputs – (M by definition) and total revenue from selling output – (M'). When the capitalist sells Q he converts commodity capital C' back into money capital M'. The money he had advanced returns to the capitalist, but with an additional profit. The other half-cycle is therefore:

$$P \rightarrow Q \rightarrow C' \rightarrow M'$$

Temporary or cyclical shrinkage of the market and the general problems of marketing affect the price at which Q (and C') is converted into M'. Now in general M' > M and C' > C. We saw above how the class relation in the sale and purchase of labour power drives a wedge between the exchange-value of labour power and its use-value. We shall return to this point below. Notice that the capitalist, having advanced M, owns all elements of P; hence the final product and its money equivalent also belong to him. Thus whatever is the difference between total revenue (M') and the costs of production (M) is taken by the capitalist. At the visible level, the entire collection of heterogeneous inputs has contributed to the final output. It is, however, the class relation in buying labour power that reveals the source of profit. This source is the surplus value expressed as the difference between C' and C but understood only if the wage bargain is put into its social context. The production process in capitalism is a way of appropriating unpaid or surplus labour. The capitalist purchases labour power as a commodity as well as materials of production, and upon purchase during the working day, the labourer is at his disposal. Thus, the productivity of labour appears as the productivity of capital. This legitimizes the capitalist appropriation of profit. Seemingly all the elements of productive capital have contributed to producing the profit. {64} {90}.

At the end of the cycle M – C – M', in a way, the labourer restores to the capitalist the wage the latter had paid him so that the capitalist can hire him again. Thus labour power reproduces its existence as labour power. The capitalist can start the cycle again with M' in his hand free to hoard it, spend it on consumption or advance it.

The value process of production is thus larger, and in a structural sense deeper, than the physical process or the exchange process. All three are different ways of looking at the real world and understanding the logic of the dynamic of capitalism. We shall continue to keep 'accounts' in all the three units of value, physical quantity and money.

The capitalist can convert money capital into productive capital only because, due to historical circumstances, labour power – the commodity produced by the 'free' labourer – has become exchangeable {43}. Without this background, and viewed only as an exchange process or as a physical production process, the exploitation of labour and the creation of surplus value are not understandable. The possessor of any use-value that takes the form of a commodity can realize its exchange value only by selling it, that is, by exchanging it for its money equivalent (or commodity equivalent). Thus in exchange, one is alienated from the commodity one possesses and acquires another. Labour power is a commodity. It is a use-value possessed by the labourer which in its commodity form – (labour power), has an exchange-value. The labourer can realize its exchange value only be selling it, by divesting himself of it or by alienating it. But there is no slavery. The labourer has to realize, personally and physically, the use value of the commodity labour power for the capitalist. For the length of the working day, the labourer agrees to give up the commodity he sells, that is, to be at the disposal of the capitalist. He loses control over the end product of the process (the labour process) in which he participates; he is *alienated* from his labour. He faces the products of past labour – the materials of production and the end product – in their *alienated* forms. This is why the exchange of labour power for wage is like all other exchanges (divestiture of the commodity to realise its exchange value), but unlike them, since the labourer *personally* has to realize the use value of the commodity he has sold to the capitalists and this is done in the process of production.

In all exchange, equivalents are exchanged voluntarily. At the visible level, this also holds true for the exchange of labour power for money. But the underlying reality of the class relation makes it an *unequal exchange*. The labourer gives up more use value than is contained in the commodity equivalent of the exchange value he receives. Profit appears as a legitimate reward for capital, but is the money expression of the gain made by the capitalist in this unequal exchange. *It is the task of the labour theory of value, the task of political economy as Marx sees it, to explain the social process by which exploitation is 'dissolved', as it were, at the level of exchange, and profits emerge at the visible level from an underlying unobservable surplus value relationship.*

V

THE THREE CIRCUITS OF CAPITAL

We can set out in some detail three ways of looking at the value and the physical processes of production following Marx's discussion in II/1. These three ways are called three circuits of capital – the commodity capital (C' – C') circuit, the productive capital (P – P) circuit and the money capital (M –M') circuit. The three circuits of capital are put together in Figure 1. In one sense, it is of no consequence which place you start the circuit at as long as you complete it. But as we have seen, the two former circuits underplay the role of money as capital. They also obscure the social relation by which the owner of money capital buys labour power. Also, surplus value is prominent in the M – M' circuit and becomes the driving force of economic activity whereas it is not apparent in the other two circuits.

The device of circular flow of income to describe the interdependence of consumption, production and exchanges is familiar in many textbooks on economics. The circuits described below are similar to circular flow except that while circular flows describe static conditions, the circuits portrary a dynamic process where accumulation and growth in real and money quantitities are taking place {74}. But even within the three circuits, as we mentioned above, the money capital circuit brings out the role of class relations in value theory more clearly than do the other other two circuits. Many of the modern approaches to Marx's value theory ignore the money capital circuit and hence minimize the difference between Marxian and other approaches to value theory.

The money capital circuit is the most important in a commodity mode of production, since production is undertaken not for

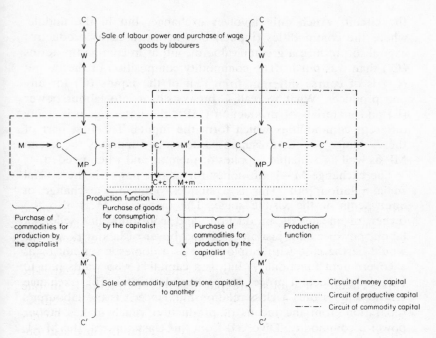

FIGURE 1

use but for profit. The capitalist wants to have his profits not in terms of final output but in terms of money. This is because he has originally advanced money capital (M) and he needs to recover his expenses and to make profit in money terms. He is then free to reinvest money in the same industry or in another industry, or to buy consumer goods. Thus the circuit of money capital begins with purchase of commodities which will form productive capital (P) in the hands of the capitalist. The circuit ends with the sale of output (C') and realization of money sum (M'). Exchange forms the beginning and the end of the process. Money lying as a hoard or spent directly on use values (consumer goods) is not capital, since it only performs its function of being a medium of exchange. Money becomes capital for Marx only when it is advanced {56}. Capital has the property of being value which generates surplus value or of being self-expanding value {57}. This self-expansion takes place not at either end of the circuit, which only involves exchange, but in the middle, where the commodities (inputs) bought are used as productive capital to produce a greater value of output in commodity terms (C') than was put in. The commodity composition of the output (C') is of course different from that of the inputs (C) for any one producer. What we call C breaks down into labour power (L) and materials of production (MP); the latter again is many different commodities which form the inputs. The first part of the exchange M – C, presupposes developed markets for L and MP as well as available supplies of them as and when needed.

The exchange M – L of money for labour power is the crucial social relation {60}. This is a simple commodity exchange of equivalents at the visible stage. The owner of M is also the owner of means of production, and confronts the seller of labour power as not just any ordinary buyer of labour power (as would be the case with employment as a domestic servant or as a government functionary) but as a capitalist who wants him to join the production process to realize his capital. This exchange relationship is thus a class relationship, since it is the labourer's separation from the means of production which makes labour power a commodity. Divorced from this class context, the M – L exchange would appear as a straightforward exchange of equivalents on a basis of equality. Divorced from this class context, it is hard to understand the role of exploitation.

The other part of the M – C exchange is the M – MP purchase. There is a difference that Marx emphasizes between labour power and other commodity inputs. Markets for commodities predate the emergence of capitalism, though they are fully developed only under capitalism. In this sense, commodity markets are not different under capitalism except that they are universal. It is the emergence of the labour market that differentiates capitalism. Another difference between labour power and other commodities can be seen from the point of view of the sellers of these commodities {64}. For the labourer, labour power is a commodity to be exchanged for money, which will be in its turn spent on consumables C – M – C. For the seller of other commodities, which become inputs, these commodities form commodity capital (C') emerging at the end of their productive process, which they are now converting by sale into money (M') to either reinvest as capital in the productive process or to spend as revenue on consumer goods. This is the reason why commodities other than labour power cannot be exploited; their surplus value is already realised by their sellers. In this sense, one can distinguish between the subjective (L) and the objective (MP) elements of productive capital. Labour power is a commodity in the hands of its seller but becomes capital in the hands of its buyer, since he can use it to create surplus value. Other commodities (MP) are capital in the hands of the seller and capital in the hands of the buyer – commodity capital to be sold in the first case and productive capital to be used in the other case.

At the other end of the circuit, the output (C') is sold for money (M'), and as an abstraction one can think of the value of C' as being C (equal in value to the inputs) + c (surplus value embodied in output), although physically the initial C and the terminal C' are different. Similarly, M' can be divided into M (equal to the original sum advanced) + m (surplus value in money form). As long as C' remains unsold it forms commodity capital, but the point is not to hoard it (except for speculation), but to sell it for a sum of money which will yield a profit. Having realized M', the end use can vary according to the individual capitalist. As a general form, we can say that in simple reproduction (that is, no net accumulation), M is again advanced for C in the second round and m is spent on consumer goods by the capitalist. Until M' is spent, it forms a hoard, but becomes capital when advanced. M can, of course, be advanced in a different industry and in expanded reproduction m can also be advanced. Again m may be such a small quantity that many circuits have to be gone through before the sum of these amounts can be invested if there are indivisibilities in the inputs.

Although the crucial social relation manifests itself in M – L exchange, the production of surplus value is accomplished in the middle third of the circuit. This is the process of production which takes the commodity inputs (C) which comprise labour (L) and materials of production (MP) – together making up of productive capital (P) and generates output (Q'):

$$C \left\{ \begin{array}{l} L \\ MP \end{array} \right\} = P \rightarrow Q'.$$

It is a purely technological relationship, although the organization of production changes as the technology changes. A 'putting out' system, whereby the capitalist advanced raw materials
to workers to transform into output, and a factory system are
different organizational forms (and these have their implications
for the value relations which we shall not go into). The output
Q need not be physical output; it can as well be services {66}.

In *Capital*, Vol. I, Marx shows how, since the owner of M
has purchased C and brought together L and MP, the production
process seems a function of capital and hence of the capitalist.
The entrepreneur of later nineteenth century economic theory
thus appears as a reflection of the ownership of M and the
productive process which is a purely technological relationship
becomes his function in capitalist production. The technology
would be invariant under another mode of production – under
socialism – but the social relationship would be different. The
apparent productivity of the entrepreneur is a by-product of the
structure of property rights.

There is, however, a difference between capitalism and previous systems. Industrial capitalism concerns itself not only with
appropriation of surplus value but also with creation of surplus
value. Thus it is not usury, speculation or market restriction that
is important in this system but the production of surplus value.
By constantly changing technology, the system aims to improve
the productivity in the $C \rightarrow P \rightarrow C'$ stage. Feudal exploitation
exists on a static technology and does not create surplus value
on the ever-expanding scale of capitalism.

The $M - M'$ circuit can, of course, be interrupted at various
stages. At the beginning, appropriate quantitities of the commodities and labour power may not be available or the sum of
money may not be advanced at all and may lie idle as a hoard.
At the end there may be no possibility of selling all of C', or M'
may be less than M. These matters are important in discussing
crises but do not affect the discussion at this stage {65}.

The importance of the $M - M'$ circuit lies in the fact that it is
most often forgotten that money is the starting and the end
point of economic activity in capitalism. In the other two circuits, money appears as a mere intermediary and can be easily
ignored. The function of money as money capital, as more than
just a medium of exchange, comes out only in this circuit.

The P – P circuit starts with productive capital and by transforming output (Q) into inputs for the second stage, returns to P. We may call it Input-Output-Input circuit. We begin therefore with labour power and materials of production already in the hands of the capitalist, though we do not ask how they came to be there. In a sense the factors of production are already in their employment at the start of a circuit. The function of money as capital is suppressed in this circuit, since the exchange C′ – M′ – C can be easily seen to be an exchange of equivalents with money performing its role only as a medium of exchange. If we can assume that at the economy level it would be always possible to exchange C′ for the requisite quantities of C, then the intermediation of money can be ignored altogether {70}.

We can regard the purpose of economic activity as consumption, since the acquisition of consumer goods occurs in the circuit at least at two distinct points. Thus the worker exchanges labour power for a sum of money only to spend it on consumer goods. In Marx's notation, this is the L – M – C exchange. The capitalist, on the other hand, having realized M′ at the end of the production process, will spend the part he does not reinvest on consumption. Let us say out of M′, he reinvests M and spends m on consumption goods. In this case instead of C′ – M′ – C we have two circuits. One is the Output-Money-Input, C′ – M – C, and the other is the circuit of surplus value in commodity form (c) converted into surplus value in money form (m) to be spent on consumption goods (c). We then have simple reproduction – no net accumulation – since the same amount (C) is invested at the beginning of each period. The end purpose of economic activity from the point of view of the worker and the capitalist is then easily seen to be consumption, but such a view is misleading according to Marx {67}.

The P – Q – P circuit does not explicitly bring out the crucial property of capital being a value producing surplus value. The difference between M – M′ is clearly brought out in the money circuit. In the P – P circuit, the initial and terminal items may be different in composition and also in value. If labour productivity in particular and technology in general are changing constantly, as Marx emphasized, the end of the process is different and perhaps not directly comparable with the beginning. Surplus value thus disappears (or is obscured) in the P – P circuit.

The $C' - C'$ circuit is similar but not identical to $P - P$ circuit. It also emphasizes the commodity aspects of economic activity {72}. The $P - P$ circuit is concerned with use-values and $C' - C'$ circuit with exchange values. As we also saw in the previous chapter, in the $C' - C'$, we look at homogeneous aggregates of material things and labour power in terms of their labour values. We start with surplus value already embodied in the output commodity capital C' and end with C' again, though the physical form may differ if the capitalist has gone into another activity. (At the economy level, this does not matter.) Both $P - P$ and $C' - C'$ circuits presume that all the heterogeneous inputs required for the production process exist in sufficient quantities and also that there is no effective demand problem in selling output. Marx describes Quesnay's *Tableau Economique* to be an example of the $C' - C'$ circuit {73}. This may seem strange, since the units in Quesnay's table are in money terms, for two reasons. In much of the first two volumes of *Capital*, Marx does not maintain the price-value distinction and often uses the value and money units interchangeably. (We shall see another example of this in the model of expanded reproduction.) But also in a stationary system, with no accumulation and no technical change, with an unchanging amount of money in circulation, a unit of money will come to represent a fixed quantity of labour hours. In such a stationary system it is legitimate to translate money freely into values, *but only in such a stationary system*.

In economics we are more familiar with the $P - Q - P$ circuit. This is the basis of Leontieff's Input-Output table, and of Sraffa and von Neumann's models.[1] In each of these, the price calculation is also developed as a dual. Prices then help aggregate net outputs (Q_i) of heterogeneous goods into an expression of national income. Now the $c - m - c$ (purchase of consumption goods by capitalists) and the $L - M - C$ (purchase of consumption goods by workers) are consumers' expenditure and the rest would be investment {71}.

We shall make use of the three capital circuits in the following chapters. They will help us to maintain our separate accounts in value (labour hours), physical units and in money units. We shall also see how many criticisms of Marxian value theory concentrate one and the other input-output circuit and how the money circuit is most often ignored.

VI

SIMPLE REPRODUCTION AND EXPANDED REPRODUCTION: A PRELIMINARY VIEW

In the previous section, the discussion of circuits had to be carried out using the same notation for inputs as for output. We mentioned at some points that the commodity composition of C′ was different from that of C. We could also have brought out the difference in the commodities purchased by capitalists in c – m – c exchange as against those purchased by workers in L – M – C exchange. We clearly need to disaggregate our circuits in many commodities. There is a second more important reason why we need to disaggregate. The role of prices, and especially of differences in relative prices, cannot be brought out in the general notation of the circuits. Even in a C′ – C′ circuit, while the capital function of money is ignored, the influence of relative prices can be brought out by disaggregation. Disaggregation of the value relations and the price relations will also be crucial in understanding the nature of the transformation problem.

Marx pioneered a two-sector representation of economic activity. His representation is an advance upon Quesnay's *Tableau* since his sectoral classifications are much more relevant to an industrial economy. Consumption and investment relationships are linked with production and distribution. In comparison with the three circuits of capital, the two-sectoral representation is, however, only a partial picture. Like Quesnay's *Tableau*, it is a C′ – C′ circuit where all the magnitudes are measured in labour values. Both the money capital and productive capital circuits are ignored. Since value measures are not directly observable by the economic decision makers (in Marx's own view), and also since value aggregates are not directly measurable, the two-sector representation leaves something to be desired. We shall, however, first look at Marx's representation.

The problem that led Marx to formulate the model of *simple reproduction*, as he called it, was the way Adam Smith defined the components of price. There was a confusion here which can be best described in modern national income accounting terms. The term 'price' was used by Marx and by classical economists to denote both price per unit of output and what we may call total revenue. Now Adam Smith said that price could be dissolved into wages, profits, and rent. At national level, this only says that national income is sum of factor incomes. But for an individual commodity, factor incomes represent only *value added*. Price per unit of output or even total revenue consists of value used up – raw materials, wear and tear of fixed capital, use of power as well. Marx called these items constant capital. (Constant because during the production process, their value did not change but was transferred from input into output). Constant capital is thus comprised of the used up part of materials of production (MP). How was constant capital recovered if price was the sum of wages, profits and rent? We can see today that Adam Smith was aggregating value added over all the commodities and that took care of used up materials. However, the use of the word 'price' for national incomes as well as for the microeconomic concept of total revenue caused much confusion. Marx's struggle to think through this problem yielded him the brilliant device of the scheme of simple reproduction and expanded reproduction.[1]

We have two sectors, or Departments, as Marx called them. Department I produces the commodity (or collection of commodities, since a Department is an aggregate of firms) which is used as constant capital. Now this can be thought of as a machinery or building – that is, fixed capital or raw materials. In measuring the value of the input which goes into final output, we will be interested in measuring the service flow of capital, as it is called in modern economics, albeit in labour value terms; there is, however, a problem here. The output of Department I in physical terms may be durable fixed capital, not all of which is used up in a given production period. Marx was quite aware of this problem and discussed the turnover of capital – the relation of flow of services to the stock of capital – in great detail in the second volume of *Capital*.

In constructing the scheme of simple reproduction, he ignored this problem. The output of Department I is materials of production which can be used as constant capital within a production period. So we are talking here of non-durable materials of production with a turnover of one period. We shall have to look again at fixed capital because it poses challenging problems to Marxian value theory in many ways. For the time being, note that ignoring the $P - P$ circuit as is done here can cause problems.

Department II produces the commodity (or collection of commodities) which is used as consumption good. The output of each Department in value terms is denoted Y_i and is the sum of constant capital (C_i), variable capital (V_i) and surplus value (S_i). We have

$$
\begin{array}{c|ll}
C_1 + V_1 + S_1 & = Y_1 & \text{Department I} \\
C_2 + V_2 + S_2 & = Y_2 & \text{Department II} \\
\hline
C + V + S & = Y &
\end{array}
\qquad (1)
$$

Reading along the row, we see the components of value of output as they are in the value production process. C_1 is the amount of constant capital used in the Department I for producing Y_1. The physical form of C_1 and Y_1 is therefore the same (assuming that each Department produces one commodity). Thus C_1 represents Department I's consumption of its own output. V_1 is the value equivalent of the consumption good received by workers in Department I. It is the commodity equivalent (in terms of output of Department II) of the exchange value of labour power bought by capitalists of Department I. This rather long definition is necessary because all the steps $M - L - C$ have been compressed in V_1. The physical form of V_1 is the same as Y_2. It represents the necessary labour component of total labour input, as S_1 represents the surplus labour component of total labour input in Department I. In physical terms, total labour input will appear as the equivalent of $(V_1 + S_1)$. Similarly, for Department II C_2 is the amount of constant capital used up (physical form same as Y_1), V_2 the variable capital (physical form same as Y_2 and the commodity equivalent of necessary labour in Department II) and S_2 is surplus labour. Notice that C_i and C in this context are different from commodity capital C in the circuit of capital context. The italics mark the difference.

Having described the two-department table, we can establish some functional relationships. We have implicitly indicated that the column and row sums are the same. Thus $C + V + S = Y_1 + Y_2 = Y$. In simple reproduction, the same value of total output is produced year after year – a system with zero growth rate. This clearly implies that the total output of Department I (Y_1) must not exceed the total usage of constant capital in the two Departments $(C_1 + C_2 = Y_1)$. Thus we have a balancing equation, $Y_1 = C$. This, together with the total identity, implies that value of output of Department II (Y_2) must equal the total amount of variable capital (V) and surplus value (S). Thus, the output of Department II has to consist of wage goods as well as goods consumed by the capitalists. After replacing the amount of constant capital consumed in each period, the entire value is spent on the output of Department II.

In order to make a further distinction between wage-goods and other consumer goods, we add a third Department to our model. In particular we can make the distinction that the third Department absorbs surplus value while Department II produces only wage-goods. A three-Department scheme will be found useful in discussing many problems in Marxian theory as well as in analysing contemporary discussions about the nature of modern capitalism. We write down the three-Department scheme as follows:

$$
\begin{array}{ll|ll}
C_1 + V_1 + S_1 & = Y_1 & \text{Machine goods} & \\
C_2 + V_2 + S_2 & = Y_2 & \text{Wage goods} & \\
C_3 + V_3 + S_3 & = Y_3 & \text{Other goods} & (2) \\
\hline
C + V + S & = Y &
\end{array}
$$

Now there is a symmetry in a situation of simple reproduction between the column sums and the row sums. But there is a crucial difference. The output of Department III (Y_3) does not enter as input into the other two Departments; its only function is to absorb the surplus value created in the system. The role of Department III can be discussed in the context of the problem of the realization of surplus value.

As we have said above, the capitalist has to sell his output in the market before he can realize surplus value $(C' - M')$. The scheme above suffers from the drawback that it is not on an $M - M'$ circuit but a $C' - C'$ circuit. We can still analyse the conditions under which the realization problem does not occur, that is, the conditions of equilibrium in simple reproduction. In the two-Department schema (1) above the output of Department I (in value terms) which has to be sold outside the Department is $(Y_1 - C_1)$, whereas the demand by Department II for the output of Department I is represented by C_2. The equality of C_2 and $(Y_1 - C_1)$ $[C_2 = V_1 + S_1]$, is reciprocated by the demand of Department I for the output of Department II $[V_1 + S_1]$ and the output of Department II sold outside itself $[Y_2 - (V_2 + S_2)]$.

The three-Department schema is then just an elaboration of the previous one, except that more inter-Departmental transactions have got to take place. The more such transactions are required, the greater the uncertainty about whether the surplus value would be automatically realized and therefore the greater the possibility of crises.

It may be useful to look at the inter-Departmental transactions as they would look in the three circuits framework. Assume M_i is the money capital advanced in the ith Department, M'_i its money revenue, Q_i its physical output. Purchase of input and its usage are equivalent by assumption. Then we have the picture as in Figure 2.

Department I has two transactions: the purchase of L and MP_1. As indicated, however, MP_1 has the same physical form as its own output. Ignoring the problem of many firms comprising Department I buying from each other, the net transaction is only one $M_1 \rightarrow L_1$. But the workers purchase consumption goods (Q_2) which appear in their value equivalent V_1 in the circuit. (The workers transaction should appear in Fig. 1 as $L_1 - M_1 - Q_2$ but it will only clutter the diagram). MP_1 is expressed as C_1 directly. When output Q_1 is achieved, we represent it in its value equivalent Y_1,

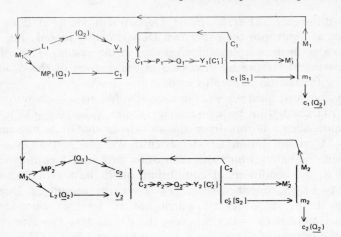

FIGURE 2   Simple Reproduction: A Circuits of Capital Representation

which is what we called commodity capital C'_1 before. C'_1 splits into C_1 and c_1. Being simple reproduction, C_1 at this stage will equal C_1 at the input stage and c_1 is the measure of surplus value S_1. In money terms M'_1 splits into M_1 equal to its starting value and m_1 which is the money equivalent of S_1 and is spent on consumption goods. Thus $c_1 - m_1 - c_1$ is now in terms of Q_2. Thus $m_1 - Q_2$ is the second transaction. In addition, the Department has to sell its output in excess of MP_1, that is $(Q_1 - MP_1)$. This is shown by the curly bracket connecting MP_1 and MP_2.

This is seen by looking at Department II. Here again we have $M_2 - MP_2$. Notice that workers' purchase of Q_2 does not represent an intra-departmental transaction for Department II except in the sense that its workforce represents a demand for its own product. But $M_2 - MP_2$ is definitely an inter-Departmental transaction. This is indicated by the physical form (Q_1) of MP_2. At the end of the process Q_2 is the total output with total revenue of M'_2 of which again m_2 is spent by Department II capitalists on their own products. This is, then, an intra-Departmental transaction. We have therefore six transactions as represented below, (a) through (f):[2]

$$\text{(a)}\quad M_1 - L_1$$
$$\text{(b)}\quad L_1 - (Q_2)$$

(c) $m_1 - c_1(Q_2)$
(d) $M_2 - L_2$
(e) $L_2 - (Q_2)$
(f) $M_2 - MP_2(Q_1)$.

The precise quantities in each transaction are not important. What does matter is the physical form which is indicated in parentheses. In physical and value terms, we set

$$MP_1 + MP_2 \approx C_1 + C_2 \approx Q_1 \approx C'_1 \approx M'_1 \qquad (3a)$$

$$L_1(Q_2) + L_2(Q_2) + m_2(Q_2) + m_1(Q_2) \approx V_1 + V_2 + S_1 + S_2 \approx Q_2$$

$$\approx C'_2 \approx M'_2 \qquad (3b)$$

Thus the integration of the simple reproduction scheme with the circuits of capital framework brings out the nature and number of transactions necessary to reach the equilibrium of simple reproduction. In the three-Departmental framework, we shall have a correspondingly larger number of transactions – ten in all. If at any stage there is a tendency to hoard, or a temporary shrinkage of the market, a crisis may result. As we have already said, in the real world each Department represents a multiplicity of products and firms, all of which will lead to further uncertainty as to whether the balancing condition will be met.

The simple reproduction scheme proves the possibility of equilibrium: in modern terms it lays down the conditions for the existence of equilibrium. It says nothing about the probability of such an outcome nor as to how stable such an equilibrium will be.

Simple reproduction is not a realistic assumption, since it is in the nature of a capitalist system not to stand still. Even when aggregate data (e.g. GNP) show zero growth, there will be changes in the value ratios due to continuous changes in tastes or technology. In any case, what we observe is a fluctuating growth rate and continuous net accumulation in capitalist countries. We recast our schema in terms of Expanded Reproduction. In each period, the surplus value is realized in money terms and reinvested in constant as well as variable capitals on an expanded scale. Thus, for example, in the context of System

(1) above, C_1 next year will incorporate a part of S_1 of this year and will therefore exceed C_1 of this year. Such expansion of C_1 and V_1 as we see here, is in value terms, and may mean an even greater expansion of physical quantities, since values are always changing, especially because a reduction in the value of labour power is always sought. The logic of the system which drives it to expand continuously is embodied in the behaviour of the rate of profit and the rate of exploitation. We shall discuss this next and postpone any discussion of Expanded Reproduction to Chapter XIV.

VII

THE RATE OF EXPLOITATION
AND THE RATE OF PROFIT

In terms of value relations, which Marx treats as crucial to understanding the class division in capitalist society, surplus value and the rate of exploitation are the key variables. At the level of observed data, profits and the rate of profit on capital are the key variables. The desire for profits drives the capitalist to seek as large a difference between M and M' as possible. On certain assumptions (which always have to be kept in mind) one can talk of the rate of profit in value terms. These simplifying assumptions comprise the conditions under which prices are strictly proportional to values in each Department and in each firm within each industry. But these assumptions are not always borne in mind, and this leads to much confusion. Also in Vol. I of *Capital*, Marx talks in terms of the (value) rate of profit. In the latter two volumes the money rate of profit is discussed, but here again Marx made a number of simple but serious errors in solving the price-value transformation problem. We shall try as far as possible to confine the term 'rate of profit' to the price domain, but add the parenthetical word (value) when we talk about the simple case. A number of puzzles regarding Marx's predictions, especially regarding 'the falling rate of profit', will be clarified (but not necessarily solved) by adhering strictly to this distinction.

The rate of exploitation (or the rate of surplus value) is the ratio of surplus value to variable capital. It measures that part of the value transferred to the final product by the labourer that can be expropriated by the capitalist. Nearly half of *Capital* Vol. I is devoted to the theoretical and historical examination of the rate of surplus value. In discussing the rate of exploitation in Parts III to VI of *Capital* Vol. I, Marx goes into detailed accounts of the length of the working day in various industries (mainly in England) and in various countries. He examines the labour process in pre-capitalist as well as capitalist epochs, looks at factory legislation, the reports of factory inspectors, and the course of technological change and growth of large-scale industry, and talks of methods of wage determination in different occupations and countries. He also, of course, discusses the conceptual basis of the rate of surplus value and its determinants.

Marx offers various measures of the rate of surplus value which in equilibrium are all equivalent. He assumes (1) that wages never fall below the exchange value of labour power and occasionally rise above it and (2) that commodities are sold at their values. [I/17/p.486]. The three measures are then in terms of product produced by the worker in his line of employment, in terms of labour time and in terms of the value of capital advanced and surplus value earned. One can also obtain the ratio with the numerator and denominator in physical money or value terms. We get the following various equivalent definitions. [I/18].

$$r = \frac{S}{V} = \frac{\text{Surplus value}}{\text{Variable capital}} = \frac{\text{Surplus value}}{\text{Value of Labour Power}} = \frac{\text{Surplus Labour}}{\text{Necessary Labour}}$$

$$(4a)$$

$$= \frac{\text{Unpaid Labour}}{\text{Paid Labour}} = \frac{\text{Surplus value}}{\text{Value of Labour Power}} = \frac{\text{Surplus Labour}}{\text{Necessary Labour}}$$

$$(4b)$$

Here (4a) is the measure we have discussed above and is S_i/V_i in any branch of activity i. (4b) takes the length of the working day and works out what portion of it would replace the exchange value of labour power and finds the remaining portion to be unpaid labour. Note that in physical composition of the numerator and denominator these measures can be different. Thus in (4a) surplus value will be embodied in the final product produced, whereas in the denominator variable capital can be expressed either in terms of the portion of the final output that will be equivalent in value to the quantity of wage goods bought by the workers or directly in terms of value of the wage goods. This was illustrated in Figure 2 (p. 44.) Thus V_I can be expressed as a portion of Y_2 bought for Department I or as a portion of Y_I set aside for paying the workers to enable them to buy V_I an equivalent of Q_2. Thus when purchase of variable capital involves an *Inter-Departmental* transaction, the terms of trade – the labour value ratios of the products of the two Departments – can be important. This will be important when technical change in one Department may be reducing the labour values (reducing the ratio Y_i/Q_i) faster than in the other Department.

The terms of trade effect can also be seen by looking at the worker's side of the bargain. Equation (4b) is a measure in terms of worker's time and can be used to express the money wage equivalent of a day's output. Suppose all workers consume one unit of Q_2 as their subsistence basket. Then necessary labour is the amount of labour time embodied in one unit of Q_2. This is given as Y_2/Q_2 say l_2. Then l_2 number of hours is necessary labour and the rest of the working day is surplus value. If length of working day is T_i hours in the ith industry (Department) we get as (4b)

$$r_i = \frac{T_i - l_2}{l_2} \tag{5}$$

Let us then assume that price per unit of Q_2 is q_2 and equivalently that per unit of Y_2 is p_2. (Note the two separate price expressions. We shall use them in the next Part extensively). Each worker needs a money wage of $p_2 l_2$ or q_2 units of money. What is then paid labour and what unpaid labour? This depends on how much time is required in each Department to produce value which has a money equivalent of $p_2 l_2$. But will this not depend on terms of trade between the Departments? A worker in Department I will need to find out how many hours he takes to produce $p_2 l_2/p_1$ amount of value. But then we look at Marx's assumption (2) that commodities exchange at their values. This would imply simply that

$$\frac{q_i}{q_j} = \frac{l_i}{l_j} = \quad \text{for all pairs i,j} \tag{6a}$$

Thus prices per unit of output are in the same ratio as the labour content. Marx was aware (as is evident at various places in his notebooks which precede *Capital*) that prices did deviate from values. Indeed, he berated Ricardo in *Theories of Surplus Value* for not making this explicit. But he assumed in many places, especially in the first two volumes of *Capital*, that prices were proportional to values. Equation (6a) implies that

$$p_i = p_j \quad \text{for all } i, j \tag{6b}$$

This means in our example that workers in Department I receive a wage of $p_2 l_2$ and have to produce $p_2 l_2/p_1$ or l_2 amount of value to pay for their subsistance basket of goods. Thus terms of trade effects vanish under assumption (2).

When prices deviate from values (as we shall see in the next section), when wages deviate from the exchange value of labour or when technical change in one part of the economy proceeds faster than others, our formulae will not all yield the same answer.

Note that if the length of the working day is uniform in all industries and the same subsistence basket of goods is consumed by all workers, then the measure (4b) will be identical across all industries. Other measures will not have this property without these two additional assumptions.

Marx mentioned two measures of surplus value – Absolute and Relative Surplus Value. Given equation (5), absolute surplus value will be increased by an increase in T_i length of working day. Marx thought of the working day as a variable quantity (I/10/223). He gave copious contemporary evidence on the variability of the working day across industries and noted how incessant class struggle was necessary to reduce the length of working day to a 'normal' uniform length. This is done in Chapter 10, 'The Working Day', in *Capital* Vol. I {27}. One way exploitation was increased by lengthening the working day even in defiance of legislation regulating its length.

If the length can be taken as fixed, then we can define relative surplus value. This will be increased if the necessary labour portion goes down. This can be due to growth of productivity in wage goods industries (Department II) or by cheap imports of wage goods – any factor that depresses the exchange value of labour power (l_2 in equation (5) above). Another way would be to raise productivity within an industry to such an extent that again the necessary labour portion of the total working day would decline.

Another factor Marx mentions as influencing the rate of surplus value is intensity of work. In the same labour time, more intense work may lead to greater productivity than less intense work.

We may briefly note that many writers on Marxian economic theory consider that Marx requires that rate of exploitation be equal across all industries and also equal for different categories of labour. There is just one sentence in Vol. III of *Capital* that lends justification to this view. Also, in his schemes of 'Simple and Extended Reproduction' in Vol. II of *Capital* and in the celebrated Transformation problem example in Vol. III of *Capital*, Marx assumed identical rates of surplus value. Nothing in the extensive discussion of Vol. I, however, (nothing in more than three hundred pages, that is) gives the impression of such an assumption. We have unequal lengths for the working day across industries both historically and theoretically. Intensity of work and technical conditions of production are shown to vary. At this stage we shall leave the question open as to whether equality of rates of exploitation is an equilibrium condition, or a simplifying assumption or a necessary part in Marx's value theory.

THE RATE OF PROFIT

The importance of the rate of surplus value is in determining the rate of profit. For the time being, we shall show its connection with the (value) rate of profit π as shown by Marx. We shall note later why this is unsatisfactory. The (value) rate of profit is related to the rate of exploitation via the organic composition of capital.

The organic composition of capital, which is also a value concept, is the proportion of constant capital in the sum of total capital advanced, or $C_i/C_i + V_i$), where i refers to any particular individual firm/industry/Department. Only under certain (unlikely) circumstances can this be approximated by the capital-labour ratio, that is, the ratio of physical quantities of men and machines, assuming that these can be added together at all ($MP_i/L_i + MP_i$); nor is this the money value of fixed capital as a ratio of the money value of fixed capital and the wage bill. The ratio is meant to show the importance of class relations, since whereas the capitalist needs labour power in the production process, he controls more easily the objective factor – materials of production. The buying and selling of MP involves transactions within the class that has a monopoly of the means of production and hence such transactions do not involve antagonistic conflicts (though there may be cut-throat competition). In purchasing labour power, the capitalist confronts the worker not just as one individual confronts another entering in exchange but as members of two different and antagonistic classes, one of which has a monopoly of the means of production of which the other has been divested of these means. The ratio has thus a qualitative, social dimension to it {82}.

Quantitatively, the organic composition of capital (g) is important because the (value) rate of profit can be related to the rate of surplus value (r) through g. Very simply, we define the (value) rate of profit (π) as the ratio of surplus value to the sum of capital advanced: $S_i/(C_i + V_i)$. In terms of only one good, we have

$$\pi = \frac{S}{C + V} = \frac{S}{V}\left(1 - \frac{C}{C + V}\right) = r(1 - g) \qquad (7)$$

The simplicity of this formula is misleading and is an invitation to its indiscriminate use. For the present we notice that the rate of profit varies directly with the rate of surplus value (r) and inversely with the organic composition of capital (g). Thus the within-class transactions that determine g depress the rate of profit and the antagonistic class transaction helps it.

Note in the context of our integration of the scheme of Simple Reproduction with the three circuits of capital that we can distinguish between various concepts. Thus the value rate of profit π in any Department is

$$\pi_i = S_i/C_i + \dot{V}_i = r_i(1 - g_i) \qquad (7a)$$

The money rate of profit ρ is

$$\rho_i = (M'_i - M_i)/M_i \tag{8}$$

Now it is a standard assumption in all schools of economic theory that the rate of profit is equalized in equilibrium across different industries. Thus $\rho_i = \rho$ in different industries. There is no reason for π_i to be the same for all i unless r_i as well as g_i are identical for all industries. Marx substituted another concept for value of rate of profit – the average rate of profit, which he defined in aggregate terms as

$$\pi = \frac{\Sigma S_i}{\Sigma C_i + \Sigma V_i} = \frac{S}{C + V} \tag{9}$$

This brings us back to equation (7), which was defined for a one-good case. The substitution of π instead of ρ for the rate of profit led to some serious problems when Marx came to relate values to prices. This is what we must now look at.

PART TWO

Value and Prices:
The Transformation Problem

INTRODUCTION

The problem of values and prices – the transformation problem – has been at the heart of the controversy regarding Marx's
theory. For many critics of Marx, his failure to show that prices
are proportional to values is a sufficient reason for abandoning
his entire apparatus. Bohm-Bawerk in his *Karl Marx and the
Close of his System*[1] was the first to point out that Marx had
asserted that prices are proportional to values in Vol. I of *Capital* and promised to show this solution explicitly, which he failed
to do. In Vol. III, Marx was stuck with an example where prices
in the different Departments were not proportional to values.
Bohm-Bawerk in his brilliant polemical work was to show that
the various reasons Marx advanced in order to salvage this
result were not adequate. Values if they were based on labour
content alone could not, according to him, explain prices and
profits in the real world. If labour values could not explain the
structure of prices and profits, then the theory of surplus value
which asserted that capitalism was based on the exploitation of
workers also fell. Clearly it was Marx's failure to take into
account the contribution of the other factors of production
which seemed to be at the heart of this failure.

A few years before Bohm-Bawerk's criticism (which had to
wait until all the three volumes of *Capital* were published),
Philip Wicksteed[2] in a celebrated debate with Bernard Shaw had
demonstrated that relative prices were in fact explained by relative scarcities and therefore by the ratio of marginal utilities
which they yielded to a consumer. Wicksteed's demonstration
did not deal in detail with Marx's theory but showed that an
explanation based on Jevons' theory of utility was a superior
logical explanation. If prices are explained by relative scarcity
rather than by labour content, then the notion of surplus value

ceases to have a rational foundation. Profits become a legitimate
income as a reward for relative scarcity of capital. (Bernard
Shaw was to admit the force of this argument and later in his
life concentrated on the Ricardian notion of land rent as
unearned surplus. To this day land nationalisation and appropriation of profits in real estate have been a part of the Labour
Party's economic philosophy. Profits in industrial activities are
regarded as legitimate.)

The importance of Wicksteed's criticism has been underrated.
In Neoclassical economics, the duality of exchange value and use
value is accepted. But whereas in classical and Marxian theory
these two are independent of each other, in neoclassical
economic theory, they are linked together causally. This was the
crucial new element in Jevons' contribution that Wicksteed used
to criticise Marx. Marx's explanation of exploitation relies on
the independent determination of the exchange value of labour
power and the use value of labour during the production process. The marginalist and the modern approach deny this independence and causally link the two via the twin prongs of dis-
utility of work and the productivity of labour. They treat labour
and capital as symmetrical with all commodities and thus do not
employ the notion of class relations in the labour market any
more than in the commodity market.

The Marxist reply to these criticisms has not been very con-
vincing. Many, like Hyndman, have been polemical and have
relied on assertions without proof.[3] Others argued for example
that Marx was speaking of values as long run or natural prices;
considerations of demand/supply which modern economics takes
into account are only relevant to short run prices. This does not
at all meet Bohm-Bawerk's point which did relate to such long
run prices. Many repeated the arguments advanced by Marx
which Bohm-Bawerk had already dealt with. There grew thereafter a gulf between Marx's theory and modern economic theory
with very little communication between them.

As we shall show later, Marx's attempt to solve the transformation problem was marred by some simple but very serious
errors. It was up to Bortkiewicz to correctly formulate the problem Marx was attempting to solve and show the nature of the
solution. Bortkiewicz correctly saw that the problem had to be
formulated separately in price terms and in value terms and

then a 'mapping' from values to prices had to be rigorously established.

Bortkiewicz solved the problem in two stages. In the first article he dealt in general with the transformation problem including the case of fixed capital. In the second article he dealt with the simpler case of all constant capital being used up within the production period (as in (1) and (2) above in Chapter VI). His two articles were published in German in 1906–07.[4] The second article is the more well-known one since it became available in English in 1948. The first one which is the less well-known one was translated in the early 1950's. Bortkiewicz's solution was mathematically elegant though he did not use any of the tools that modern developments in linear algebra have made available to economics. Nowadays, especially for the case of fixed capital which he dealt with, mathematical economists prefer the von Neumann model of joint production as a much more powerful formulation. The linear model, whether with or without joint production, has a number of parallels with Marx's formulations and hence the mathematical properties of the linear model can be directly used to analyse Marx's model.

During the 1930s, there was a revival of interest in Marxian economics but this was more in the macroeconomic contributions of Marx. This was because Keynes' General Theory had provided economists with a 'new pair of glasses' for reading Marx. There was much interesting writing on the Marxian theory of cycles and of Marx's pioneering contribution to national income analysis. The value problems was ignored in all these discussions.

In the late 1940s, Witernitz proposed a solution of the value price transformation problem using the notion of linear models.[5] Samuelson in his 1957 article explicitly treated the value scheme as an input-output model and confirmed many of the criticisms of Bohm-Bawerk and the analysis of Bortkiewicz. This was that values and prices could be proportional only if either (i) equal rates of exploitation among industries and equal organic composition of capital prevailed, or (ii) zero rate of exploitation and zero rate of profit prevailed everywhere. We shall demonstrate this later.

There has been an upsurge of interest in Marx again in the 1970s. Samuelson has returned to the question of the transformation problem in his 1971 article in the *Journal of Economic Literature*. This article, which we shall discuss in greater detail later, argues that the value price transformation is an unnecessary step, that the value scheme is applicable only to very simple economies and is an erroneous view of the economic system. Morishima, on the other hand, has arrived at somewhat different conclusions using the same tools. Starting with a clear distinction between the value and the price models, he has tried to formulate Marx's propositions in a mathematically rigorous fashion. His analysis, which we shall examine later, concludes with the message that the labour theory of value can be superseded today by better mathematical formulations [Morishima (1973)].

There have been two new areas of debate opened up since we received this problem in Desai (1974). Baumol has proposed an interpretation of Marx's solution of the transformation problem that shifts the emphasis away from quantitative price calculations. This led to a symposium between Samuelson, Morishima and Baumol in the *Journal of Economic Literature* (1974). Another strand has been what is called the 'Neo-Ricardian' critique of Marx. In a number of articles Steedman has developed the argument that value calculus is clumsy and unnecessary and that Sraffa's model as presented in *Production of Commodities by Means of Commodities* is a much better model for approaching the wage-profit division problem of a modern capitalist economy. In a way the preference for Ricardo's approach over Marx's for an explanation of the rate of profit in these articles is anticipated by Bortkiewicz who championed Ricardo above Marx. Steedman has raised the possibility that values may not even be positive and that negative value and surplus value can be shown to coexist with positive profits. This has led to an extended debate and was the subject of an exchange between Wolfstetter (1976), Morishima (1976) and Steedman (1975, 1976), in the *Economic Journal*. This debate – indeed, the whole issue of joint production – is mathematically demanding but it raises extemely important issues as we shall see in Chapter XIII.

We shall first outline the problem as posed by Marx and the mistakes he made in the process of solution. The mistakes are not so much mathematical as conceptual – a confusion over the question of commodity fetishism. But Marx's original numerical example related to five activities (individual capitals) and distinguished between fixed capital and its rate of turnover. This has been somewhat ignored in later discussion because attention has been paid exclusively to the second of Bortkiewicz's two articles. We shall therefore outline the solution of the problem in two stages. First, dealing with Bortkiewicz's second article assuming no fixed capital, and then the more general approach of the first article. There we shall also see the way Bortkiewicz posed the Marx/Ricardo contrast. We then survey the contributions of other writers.

VALUES AND PRICES: THE PROBLEM AS POSED BY MARX[1]

The simplest way to pose the transformation problem is as follows. Marx states that surplus value can be generated only by living labour i.e. by the exploitation of the labourer by the capitalist. If that is true, surplus value and hence profit should be higher in those industries where the ratio of labour power to materials of production is high and vice versa. But everyone, including Marx, accepts that the rate of profit is equalised across industries in equilibrium. Here is a basic contradiction.

In Part I of *Capital,* Vol. III, Marx begins by relating the rate of surplus value to the rate of profit. He considers variations in r, C and V and the various forces determining them. In Part II he moves to the question of conversion of divergent profit rates in different industries. This is the transition from our equation (7) to equation (9). Marx begins by assuming equal rates of exploitation justifying it partly on Adam Smith's chapter X where relative advantages of different occupations are discussed and partly on the ground that though rates of exploitation may differ in the real world, it is 'incidental and irrelevant in a general analysis of capitalist production'.

We then have Table 1 which sets out the problem without fixed capital. There are five spheres of production which indicate the average normal organic composition of capital invested in each sphere. The working day is also assumed constant which along with the rate of exploitation being equal and constant implies constant wages (equal to necessary labour). Having made these assumptions explicit, Marx proceeds to base the five spheres on differences in proportion of C to V keeping total capital at 100. The rate of exploitation is also 100 per cent. So we get as far as the production of values is concerned

$$Y_i = C_i + (1 + r)V_i \qquad (10a)$$

$$= \left[\frac{g_i + (1 + r)(1 - g_i)}{(1 - g_i)} \right] V_i = \frac{k_i}{(1 - g_i)} V_i \qquad (10b)$$

Here $k_i = g_i + (1 + r)(1 - g_i) = 1 + \pi_i$, since

$$\pi_i = r(1 - g_i) \qquad (7)$$

As we can see there is a wide divergence in the rate of profit as between different spheres from 5 per cent – 40 per cent. *So if commodities are sold at their values* i.e. if Y_i represents total revenue as well as total value $(p_i = 1)$ then rates of profit diverge. As Marx then puts it 'There is no doubt, on the other hand, that aside from unessential, incidental and mutually compensating distinctions, differences in the average rate of profit in the various branches of industry do not exist in reality, and could not exist without abolishing the entire system of capitalist production' (III/8/153). But then Marx says that the amount of capital advanced is what capitalists look at. This is the cost price. It is the same average profit rate on cost price that competition establishes according to Marx.

Cost price is calculated as $C_i + V_i$. [Note however that cost price should have a monetary dimension. It is really M_i in Marx's notation of earlier volumes. $C_i + V_i$ are in value units.] Average profit rate is then calculated on the notion that the *total of profits for the entire system is equal to total surplus value* and then the ratio of total profit to total capital advanced forms the average profit rate. (The identity of 'mass of profits with mass of surplus value' is a basic assumption in all of Marx's work: in *Theories of Surplus Value* as well as in *Capital*. We shall examine its validity later on.) Thus we have equation (9) which is

$$\pi| = \frac{\Sigma S_i}{\Sigma C_i + \Sigma V_i} = r(1 - g) \qquad (9)$$

In this case r being identical, we can express π in terms average organic composition g. Prices or rather total revenues are decided by the average rate of profit acting as a mark-up above capital advanced.

$$P_i = p_i Y_i = (1 + \pi)(C_i + V_i) \tag{11a}$$

$$= [1 + r(1 - g)] \left[\frac{(g_i + (1 - g_i)}{(1 - g_i)} \right] |V_i$$

$$= \frac{[1 + r(1 - g)]}{(1 - g_i)} V_i \tag{11b}$$

Though Marx does not work out the prices for the no fixed capital case, we illustrate the method in Table 1. The average rate of profit is 22 per cent and price is calculated as a cost price times a mark-up factor $(1 + \pi)$. Then it is clear that prices deviate from values. The last column shows the deviation. This is also shown by calculating p_i, price per unit of value embodied in the ith commodity. Dividing (11b) by (10b) we get

$$\frac{P_i}{Y_i} = p_i = \frac{[1 + r(1 - g)]}{k_i} = \left[\frac{1 + r(1 - g)}{1 + r(1 - g_i)} \right] \tag{12}$$

Thus unless $g_i = g$ in every sphere, some p_i will be greater than one and some less.

$$p_i \gtrless 1 \text{ as } g_i \gtrless g. \tag{13}$$

Before we discuss this further, let us look at the case Marx did provide a solution for. The rate of profit is calculated on total capital advanced fixed as well as circulating and not just on capital used up during production which is reflected in costs of production (cost-price). Thus profit rate is not a mark-up above costs but above total capital advanced. Different spheres will use capitals of different durability – of different rates of turnover. To make this explicit, Marx gives an example with the same total capital advanced as before but different rates of turnover. We have called fixed capital K_i. The constant capital used up is C_i as before and K_i/C_i is of course the rate of turnover. Profit rate is then calculated as

$$\pi_i = \frac{S_i}{K_i + V_i} \tag{7a}$$

and average rate of profit as

$$\pi = \frac{S_i}{\Sigma K_i + \Sigma V_i} \tag{9a}$$

Let the rate of turnover be t_i. Then we get

$$\pi_i = \frac{r(1 - g_i)}{t_i g_i + (1 - g_i)} \tag{7b}$$

which reduced to (7) when $t_i = 1$. And defining ω_i as weights V_i/V we have

$$\pi = \frac{r \sum_i \omega_i(1 - g_i)}{\sum_i (t_i g_i + (1 - g_i)\omega_i)} \tag{9b}$$

Marx then calculated prices as the value of capital advanced times $1 + \pi$. So we get

$$P_i = p_i Y_i = (1 + \pi)(K_i + V_i) \tag{14}$$

$$= [1 + r\Sigma\omega_i(1 - g_i)] \left\{ \frac{t_i g_i + (1 - g_i)}{\Sigma(t_i g_i + (1 + g_i)\omega_i)} \right\} V_i \tag{15}$$

The expression for P_i in the case of fixed capital is not as transparent as in the case with no fixed capital. The first expression in square brackets gives us aggregate surplus value as a proportion of total variable capital. The second expression in curly brackets gives the organic composition of capital of the ith sphere as a proportion of the average organic composition.

It is perhaps worth manipulating (15) a bit more to bring out the expression for unit price p_i. Since $\Sigma\omega_i = 1$ and $k_i = 1 + r(1 - g_i)$

$$p_i = [1 + r\Sigma\omega_i(1 - g_i)] \left\{ \frac{t_ig_i + (1 - g_i)}{\Sigma(t_ig_i + (1 - g_i)\omega_i)} \right\} \frac{1}{[1 + r(1 - g_i)]}$$

(16)

$$= [1 + r(1 - \Sigma\omega_ig_i)] \left\{ \frac{1 + (t_i - 1)g_i}{1 + \Sigma(t_i - 1)\omega_ig_i} \right\} \frac{1}{1 + r(1 - g_i)}$$

Now using ω_i as weights we can see that $g = \Sigma g_i\omega_i$: the average organic composition of capital is a weighted average of individual organic compositions, the weights being V_i/V. So we can similarly define and average t_g where $t_g = \Sigma t_i\omega_ig_i$. There

$$p_i = \frac{[1 + r(1 - g)]}{[1 + r(1 - g)]} \left\{ \frac{1 + t_ig_i - g_i}{1 + t_g - g} \right\} = \frac{[1 + r(1 - g_i)]}{[1 + r(1 - g_i)]}$$

(17)

$$\left\{ \frac{1 - g_i(1 - t_i)}{1 - g(1 - t)} \right\}$$

In equation (17) on the right hand side, the first expression is the same as in the case without fixed capital (see Equation (12)). The second expression brings out the influence of turnover of capital in each sphere as well as that in the average sphere. In the case with no fixed capital $t_i = 1$ and indeed we can take this as a maximum value of t_i. Hence $t \leqslant 1$ and so $t_g \leqslant g$. We see again that except by fortuitous circumstances $p_i \neq 1$ unless various equalities for t_i and g_i are satisfied. Prices in general then deviate from value. Commodities exchange at ratios which differ from their value ratios. This is so with and without fixed capital.

Marx called his prices *prices of production*. He defines it as follows 'Hence, the price of production of a commodity is equal to its cost-price plus the profit allotted to it in per cent, in accordance with the general rate of profit, or in other words, to its cost-price plus the average profit' (III/9/157). The equal-isation of divergent rates of individual profit into an average profit was done, Marx said, by competition. Thus individual capitalists do not secure the surplus value produced by them but get the average profit. This average profit depends on the total surplus value produced by the whole economy and the pro-portionate share of an individual sphere's advanced capital in total capital advanced. Thus the profit added to the cost price is independent of the particular sphere of production.

The deviation of P_i from Y_i is also by definition the gap be-tween profits R_i and surplus value S_i of the ith capital. Thus com-petition and price calculus distribute total surplus value in such a way as to give equal rates of profit on advanced capital. Thus the source of profit-surplus value is in living labour measured by V_i when working day and wages are constant but the profit received by a firm is proportionate to $K_i + V_i$. Thus the origin of profit is masked by the pricing process. Each capitalist thinks profits are due to both elements of capital constant and variable since the rate of profit is invariant to individual organic com-position of capital.

Notice that in Marx's example not only is total profit equal to total surplus value by assumption but total value is also equal to total price. The former is more basic since, as we have said above, it permeates all of Marx's work. The latter is a con-sequence of the price calculation. Thus

$$\Sigma R_i = \Sigma S_i \tag{18}$$

and

$$\Sigma P_i = \Sigma Y_i \tag{19}$$

Equation (18) is only a rewriting of (19), (9a) or (9b) in levels rather than rates. Equation (19) is a consequence of (18) as can be seen from, say (10a) and (11a). From (10a)

$$\Sigma Y_i = \Sigma C_i + (1 + r)\Sigma V_i$$
$$= (\Sigma C_i + \Sigma V_i) + r\,\Sigma V_i$$

and from (11a)

$$\Sigma P_i = (1 + \pi)(\Sigma C_i + \Sigma V_i)$$

But by (9) or (18)

$$r\Sigma V_i = \pi(\Sigma C_i + \Sigma V_i)$$

We shall see later that both these identities (18) and (19) can be satisfied only by accident.

The assumption prices being proportional to values in Volume I and II of *Capital* and prices deviating from values in Volume III was held up as a great contradiction, a fundamental flaw in Marx's system especially by Bohm-Bawerk. There is much internal evidence in *Capital* and *Theories of Surplus Value* that Marx did not think of price-value deviation as an anomaly but a fundamental part of capitalist system. It was a crucial element in the mystification of true relations, an example of the exchange process masking the production process.

The problem with Marx's calculation is not, however, that prices deviate from values. That they must, in any but very simple commodity mode of production. The problem is that Marx did not pursue his distinction between values and prices thoroughly enough. The mystification due to the exchange process is even more thorough than that emphasised by Marx. Marx's fundamental error was to treat value relations as if they were observable and directly measurable. By writing down the scheme as in Table I, value categories are treated as if the individual capitalist and the worker could directly perceive the relations of exploitation. We saw in Chapter VI in our integration of the scheme of Simple Reproduction with the three circuits of capital how much of the intermediation of prices and money was obscured by the $C' - C'$ circuit used in that scheme. Table I is again a $C' - C'$ circuit. Monetary aspects are ignored, or worse, confused by calling value aggregates such as $C_i + V_i$ cost-price. The importance of the $M - M'$ circuit lies in the fact that the capitalist has to sell his output he has to realise surplus value – convert it into money. What the capitalist sees is not the *value* of constant capital (stock or flow) or of variable capital; he sees material costs and a wage bill, he buys the physical commodities MP_i and L_i. These are directly equivalent to each other only if values and prices are proportionate. We saw this also in the different expression for the rate of surplus value in Chapter VII above.

A capitalist economy is a monetary economy above all. The capitalist invests a sum of money M and obtains revenue in money terms M'. The relevant magnitude that he looks at is the money rate of profit ρ expressed as in equation (8).

$$\rho_i = (M'_i - M_i)/M_i \qquad (8)$$

What competition equalises is ρ_i across different activities because once capital is back in its money form M', it is freely mobile between different activities. Neither $(C_i + V_i)$ nor $(K_i + V_i)$ are expressions for M_i unless $p_i = 1$ for all i, unless that is values equal prices. It is not legitimate to start off the input calculation with implicit assumption $p_i = 1$ and then arrive at output price calculation where $p_i \neq 1$.[2] This argues that the items listed as cost-price and price (revenue) will not bear interpretation as monetary magnitudes. They are all in labour value terms and represent labour values. What the procedure of charging an average rate of profit on capital advanced accomplishes is a reshuffling of the value produced into value received. Capitalist i advances $K_i + V_i$ amount of value (implicitly bought with the money he had) and at the end of the production process Y_i is the value he turns on the market. He gets back however P_i if average (value) rate of profit is equalised across industries.

Interpretation P_i as money sums or as value sums are therefore two alternatives. Recently, Okishio and Morishima have each advanced an iterative (monetary interpretation of Marx's procedure. Shaikh has also independently advanced that interpretation in an unpublished paper.[3] This starts with the anomaly we pointed out above that inputs are priced at $p_i = 1$ but by the end of the calculation $p_i \neq 1$. The answer then is to go back and reprice the inputs at new prices and repeat the procedure until both input and output prices come out equal i.e. until the iteration process converges. We can not demonstrate this in Marx's example because it is not clear what the physical commodity output of each sphere is – i.e. whether it produces Department I good or Department II good etc. Fixed capital is also excluded

TABLE 1

Marx's Example (Without Fixed Capital)

Capitals (Spheres)	Constant Capital C_i	Variable Capital V_i	Surplus Value S_i	Rate of Profit π_i	Value of Prod. Y_i	Cost Price $(C_i + V_i)$	Average Rate of Profit π	Price of Production P_i	Deviation
1	80	20	20	20%	120	100	22%	122	+2
2	70	30	30	30%	130	100	22%	122	−8
3	60	40	40	40%	140	100	22%	122	−18
4	85	15	15	15%	115	100	22%	122	+7
5	95	5	5	5%	105	100	22%	122	+17
Σ	390	110	110		610	500		610	

Capital III/9/155.

TABLE 2
Marx's Example with Fixed Capital

Capitals (Spheres)	Fixed Capital K_i	Variable Capital V_i	Used up Constant C_i	Surplus Value S_i	Value of Product Y	Rate of Profit π_i	Cost Price $C_i + V_i$	Average Rate of Profit π	Price of Production P_i	Dev.
1	80	20	50	20	90	20%	70	22%	92	+2
2	70	30	51	30	111	30%	81	22%	103	−8
3	60	40	51	40	131	40%	91	22%	113	−18
4	85	15	40	15	70	15%	55	22%	77	+7
5	95	5	10	5	20	5%	15	22%	37	+17
	390	110	202	110	422	—	312		422	

Capital III/9/156–7.

so far from the proofs offered by Morishima and Okishio. When we come to Bortkiewicz's solution we shall see that if the price-value distinction is correctly maintained, the correct answer can be arrived at (in the circulating capital case) immediately without iteration. While Marx took a five industry example, Bortkiewicz took a three Department scheme as in (2) above. This meant that he only needed to solve a quadratic equation after some further assumption whereas Marx would have had to solve at least a fourth-degree polynomial. This though not impossible at the time given the state of mathematical knowledge would have been extremely arduous.

X

BORTKIEWICZ'S SOLUTION: THE SIMPLE CASE

Bortkiewicz wrote two long articles on Marx's transformation procedure, as we said in Chapter VIII above. The more well-known article provides a numerical example and the mathematical formulation for correctly solving Marx's problem when no fixed capital is assumed. The other article which we shall discuss in the next chapter offers a much more general solution but apart from reproducing Marx's example which we gave in Table 2 does not compute the correct solution. This may have been due to the fact that given the five industries but no idea of the nature of their output, we cannot link output and input prices without some further arbitrary classification of the five industries into three Departments. We shall take this question up as well in the next chapter.

Bortkiewicz like Marx starts with a $C' - C'$ circuit on the value side but correctly sets up the corresponding $M - M'$ circuit. Both inputs and outputs are consistently priced. He does not however bother with the physical forms of things, that is, the $P - Q - P$ circuit or the input output table. Purely as an expository device, we shall do this after we have looked at Bortkiewicz's solution.

As we can see in Table 3, there are three Departments and we have Simple Reproduction. Note that Marx did not worry about reproduction problems in the Chapter on Transformation. Bortkiewicz thus integrated material from Vol. II and Vol. III of *Capital* to make the price-value problem tractable. This device enabled him to ignore the input-output table $- P - Q - P$ circuit – which in many modern solutions is taken as a starting point.

The three Departments and their commodities are the same as we described in Chapter VI equation (2). We then immediately set up the pricing equations

$$M'_1 = p_1 Y_1 = (1 + \rho)(p_1 C_1 + p_2 V_1) = (1 + \rho)M_1 \qquad (20a)$$

$$M'_2 = p_2 Y_2 = (1 + \rho)(p_1 C_2 + p_2 V_2) = (1 + \rho)M_2 \qquad (20b)$$

$$M'_3 = p_3 Y_3 = (1 + \rho)(p_1 C_3 + p_2 V_3) = (1 + \rho)M_3 \qquad (20c)$$

Being simple reproduction and Departmental scheme Y_1 is C, Y_2 is V and Y_3 is the industry which produces goods bought by capitalists. (Note we cannot say Y_3 is S. The physical forms of Y_3 and S are different.) Here we can see the $M - M'$ circuit explicitly since $p_1 C_i + p_2 V_i = M_i$ and $p_1 Y_i = M'_i$. We assume equilibrium and therefore no problem in selling what is produced.

The value equations are as in (10a) and (10b) above, reproduced here:

$$Y_i = C_i + (1 + r)V_i \qquad (10a)$$

$$= \frac{g_i + (1 + r)(1 - g_i)}{(1 - g_i)} V_i = \frac{k_i}{(1 - g_i)} V_i \qquad (10b)$$

In addition one can impose either equation (18) or equation (19) as an identity, but not both. This is because we have in (20a)–(20c) four unknown p_1, p_2 p_3 and ρ. So only one more equation is necessary. In the article under discussion Bortkiewicz mentions identity (19) – equality of total values and total prices but as we see from Table III, his solution satisfied equation (18) rather than (19) i.e. total surplus value and total profits are each 200 but total value is 875 and total price 1,000. We shall bring out this difference later on. In the next chapter we shall see the general formulation of this question. In general, Bortkiewicz thought of (19) as arbitrary because as he shows it depends on the commodity chosen as a standard of measurement.

He assumes that Department III produces gold – the money commodity. Thus the profits are received in money terms. Gold output is enough to enable capitalists to hold their profits in gold.

Substituting (10b) into (20a)–(20c) and using the definition of

g_i we get

$$p_i k_i = (1 + \rho)[p_1 g_i + p_2(1 - g_i)] \qquad (21)$$

Since Y_3 is value of Gold production, Bortkiewicz took $p_3 = 1$. (There is a problem here as we shall see below.) Then, let us define $p_i/p_3 = p'_i$; p'_i are prices in terms of gold. Put $p_1/p_2 = p'_1/p'_2 = x$. Then we get

$$xk_1 = (1 + \rho) \ [xg_1 + (1 - g_1)] \qquad (21a)$$

$$k_2 = (1 + \rho) \ [xg_2 + (1 - g_2)] \qquad (21b)$$

$$k_3 = (1 + \rho) \, p'_2[xg_3 + (1 - g_3)] \qquad (21c)$$

These are the three equations. In addition we may have (18) or (19). These are various ways to express (18) and (19) concisely. Recall that (18) can be expressed as

$$\Sigma S_i = \Sigma R_i = \rho \Sigma M_i | = \rho \Sigma (p_1 C_i + p_2 V_i)$$

Using the definition of x and ω_i and some manipulation we get

$$\rho p_2 \Sigma \left\{ \frac{1 + g_i \, (x - 1)}{(t/1 - g_i)} \right\} \ \omega_i = r \qquad (18a)$$

Equation (19) can be compressed using weights $\omega^*_i = Y_i/\Sigma Y_i$ as

$$\Sigma p_i \omega^*_i = 1$$

We can now solve for p_i and ρ as follows. There are various ways of approaching a solution. Note that dividing (21a) by (21b) we get a quadratic in x and $(1 + \rho)$ entirely disappears

$$\frac{xk_1}{k_2} = \frac{xg_1 + (1 - g_1)}{xg_2 + (1 - g_2)}$$

$$x^2 g_2 k_1 + x[k_1(1 - g_2) - g_1 k_2] - (1 - g_1)k_2 = 0$$

This will give a solution of x in the parameters g_i and r (since k_i is a function of g_i and r). Given the two real roots $\hat{x}_1$, $\hat{x}_2$ we can choose the positive $\hat{x}_i$. We substitute $\hat{x}_i$ in (21b) or (21a) to solve for $(1 + \rho)$. Another method is to express (21a) as

$$x = \frac{\lambda(1 - g_1)}{(k_1 - \lambda g_1)} \qquad \text{where } \lambda = (1 + \rho)$$

Then substitute this into (21b) which can be expressed as

$$\frac{k_2 - \lambda(1 - g_2)}{\lambda g_2} = x$$

This will give a quadratic in λ which will have two real roots, one of them positive. In these solutions we treat g_i and r as known and solve for p_i and ρ. The precise solution for x or ρ is only a complicated expression not involving any interesting concept. The only thing worth noticing is that we can leave out Department III altogether and get $(1 + \rho)$ in terms of g_1, g_2 and r. Department III does not enter the calculation of profit rate as it does not produce any good which is used as inputs – M_i involves only p_1 and p_2 not p_3. This will not be so in Marx's way of calculating π because as long as any industry produces surplus value it will contribute to forming π. We come back to this in the next chapter. Having obtained x and ρ we can get p'_2 from (21c). Once x and p'_2 are known, p_i can be derived straightaway.

The numerical solution assuming $p_3 = 1$ is given in Table 3. We indicate prices as p'_i to make clear that these are in terms of p_3. Notice that profits of each Department deviate from surplus value with Department I gaining at the expense of the other two Departments. The rate of profit $\rho = 25$ per cent whereas $\pi = 29.6$ per cent and r is assumed to be $66\frac{2}{3}$ per cent. Note also that the dissolution of value magnitudes is even more complete in Bortkiewicz's solution. Thus the organic composition as measured in value terms for Department I is $225/315 = 0.714$ but if we use cost magnitudes $p_1C_i/M_1 = 0.75$ $g_2 = 0.454$ but in money terms $p_1C_2/M_2 = 0.50$. The ratio of profits to wages or to total revenue does not measure the rate of exploitation etc.

We now come to the important question of the identities (18) and (19). Sweezy noted that while Bortkiewicz mentions (19) as a condition, his solution does not satisfy it. We can now explain various anomalies due to Bortkiewicz's procedure. [Sweezy (1968), Desai (1974/75).]

Note first that in solving for p'_i and ρ_1 we have not used (18) or (19) and neither did Bortkiewicz. The equality of total profits and total surplus value is however satisfied in the solution. How can we explain this? We can show that, given Simple Reproduction, the requirement that all profits are spent on the output of Department III has automatic consequence for p_3. This is because the equilibrium condition requires

$$\Sigma R_i = p_3 Y_3 = p_3 \Sigma S_i$$

As soon as $p_3 = 1$ is chosen total profits are equal to total surplus value without imposing such a condition. Alternatively if one impose such a condition as (18), in Simple Reproduction $p_3 = 1$. This is independent of whether Department III produces Gold or racehorses.

We can indeed say further that Bortkiewicz himself confused the physical and the value processes of production when he imposed $p_3 = 1$. Let us grant that Department III produces the money commodity – Gold and that it is the numeraire. But the relevant price is not p_3 which is price per unit of value embodied in Gold. The price which is set at unity is price per unit of *physical* output – what we labelled q_3. Now $p_3 = q_3/l_3$ as in general $p_i = q_i/l_i$, l_i being the labour content per unit of physical output Q_i. If $l_3 = 1$ then $p_3 = q_3$ and the normalization does not disort. Otherwise if $l_3 > 1$ it blows up relative prices p'_i and $l_i < 1$, it scales them down. Choosing a numeraire and setting its price equal to one is standard procedure but it is not the proper price which is normalized here.

We can solve for absolute p_i by applying either (18) or (19). We can write (21c) as

$$p_3 k_3 = (1 + \rho) p_2 (x g_3 + (1 - g_3)) \qquad (21c')$$

Thus having solved for x and ρ as above from (21a) and (21b), we can solve for p_2 from (18) and p_3 from (21c'). But we already know that $p_3 = 1$ as soon as (18) is imposed in Simple Reproduction with the condition that all profits are spent on Department II products. If profits are spent on Y_2 and Y_3 or invested, this will no longer be so and p_3 will no longer equal one.

If we impose (19) along with (21a)–(21c), given x and ρ we solve for p_2 and p_3 from (21c) and (19) or (19a). This is done in Table 4. There we show that Bortkiewicz's procedure yields one set of prices when we impose $\Sigma R_i = \Sigma S_i$ and another when we have $\Sigma M'_i = \Sigma Y_i$. We also give prices obtained by Marx's procedure. *These are all prices of production*, equilibrium prices around which day-to-day market prices will resolve. *Bortkiewicz prices are the ones that Marx's prices will converge to* when the iterative procedure suggests by Okishio, Morishima and Shaikh has been carried out. Note that our demonstration that $p_3 = 1$ when $\Sigma R_i = \Sigma S_i$ and $\Sigma R_i = p_3 Y_3$ is true for Bortkiewicz's prices and not for Marx's calculated prices.

We have discussed normalization rules and alternate identities in some detail. Usually normalization conditions are thought to be quite arbitrary and nothing much hinges on them. We hope to have solved the puzzle that Sweezy pointed out concerning the divergence between ΣY_i *and* $\Sigma M'_i$. We have also shown that $p_3 = 1$ is not necessarily a reasonable normalizing rule and that it automatically yields the profit–surplus value identity in Simple Reproduction where profits are spent on the luxury good. The importance of these rules is due to the fact that in analyzing real world events we shall be observing p_i and ρ. From such information, we shall have to infer about the Marxian parameters r and g_i. We shall then have to choose one of these two normalizations depending on which reveals more accurately the social relations underlying exchange. Applying the wrong rule will lead to wrong inference about the size of exploitation. These considerations become only more important when we admit accumulation, technical change, money hoarding etc.

Normalization rules thus share the dual character that we noted in the notion of abstract labour. There is here simultaneously an abstraction and a social process. The equality of total profits and total surplus value is a very basic condition. It implies that all profits come from surplus value alone. Profits here being defined in a broad sense including rent and interest. But there is also a converse implication. This is that surplus value goes to profit receivers alone. The latter statement crucially depends on wage being equal to the exchange value of labour power. But wages have in the developed capitalist countries departed considerably from exchange value of labour

TABLE 3
Bortkiewicz's Example (No Fixed Capital)

Dept.	C_i	V_i	S_i	Y_i	P_i	$p_1'C_i$	$p_2'V_i$	M_i	R_i	M_i'	$M_i'(p_3 \neq 1)$
I	225	90	60	375	408.3	288	96	384	96	480	420
II	100	120	80	300	285.2	128	128	256	64	320	280
III	50	90	60	200	181.5	64	96	160	40	200	175
Σ	375	300	200	875	875	480	320	800	200	1,000	875

TABLE 4
Prices as Derived by Marx and Bortkiewicz Procedures

	Marx Procedure $P_i/Y_i\{\Sigma R_i = \Sigma S_i\}$	Bortkiewicz Procedure $M_i'/Y_i\{\Sigma R_i = \Sigma S_i\}$	Bortkiewicz Procedure $M_i'/Y_i\{\Sigma Y_i = \Sigma M_i'\}$
I	1.089	1.28	1.12
II	0.951	1.07	0.936
III	0.907	1.00 (by assumption)	0.875

In curley brackets, we state the normalization identity which holds in each price calculation.

power *in fact*. But *in theory* as well, since all commodities sell at a price which departs from value, there is no reason why labour power should not do the same. This will create conceptual and historical difficulties but such difficulties have to be faced. We shall have to come back to this at a later stage but some brief note should be made of the problem here.

Money wage is the price per unit of labour power, thus belonging to the $P - Q - P$ circuit. Wage W is thus q_i price per unit of labour power. We can adopt the normalization that the corresponding price per unit of value contained in labour power $p_L = 1$. In early capitalism $q_L = p_L$ i.e. the labour value content of an hour of unskilled labour is unity. As accumulation and development take place, the labour content of average labour power rises so that q_L/p_L is now a multiple of its initial value. Alternately we may conceptually divide the wage into exchange value of labour power and an additional component. This additional component has then been clawed back from profits as a result of class struggle. Wages rise above subsistence level, not automatically due to technical progress and accumulation (these only make it possible for wages to rise) not out of charity on part of capitalists but due to strikes, unionization, political action etc. – manifestations of class struggle on part of workers. Thus while profits still come from surplus value not all surplus value may go to profits.

The other normalization rule – equality of total value and total price – is much more flexible, for here the role of the price system is to reshuffle all value into wages, profits and material costs.

Before we go on to Bortkiewicz's general solution, note that Bortkiewicz's correct solution *confirms* Marx's views that prices of production depart from values. It also in general agrees with Marx's finding that if $g_i \gtrless g$ than $p_i \gtrless 1$. The major change now is that we no longer look at g_i or g but the money equivalent $p_1 C_i/M_i$ – the share of material costs (or of value of fixed and circulating constant capital in general) in total costs (in total value of capital advanced). This ratio – call it pg – again tells us the same story $(pg)_i \gtrless pg \rightarrow p_i \gtrless 1$ as can be checked from Table 3 and 4. In terms of p_i being above or below 1, Marx's calculations and Bortkiewicz's (once $p_3 = 1$ has been dropped) agree with each other.

XI

BORTKIEWICZ'S SOLUTION: THE FIXED CAPITAL CASE

As we saw in Chapter IX, Marx originally posed the problem with the assumption of fixed capital, each sphere of production earning an equal rate of profit on all the capital advanced not only as a mark-up on the costs of production. In his first article, Bortkiewicz solved this problem in a general fashion though he did not implement it numerically. This article of Bortkiewicz anticipates much of the recent work on Marxian value theory. Bortkiewicz also puts into the centre of his attention the comparative merits of Ricardo and Marx regarding their theory of value and of profit. Bortkiewicz is indeed an early neo-Ricardian (or a late post-Ricardian perhaps). In this his work parallels closely and derives from Dimitriev's work as he himself acknowledges.[1] Dimitriev demonstrated that the criticisms of Ricardo's theory were ill-founded, and offered a rigourous mathematical derivation of Ricardo's theory of value. Dimitriev's treatment shows why Ricardians could not meet the criticisms of their opponents; the mathematical tools necessary for this purpose had not been discovered during much of the nineteenth century. Ricardo was not wrong but the way of proving him correct was not around until late nineteenth century.

We can say the same about Marx's theory. Bohm-Bawerk's critique, though a brilliant polemic, fails to appreciate the mathematical character of the problem. Bortkiewicz had the appropriate tools to solve the problem. Marx was not wrong, he made mistakes. He could not have got the right answer from the tools available to him.[2]

Bortkiewicz begins by reviewing Marx's solution of the transformation problem. In the notation we used in Chapter IX, he derives a version of the profit rate as

$$\Pi = r(1 - g^*)_1 = r \left[1 - \frac{tg}{tg + (1 - g)} \right] \tag{22}$$

From this he gets a version of our equation (17)

$$P_i = Y_i + (K_i + V_i)(t_i g_i - tg)r \tag{23}$$

He shows the contradiction involved in assuming input prices proportional to values but not output prices. He concludes the first part of his article by saying, 'He (Marx) made the mistake of carrying over certain magnitudes without attention from the table of values into that of prices. In transforming values into prices, it is inadmissible to exclude from the recalculation the constant and variable capital invested in the various spheres of production' (Bortkiewicz, 1906–07 p. 9).[3]

Bortkiewicz then goes on to show that 'the theory of equality of total value and total price' – equation (19) – is wrong. His arguments amount to saying that such an identity will very much depend on the good chosen as a measure of value. This has to some extent been already brought out above, that is, that choosing $p_3 = 1$ violates equation (19). Another way to show this is to see that (19a) is not dimension-free on both sides. If all prices were to double, that is, all q_i and hence all p_i, the left hand side of (19a) would double but the right hand side would not. The p_i in this sense should be homogenous of degree zero but are not. There is, however, an implicit normalization – wage equals exchange value of labour power – that one can use. This makes $q_L = p_L = W = 1$. Then all prices will be defined in wage units.

To begin with, Bortkiewicz assumes that constant capital is produced by direct labour alone. In input/output terms, this is assuming a triangular matrix. This assumption is already implicit in aggregating the economy into Departments. Thus each Department buys (in physical terms – see Figure 2) Q_1 and L – constant capital and labour. Output of Department II is used as an input only indirectly when workers purchase Q_2, though in the value measure C_i and V_i are entered as inputs directly. This triangularity assumption can be relaxed, though at the cost of making the formulae complicated.

VALUE EQUATIONS

Bortkiewicz begins by writing down value equations for each commodity. The units in which value is measured are kept quite general, that is, not necessarily in labour hours. Then

$$e_i = (1 + r) \, \overline{w}^{\,\backslash} l_i \tag{24}$$

e_i is the value per (physical) unit of commodity i, l_i is 'the number of units of labour e.g. labour days embodied in it', $\overline{w}$ the wages e.g. per working-day and r is of course the rate of surplus value. To begin with, (24) involves an assumption 'that only variable capital is engaged in this production'. If constant capital is used, l_i will represent 'the whole amount of labour employed in the production of the commodity concerned both directly and indirectly' (pp. 13–14).

Let us examine this definition carefully. l_i is total labour content per unit of the commodity. Since e_i can be measured in any units, let us say it is measured in labour hours. Then, since l_i is total labour, we get

$$e_i = l_i = (1 + r) \, \overline{w} l_i \tag{24a}$$

This then defines $\overline{w} = 1/(1 + r)$ and then (24) is consistent with our earlier definition of value process.

For n commodities, we have n equations of the form (24) but we have $(n + 2)$ unknowns e_i, r and $\overline{w}$. So we have a normalizing equation which chooses the commodity which serves as a measure of value – call it λ. Then

$$e_\lambda = 1. \tag{25}$$

Thus, in what we said above λ is labour – 'the industry' producing the use value (labour) – and – the commodity (labour power). The final equation is for the real wage assumed to be given. This real wage consists of proportions μ_i of all the n goods – some μ_i being zero, for example for Department I and Department III goods. We then have that the value of wage is

$$\Sigma \mu_i e_i = \overline{w} \tag{26}$$

Thus $\overline{w}$ is now clearly the exchange-value of labour power expressed in the units of the λ commodity.

Now we have $(n + 2)$ equations for an equal number of unknowns. Substituting (24) into (26) we solve for r. Thus

$$(1 + r)\overline{w}\, \Sigma\mu_i l_i = \overline{w} \qquad (27)$$

Now define $\Sigma_{|\mu_i|} l_i = U$. U clearly means the amount of labour embodied in the complex of goods forming the real wage. U is what Marx calls 'the necessary labour'. Then from (27) we have

$$r = (1 - U)\,/U \qquad (28)$$

Thus the definition of the rate of surplus value is consistent with our equations (4a) and (4b) as well as (5). To find $\overline{w}$, we take the λ industry and get

$$(1 + r)\, wl_\lambda = 1.$$

Thus

$$\overline{w} = U/l_\lambda \qquad (29)$$

Thus, in the numeraire industry, the value of the wage is decided. Value-ratios between commodities can be determined independently of $\overline{w}$ and r. Since given $e_\lambda = 1$, we have

$$e_i = l_i/l_\lambda \qquad i = 1, \ldots, n \qquad (30)$$

Thus exchange-values are determined by relative labour content.

Before we go on to prices, let us briefly check the equations (24) – (30) with Bortkiewicz's example in Table 3. In the value part of the table, labour hours are the units of measurement. Only three goods are produced and workers spend their wage on Department II good – Q_2. Thus by (26) we have

$$e_2 = l_2 = \overline{w}.$$

We do not in general know l_2 or $\overline{w}$. Given $r = 2/3$ we have U = 0.6. Now U = l_2 by definition. Hence $e_2 = l_2 = (1 + r)\,\overline{w}U$ and $\overline{w}$

$= U/l_\lambda$, λ being labour. Total value of wage goods consumed is Y_2 and total direct labour bought is $(S + V)$. So if l_i is total labour, we get $\overline{w} = Y_2/(1 + r)V = 1/(1 + r) = 0.6$. For Marx the wage rate was paid for the total length of working-day but the value equivalent of the wage rate was fewer hours than the working day, $\overline{w} < 1$. Since $\overline{w} < 1$ $l_\lambda = 1$ the labour content of labour power is one hour of labour.

PRICE EQUATIONS

Let q_i be the price per physical unit of the ith commodity. Bortkiewicz defines τ as the turnover period 'as starting with the moment when wages are paid and ending at the moment of the sale of the commodity to its final buyer'. To begin with, assume that wages are paid in one lump at a point of time. Then W is the money wage rate and ρ the profit rate

$$q_i = (1 + \rho)^{\tau i} \, Wl_i \tag{31}$$

Wl_i is wage bill per unit of output. Thus, while values are proportional to labour content l_i, prices are not unless τ_i is equal for all goods.

If wages are spread out over time periods $1, \ldots, m$, then we have

$$q_i = Wl_i \sum_{j=1} (1 + \rho)^{\tau_{ij}} \big/ \alpha_{ij} \tag{32}$$

$\Sigma \alpha_{ij} = 1$, α_{ij} being the proportion of wages paid in the jth time period.

The conversion of fixed capital into flow services and money costs of flow services embodied in q_i is then discussed by Bortkiewicz. He uses the standard neoclassical method of relating price of capital goods to the discounted sum of its future services. Thus let q_{kt} be the price of the capital good in year t after its construction. Then

$$q_{ko} = (1 + \rho)^{\tau_k} \, Wl_k \tag{33}$$

Then the cost of fixed capital in the tth year is

$$b_t = (1 + \rho)q_{k, t-1} - q_{kt} = \rho q_{k, t-1} - \Delta q_{k, t}. \qquad (34)$$

$\rho\, q_{k, t-1}$ is the 'interest charge' and Δq_{kt} is the capital gain.[4] If the capital good has length of life I, then we relate b_t to the portion of wages which can be apportioned to the tth.

$$b_t = Wl_k(1 + \rho)^{\tau_k + 1}\beta_i \qquad (34a)$$

$$\sum_{i=1}^{I} \beta_i = 1.$$

Marxian economists tend to be mistrustful of neoclassical calculation. Notice however that in the price domain it is entirely legitimate, indeed efficient, to use neoclassical calculus since that is the way capitalists calculate. (The equations above assume complete certainty but we cannot go into that problem now.) Thus if fixed capital is included we add b_t to the appropriate time period in calculating q_i. If the wages in constructing fixed capital are spread out, we get a complicated version of (33) as (32) is a complicated version of (31).

Bortkiewicz's aim in writing (32) and (33) separately was to make clear that variable capital and constant capital were similar in as much as the length of turnover (period of production) is involved. Fixed capital just has a longer period of production. This, he says, is an illustration of 'Ricardo's theorem that all differences between commodities with regard to the greater or smaller contribution made by fixed capital in their production can be traced back to differences in the length of their periods of production' (p. 20). The distinction constant/variable capital is therefore unnecessary, according to him.

Given in equations (32) we have $(n + 2)$ unknowns q_i, ρ and W. The α_{ij}, β_i and τ_{ij} are all known parameters. We again take a commodity as numeraire

$$q_\lambda = 1 \qquad (35)$$

and define money wage as

$$\sum \mu_i q_i = W. \qquad (36)$$

Equation (36) can be reduced again using (32) as before. We get

$$W \sum_i \mu_i l_i \sum_j (1 + \rho)^{r_{ij}} \alpha_{ij} = W.$$

This can be rearranged

$$W \sum_j (1 + \rho)^{r_j} u_j = W \tag{37}$$

where $u_j = \sum_i \mu_i l_i \alpha_{ij}$ and $\Sigma u_j = U$.

U is the same as before. Equation (37) is a polynomial in $(1 + \rho)$ and will have as many roots as the longest production period. The solution requires, according to Bortkiewicz, 'methods of higher algebra'. To determine W again we take the λth industry and

$$W l_\lambda \sum_j (1 + \rho)^{r_{\lambda j}} \alpha_{\lambda j} = 1. \tag{38}$$

We know ρ so we can solve for W.

Thus equations (24) – (26) solve for e_i, $\overline{w}$ and r and equations (32), (35) and (36) (plus the b_i for fixed capital) solve for q_i, W and ρ. Bortkiewicz does not use either equations (18) or (19) – total profits equal total surplus value W total value equals total price equations. The common link between the value and price domain is the commodity-complex which forms the real wage rate.[5]

Bortkiewicz develops a simpler expression for the relationship between ρ and r. If ρ is small, then we can approximate (37) by the first order terms of a Taylor series expansion. We get

$$q_i = W l_i \sum_j (1 + \rho \tau_{ij}) \alpha_{ij} \tag{39}$$

Define the weighted average of periods of production as

$$d_i = \sum_j \tau_{ij} \alpha_{ij} \tag{40}$$

Then

$$q_i = W l_i (1 + \rho d_i) \tag{41}$$

Since $q_\lambda = 1$, we get

$$1 = Wl_\lambda(1 + \rho d_\lambda); \text{ and} \tag{45}$$

$$q_i = \left[\frac{1 + \rho d_i}{1 + \rho d_\lambda}\right]\left(\frac{l_i}{l_\lambda}\right) = \left[\frac{(1 + \rho d_i)}{(1 + \rho d_\lambda)}\right] e_i$$

Recall that if e_i are labour values, we have

$$q_i/e_i = p_i \gtrless 1 \rightarrow d_i \gtrless d_\lambda \tag{46}$$

This is a similar result to Marx's about price value divergence, but we compare average periods of production of the ith commodity with the numeraire rather than g_i with average g for the economy. [Compare (45) and (46) with (17).]

If we then define δ as the average period of production for the commodity-complex forming the real wage, that is,

$$\delta = \Sigma u_i \tau_i/U, \text{ we get from (37),}$$
$$(1 + \rho\delta)U = 1. \tag{47}$$

or

$$\rho = \frac{(1 - U)}{U\delta} = \frac{r}{\delta} \tag{48}$$

Equation (48) is a fundamental expression for the relation between the rate of profit and the rate of surplus value. It is valid only for small values of ρ and is an approximation. We shall see in later chapters that this is an expression for what Morishima calls the 'Fundamental Marxian Theorem' proved independently by Okishio. Equation (48) can also be derived by noting that for λ industry

$$W = \frac{(1 + \rho\delta)}{(1 + \rho d_\lambda)} \; \overline{w} \tag{49}$$

and

$$Wl_\lambda(1 + \rho d_\lambda) = 1 \tag{50}$$

Since $\overline{w} = Ul_\lambda$ by (29), from (49) and (50) we get (48).

Bortkiewicz goes on to develop a comparison of Ricardo and Marx, demonstrating his preference for Ricardo. Before we follow that discussion, let us verify the price equations.

We again take the example of Table 3. Note first that by virtue of his model, Bortkiewicz clearly employed a different numeraire in value and price equations when he put $p_3 = 1$. Values are measured in labour and prices in gold. We shall see that putting $\Sigma Y_i = \Sigma p_i Y_i$ restores a common measure.

By equation (36)

$$W = q_2 = p_2 l_2$$

and

$$w = l_2 \text{ as we saw before.}$$

Thus

$$W/\overline{w} = p_2$$

Now the total money wage bill of the three Departments can only equal $M'_2 = p_2 Y_2 = p_2 l_2 Q_2$. WL is the total wage bill, then WL $= p_2 \overline{w} L = p_2 Y_2$. Here again $\overline{w} = Y_2/(1 + r)V = 1/(1 + r)$. Then money wage

$$W = P_2/(1 + r)$$

In a way by neglecting the physical circuit $P - Q - P$, Bortkiewicz does not provide information on q_i or l_i. We have only p_i and Y_i. In an input/output table, however, total labour supplied would appear as ΣL_i independently of the split between necessary and surplus labour. Thus the size of aggregate labour input is not measured by the value of the wage-good output. It is measured independently (it can be observed directly). We then compute the value of wage goods consumed to derive a measure of r. This is, of course, complicated if the wage exceeds the exchange-value of labour power. But value calculus is *ex post*; it is a device to lay bare the class-relation, not a predictive tool for behaviour of capitalists. It may be used for socialist planning but that is a different matter.

Of course the money wage is higher if $p_3 = 1$. Thus $M'_2 = £320$ in gold and $W = £320/500 = £0.64$ in gold. When $p_3 \neq 1$, $M'_2 = £280$ and $W = £0.56$. Now if $\Sigma M'_i$ is the total money supply, then the ratio of total money supply to total value produced defines the value of a unit of money – the general social labour it can command. Aggregating all Y_i means a unit of Y represents not a particular commodity but general social labour. Thus $M' = p_Y Y$ where $M' = \Sigma M'_i$ and $Y = \Sigma Y_i$. p_Y is then the price of production of general social labour. One unit of money 'commands' $1/p_Y$ units of social labour $-1/p_Y$ is the purchasing power of money. Thus gold money ($p_3 = 1$) has a lower purchasing power than is the case when $p_3 \neq 1$.[6]

The notion of price of social labour thus shows that if values are measured in labour $e_L = 1$, we need $p_Y = 1$. This is the significance of the condition $\Sigma Y_i = \Sigma M'_i$. This concept also enables one to keep 'accounts' in social labour units. Thus a Department advanced M_i/p_Y units of labour and recovers M'_i/p_Y units of labour. Thus $(M'_i - M_i)/p_Y$ is a measure of 'real' profit in terms of social labour. This is again an example of how equal exchange in the price domain is unequal exchange in the value domain.

MARX AND RICARDO

At various points in his article Bortkiewicz examines Ricardo's theory, especially in view of Marx's criticism of Ricardo in Part II of Theories of Surplus Value. We shall now look at these criticisms.

Bortkiewicz considers equation (48) to be the correct expression of the relationship between ρ and r and an indication of Ricardo's theory of the antagonism between wages and profit. Marx's formula, such as equation (22) he considers erroneous. The method of comparing individual and average organic composition of a capital is an error, 'a consequence of the fallacious method which he used for the transformation of values into prices. Ricardo, contrary to Marx, saw the relationship quite plain' (p. 27).

Ricardo was not interested so much in price-value divergence equation (46), which Marx accused him of ignoring, but the effect of changing ρ on p_i. The divergence between prices and values arises as soon as $\rho \neq 0$. This is the way Ricardo saw the problem. Marx arrived at price-value divergence in the course of examining the way in which unequal individual rates of profit are equalized by competition. Ricardo, on the other hand, starts with equal rates of profit as an empirical and theoretical datum. Ricardo, according to Bortkiewicz, was aware of the price-value divergence; he failed only to keep distinct the question of price-value divergence (ρ non zero) from that of variation in the divergence when the profit rate changes.

Marx criticized Ricardo for taking the rate of profit as given rather than showing its necessity and determining its size. Marx tried to show the necessity by value calculation. But the real wage definition, such as equation (37), will yield the rate of profit. Marx, however, according to Bortkiewicz tried 'to reduce the rate of profit to a certain mathematical expression' but as equation (37) is a high order polynomial 'it is quite impossible to represent the rate of profit (ρ) as an explicit function of these magnitudes on which it depends' (p. 37). It is only when one approximates (37) as in (48) that we get a simple expression such as Marx looked for.

Another important strand of difference is revealed by a comparison of (48) and (22). For Ricardo, profit rate is influenced by the rate of surplus value and the conditions of production in the wage-goods industries, and those which provide inputs to them. What Sraffa calls non-basic industries, for example Department III, enter nowwhere into it. For Marx's calculation of the average rate of profit, all surplus value produced by basic or non-basic industries enters into determining the profit rate. The particular use-value produced by the industry is irrelevant for Marx. This parallels the different definitions of productive labour employed by Marx as against Adam Smith and Ricardo.

If (48) is correct, then non-basic industry cannot determine the profit rate.

If it is indeed true that the level of rate of profit in no way depends on the conditions of production of those goods which do not enter into real wages, then the origin of profit must be clearly sought in the wage-relationships and not in the ability of capital to increase production. For if this ability were relevant here, then it would be inexplicable why certain spheres of production should become irrelevant for the question of the rate of profit (p. 33).

According to Bortkiewicz, when Ricardo spoke of the inverse relationship between wages and profits, he meant by wages 'neither money wages, nor real wages but the amount of labour which is needed to produce the complex of goods forming real wages. In Marxist phraseology, this is the (absolute) value of labour power' (pp. 34/35). Thus δ is a proxy for the value of labour power. If δ rises, the value of labour power rises and vice versa.

Let us consider the problem of non-basic industries and their role in formation of profit. Marx incontestably made errors in calculating the prices of production. There is, however, the problem of realization of value, which is always ignored by Ricardo, as Malthus tried unsuccessfully to point out. Values that are produced have to be realized. Markets have to be cleared. We said in Chapter VII that the Simple and Extended Reproduction Schemes were constructed by Marx to study the conditions under which all markets will be cleared – all value realized. If the non-basic industries do not sell their products, then value and surplus value cannot be realized in the economy. If the non-basic industry does not exist, as can be seen from Table 3, markets have to be found for 50 units of C and 90 units of V (their physical equivalent) either in accumulation or in international trade. We shall come up with this problem again in Part III. An equation such as (31) or (32) implicitly assumes that all that is produced is sold. If we define ξ_i as the proportion of sales to output in the ith industry, it is obvious that $\xi_i = 1$ is assumed in (31) and (32) for all i. This is also true of price equations (20a)–(20c) in Chapter X. Though the realization problem is not explicitly raised, its solution is implicit in the Simple Reproduction Scheme and Department III is necessary to realize values. Equilibrium relations will fail to hold otherwise.[7]

We postpone Bortkiewicz's consideration of the Falling Rate of Profit and technical change to a later chapter. We conclude with the one positive evaluation of Marx amongst all his criticisms that Bortkiewicz had.

If, however, there is any generally significant point on which Marx is to some extent superior to Ricardo, then it is the theory of the Origin of Profit *(p. 51)*.

He goes on to explain this superiority further:

For, in trying to make clear the origin of profit, Marx had the lucky inspiration to construct a model in which profit exists, without any norm other than the (original) law of value being decisive for the relationship in which products are exchanged for each other. Such a model made it obvious that profit could neither have its first cause in the mark-ups which were a phenomenon in an exchange economy, nor needed to be regarded as a counterpart of the productive services of capital. In other words, by making value-calculation precede price-calculation, Marx succeeded – much more sharply and emphatically than Ricardo had done – in determining the theory of withholding (that is, exploitation) against other theories of profit and in shaking off any common feature [*p. 52, interpolation in square brackets ours*].

Thus seventy years ago, Bortkiewicz provided a general solution of the price-value problem, dealing with fixed capital and long periods of production. He derived a fundamental expression for the relation between profit rate and exploitation and provided a Ricardian critique of Marx. At the same time, he put Marx's value-price calculation on a sound basis against attacks of economists such as Bohm-Bawerk. We have dealt in some detail with his contribution, for, apart from historical priority, he puts succinctly points which are still confused in many debates.

XII

ALTERNATIVE APPROACHES TO THE TRANSFORMATION PROBLEM

Debates on the Transformation Problem are still going on more than eighty years after the publication of the third volume of *Capital* and seventy years after Bortkiewicz's answer. The misunderstanding caused by Böhm-Bawerk has stimulated some of it. He asserted that price-value divergence was a contradiction in the Marxian value theory and that the theory that surplus value was the origin of profit fell due to this divergence. He gave the impression of an anomaly in Marx's work, left perhaps unrepaired due to its incomplete nature.

Today, when we have available *Theories of Surplus Value* (*TSV*) as well as earlier works, it is plain to see that Marx was completely aware of the value-price divergence and thought that the obscuring of value relations was due to this divergence. His criticism of Ricardo in Part II of *TSV*, and his use of price-value divergence in the chapters on Rent in Part VI of *Capital* Vol. III, give the clear impression that price-value divergence is part and parcel of the behaviour of prices in a capitalist system.

This has of course been partly indicated by Bortkiewicz. Marx made the error of confusing value and price calculus. But the theory of profits as arising from surplus value is on solid grounds, as Bortkiewicz shows. Thus the price value divergence does not invalidate the Marxian theory. The rate of profit and prices can be shown to be systematically determined, that is to be functions of the rate of exploitation, rates of turnover and the organic composition of capital. What is more, as we shall see below, Bortkiewicz's derivation of equation (48) linking ρ to r has recently been proved by Okishio, Morishima and Wolfstetter. This theorem, called the Fundamental Marxian Theorem by Morishima, states that a positive rate of exploitation is a necessary and sufficient condition for a positive rate of profit.

Yet the controversy persists. In this chapter we shall outline many of the strands in the controversy. The best way to guide oneself through these debates is to review the nature of the three circuits of capital and their associated three dualities. Recall from our Chapter VII and Figure 2, the following:

(1) Money Capital Circuit – $M - M' - M$: prices q_i, money revenue, profits, costs and wages.

(2) Commodity Capital Circuit– $C' - C - C'$: Values – Y_i, V_i and C_i; parameters g_i and r.

(3) Productive (Physical) Capital Circuit – $P - Q - P$: Heterogeneous products Q_i, Labour L_i.

Now we get an Output-Value duality by linking (2) and (3). The $P - Q - P$ circuit can help compute l_i; it also has information on τ_i in an ideal situation. We can go from (3) to (2). Only (3) and (1) are directly observable, so we have to go from the observable to the unobservable. In Bortkiewicz's value calculus we used l_i. We get a Price-Value duality by linking (1) and (2). This, however, gives us not q_i but p_i. We have no knowledge of q_i unless we get information on l_i from (3). But in Marx-Bortkiewicz examples of Tables 1 to 4, we calculate p_i and ρ given g_i and r then M_i, M'_i follow. The third duality is the Output-Price duality. This goes from (3) to (1). This is a link between two observable circuits. Here the explanation of prices and profits does not involve r and g_i causally or in the mathematical manipulations. We get as our answers q_i and ρ.

Many economists have therefore felt that one of the three is redundant, and the attack has mainly focused on the value calculation. The detour from the observable physical data in the $P - Q - P$ circuit to the $C' - C - C'$ circuit only to arrive at $M - M' - M$ is thought to involve one calculation too many. Why not go directly from (3) to (1)?

One technical problem that strengthens this argument is the link between value and price. As we saw in Chapter XI, a given real wage with given commodity-composition that the worker purchases is what links prices and values. Marx had used equation (18) and equation (19), but if we move from π to ρ, we have only one of them as a link. Now in most modern discussions both (18) and (19) are ignored. Given a commodity-complex that serves as a real wage, the link is immediately established. The real wage can be specified either as a wage in value terms ($\overline{w}$) or in money terms (W). The physical data contain W and L_i. Without, therefore, making what to some is an 'arbitrary' or redundant distinction between necessary and surplus labour, we can go from $P - Q - P$ to $M - M' - M$.

The issue at stake, however, is not the quickest way to solve for prices – q_i in terms of input output coefficients and unit labour costs or p_i in terms of r and g_i. The detour through the unobservable value circuit was for Marx a way of locating the origin of profit in surplus value – in exploitation of one class by another. The exploitation of profit in the output-price duality is in terms of technical productivity – the ability of the economy to produce economic surplus. Marx, on the other hand, started with the notion that the natural conditions had to be such that the product of a day's labour – *in all modes of production* – yielded a surplus above subsistence requirements to reproduce labour power, that is return to work another day. (I/7).

Once natural conditions had established the limits, the interesting questions to him were the size of the actual product, its distribution and reproduction. The latter aspects take place in context of different social relations in all modes of production. The main concern was the way social relations were designed to legitimize the seizure of surplus produced by labour (in co-operation with Nature) by a class rather than by the whole society. In capitalism, it was the ownership of conditions of labour (and also of Nature via ownership of land) and the commodity form of wage labour that gave the surplus a value form and legitimized via exchange as profits. Thus for Marx it is as a theory of the origin, distribution and reproduction of profits that the value calculus is important.

Two opposing strands of criticism have converged in the rejection of value calculus. The modern economic tradition (the neoclassical school is a rather inappropriate name for it for various reasons) traces the origin of profit in its intertemporal aspect through either the saving behaviour of individuals and the related concept of time preference, or the productivity of capital-intensive (or roundabout, that is, time consuming) methods of production or a synthesis of both. This is at one and the same time a theory of profit (or interest) as an abstract economic category and a theory of profit as the source of income of a class of people. The fact that one can have the abstract categories, for example the social rate of time preference or the productivity of capital for society as a whole, without having profit as an income of a class of people is never clearly recognized. Indeed there is often deliberate confusion created by justifying income of owners of capital from the productivity of capital.

The other strand is what is called in the UK the Neo-Ricardian one. (This is again an inadequate appelation but it has now gained some circulation.) This strand, it may be recognized, is politically sympathetic to Marx and the task he set himself of developing a critique of political economy. It regards value-calculus as an obstacle, a shibboleth, a millstone round the neck of the socialist political movement. [Such, political aspects cannot be ignored in Marxian economics.] It accepts that the origin of profit is in expropriation of surplus product but regards the value calculus as irrelevant. As we saw in Bortkiewicz's discussion, the profit-wage antagonism can be derived from Ricardo's theory of prices and profit. The crucial element is then the determinants of the real wage rate (or indeed the money wage rate since prices are solved as part of the theory).

The doubts about value-calculus cannot, therefore, be dismissed any longer in crude terms of bourgeois ideology or narrow self-interest. Many who were leading exponents of Marxian economics in the past forty years, such as Maurice Dobb, Ronald Meek and Joan Robinson, among others, agree with the Neo-Ricardian position. The catalyst for this debate of course has been Piero Sraffa's *Production of Commodities by Means of Commodities*. We shall therefore have to look closely at Sraffa's book.

In this chapter we shall conduct the discussion without employing any matrix algebra. We shall also ignore fixed capital. In the next chapter, when we take up the issue of fixed capital (joint-production), matrix algebra will be indispensable, though as far as possible nonmathematical explanations will be given.

SAMUELSON

We first take up Samuelson's critique of the Transformation Problem. Samuelson first wrote on Marx in 1957 and then again in 1971 and 1974. Samuelson has sought to establish two propositions.

i. that except for 'rude' economies, the non proportionality of values and prices can be trivially established. For example, a comparison of Bortkiewicz's equation (24) and (31) or the approximation in (45) shows the importance of the compounding of profit rate ρ in calculating prices.
ii. that the value calculus is redundant since prices and profit rate can be derived directly and related to a given (subsistence) wage rate.

Samuelson's example in his 1957 article is summarized below in Table 5. We have two commodities (or Departments). Samuelson directly identifies variable capital with wage bill expressed as $W.L_i$. Similarly constant capital is identified with the money cost of the capital good input. We then have an input-output table.

Here we see that the entries in Samuelson's input-output table are from the money circuit. Q_{ij} is the amount of Q_i used by

TABLE 5

Samuelson's Tableau

Dept.	I	II	Final Demand	Total Gross Output
I	p_1Q_{11}	q_1Q_{12}	0	$q_1Q_1 = M'_1$
II	0	0	q_2Q_2	$q_2Q_2 = M'_2$
Wages	WL_1	WL_2		
Interest	$\rho(WL_1 + q_1Q_{11})$	$\rho(WL_2 + q_1Q_{12})$	—	—
Total Costs	M'_1	M'_2	—	—

Department j, q_i is the price per unit of Q_i and so on. Notice, however, that since interest on profits is included in total costs, the column sum is the same as the row sum M'_i. Since the Tableau is one of Simple Reproduction in money terms we get the implicit balancing condition

$$q_2Q_2 = W(L_1 + L_2) + \rho(WL + M'_1)$$

Thus $W(L_1 + L_2)$ is called variable capital, directly equating value and money categories. Marx's notion of variable capital was designed to split total labour input into a necessary component (equal to $Y_2 = l_2Q_2$) and surplus labour $(L - l_2Q_2)$.

To solve for prices q_i Samuelson derives the implicit technological information in the Tableau above. Thus define

$$Q_{ij}/Q_j = \alpha_{ij} \tag{51a}$$

$$L_j/Q_j = \alpha_{oj} \tag{51b}$$

α_{ij} and α_{oj} are technical (input-output) coefficients. The technology or $P - Q - P$ circuit is then described by Samuelson as

$$\alpha_{01}Q_1 + \alpha_{02}Q_2 = L \tag{52a}$$

$$\alpha_{11}Q_1 + \alpha_{12}Q_2 = Q_1 \tag{52b}$$

(In general, strict equating of the two sides of the equation is not necessary. It is sufficient that the left hand side is less than or equal to the right hand side.) Now we can solve for q_i in terms of α_{ij} and α_{oj}, W and ρ. The solutions are then provided by relating price to unit cost. These are equations similar to Bortkiewicz's equations (20a) – (20c) above.

$$q_i = (\alpha_{oi}W + \alpha_{1i}q_1)(1 + \rho) \ i = 1, 2. \tag{53}$$

Thus, we get

$$\frac{q_1}{W} = \frac{\alpha_{ol}(1 + \rho)}{[1 - (1 + \rho)\alpha_{11}]} \tag{53a}$$

$$\frac{q_2}{W} = \frac{\alpha_{02}(1 + \rho)[1 - \alpha_{11}(1 + \rho)] + \alpha_{01}'(1 + \rho)\alpha_{12}(1 + \rho)}{[1 - (1 + \rho)\alpha_{11}]} \quad (53b)$$

Thus q_i are solved in terms of $P - Q - P$ circuit. Note that the two crucial unknowns ρ and W are assumed to be given. If the real wage is given 'from outside', then the l.h.s. of (53b), which is the reciprocal of the real wage, will help solve for the profit rate in much the same way that Bortkiewicz's equation (37) did.

Given a real wage rate, one can also link the $P - Q - P$ circuit to $C' - C'$ circuit as we show very simply here. Department I produces one unit of Q_1 from inputs of α_{11} units of Q_1 and α_{01} units of labour. Thus α_{01} units of labour give $(1 - \alpha_{11})$ net output. A unit of Q_1 then requires (embodies) $\alpha_{01}/(1 - \alpha_{11})$ units of labour. This is the direct and indirect labour content of a unit of Q_1. For Q_2 we have α_{02} units of labour and α_{12} units of Q_1, the latter then embody $(\alpha_{12}\alpha_{01})/(1 - \alpha_{11})$ units of labour. So Q_2 has $[\alpha_{02}(1 - \alpha_{11}) + \alpha_{12}\alpha_{01}]/(1 - \alpha_{11})$ units of labour embodied in it. Thus

$$l_1 = \alpha_{01}/(1 - \alpha_{11}) \quad (54a)$$

$$l_2 = [\alpha_{02}(1 - \alpha_{11}) + \alpha_{12}\alpha_{01}]/(1 - \alpha_{11}) \quad (54b)$$

Given (54a) and (54b) we can compute the $C' - C'$ circuit. W will buy W/q_2 units of Q_2 whose labour value is $(Wl_2)/q_2$ or W/p_2. Thus

$$r = (1 - W/p_2)/(W/p_2)$$

is the measure of the rate of exploitation. So given the definitions above we say that if $1 > W/p_2$ there is exploitation. Let us explore this further. We have

$$q_2 - Wl_2 = q_2 - \frac{W[\alpha_{02}(1 - \alpha_{11}) + \alpha_{12}\alpha_{01}]}{(1 - \alpha_{11})} \quad (55)$$

We require $q_2 > Wl_2$ if $r > 0$. Notice, however, from the definition of q_2/W in (53b) that $q_2 = Wl_2$ if and only if $\rho = 0$. Thus

$r = 0$ if $\rho = 0$. [Indeed, the converse is known as Fundamental Marxian theorem. If the labour content of the goods that the hourly wage rate buys is less than an hour of labour than r is positive. A positive r is necessary and sufficient for a positive ρ.] The equivalence of the three circuits can thus be established using the given wage rate. We can go from one to the other. It also illustrates that the same data which to a neoclassical economist involves one theory of profit can be *transformed* to illustrate Marx's theory. Different structural explanations reduce to the same data. Econometrics has made us aware of the notion of identifiability. We have here a reason for the perpetual debate, since the original model is under-identified. Different structures are reconcilable to the same *phenomena*. Such under-identifiability is of course inherent in the notion of fetishism.

This under-identification can be illustrated using the chart of the three circuits of capital (see Figure 3). (We have already used this device before, so no further explanation will be given here.)

In Figure 3, we have made explicit that the capitalist in Department I buys physical inputs Labour (L_1) and machines (Q_{11}). The price involved in these transactions is indicated on each connecting line. Now (L_1, Q_{11}) is exactly again what the capitalist regards as Productive Capital. He does not perceive the goings on in the left-hand box in Figure 3. This is the split of L between paid labour (V_1) and surplus labour (S_1). The entire system of social relations is required to accomplish that split. No individual capitalist, *by himself*, can do this. [The exploitation of Man Friday by Robinson Crusoe is based on cruder weapons of power and not the market place.] So the capitalist sees the

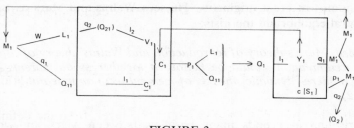

FIGURE 3

money and the productive capital circuit

$$M - P - Q - M' - M - P$$

The gap between the use value of L and its exchange value is then obscured. The link between $P - Q$ and $M - P$ can then be rationalized in terms of prices of inputs being proportional to marginal products and so on. Nor does the capitalist compare output Q in terms of labour values and notice the gap between C' (Y) and C which equals surplus value in Marx's theory. Thus the right-hand box in Figure 3 is also invisible.

MORISHIMA

In his book *Marx's Economics: A Dual Theory of Value and Growth*, Morishima has dealt with various aspects of Marx's theory. He notably deals with the transformation problem in Simple Reproduction but also in its dynamic context. He derives the conditions for which Marx's formula for rate of profit (π) is valid for ρ and also the conditions under which aggregation of industries into Departments is valid. He then goes on to consider Marx's theory of accumulation and crisis and the general validity of Marx's value theory when fixed capital is present in the production process. Here we shall consider the transformation problem and the rate of profit. We shall leave the joint production problem until the next chapter and consider accumulation in the next part.

Morishima attempts to show that modern mathematical tools can be used to formulate Marx's theories rigorously and that such an attempt would confirm Marx's status as an outstanding economist of great originality. He sees Walras and Marx as two general equilibrium theorists:

Indeed, Marx's theory of reproduction and Walras' theory of capital accumulation should be honoured together as the parents of the modern dynamic theory of general economic equilibrium (p. 2).

Morishima also finds many parallels between Marx and von Neumann, as we shall see later.

Morishima views Marx from the point of view of modern economic theory and wishes to re-integrate Marx into modern economics. He does, however, view Marx with great sympathy and attempts to construct a rigorous foundation for value theory. Though Morishima makes no reference to Dimitriev or Bortkiewicz, we shall find much similarity among their arguments.

Morishima begins by carefully distinguishing between value as crystals of abstract human labour and value as determined by social necessary labour time required for the production of a commodity. (Philosophically minded readers may see here that the distinction is between 'substance of value and magnitude of value'. Morishima, however, treats both as magnitudes and proves their equivalence.) Let us say, following Morishima, that corn is produced using seed (corn) and compost as well as labour. Then as before let α_{ij} be proportions required of physical input per unit of physical output. Then values as crystals of abstract labour are given as

$$l_1 = \alpha_{11}l_1 + \alpha_{21}l_2 + \alpha_{01} \qquad (56)$$

$\alpha_{11}l_1$ being labour embodied in corn input, etc. This formula is familiar from our discussions above such as in equation (54a).

The other definition is the input-output one. This says that to produce one unit of net output of corn, we must produce Q_1 units of corn employing α_{01} units of labour per unit and Q_2 units of compost employing α_{02} units of labour. Then

$$X_1 = Q_1\alpha_{01} + Q_2\alpha_{02} \qquad (57)$$

In Samuelson's case only Q_1 is material input. Then both (56) and (57) lead to (54a), since to produce one net unit of machine we have to produce $1/(1 - \alpha_{11})$ units of gross output of machines.

Morishima then shows that X_1 and l_1 can be shown to be equivalent where we have no fixed capital, identical production processes for all commodities, only one method of production per industry (no choice of techniques problem) and only labour as nonproduced factor of production. We shall not go into the proof here but other illustrations will follow when we discuss Sraffa's model.

An important additional assumption is that the capital goods industry is *productive*. This means that in producing capital goods there is overall net positive output in the system. Thus if corn requires corn and compost as in (57) and compost requires again corn and compost, then with one unit of corn and compost each as total input, we must get positive output of either corn or compost or both. Marx took this to be an obvious fact, though he specifically mentioned productivity of labour in subsistence goods being such that some part of the labour force can be left to produce other things. Note that in Simple Reproduction tableaux we have zero net output of Department I good as all that is produced is used up as inputs. We have, however, either positive net output of Department II in a two-Department Scheme, such as in (1) where $Y_2 = S + V$, or the positive net output of Department III in a three-Department Scheme. Now the condition of productiveness says that Department I must not consume all of its output as inputs (that is, $Y_1 > C_1$ if we measure things in value terms). This is a harmless condition but we shall see that in joint production this will be strictly required. If capital goods industries are not productive, then values can be negative. This is easily demonstrated in Samuelson's example, since non-productiveness means $\alpha_{11} > 1$ giving $l_i \leq 0$ by equation (54a).

The stress here is on capital goods industries only because, as in the $P - Q - P$ circuit, we start with physical inputs only. The fact that labour consumes wage goods, and that in buying L_i the capitalist is really advancing V_i, can be ignored. Both Department I and Department II goods are produced with Department I machines and labour as inputs. Department II goods are not *direct* inputs.

The condition of productiveness can also be written as its dual the condition of profitability. The average cost of producing a unit of Q_i is

$$ac_i = \sum_j \alpha_{ij} q_j + Wl\alpha_{0i}$$

Then profitability means

$$q_i > ac_i \tag{58}$$

Now since W is positive (or non-negative), we get for Department I

$$q_1 > \sum_j \alpha_{ij} q_j \tag{59}$$

Check that for Samuelson's case, this again comes out as $1 > \alpha_{11}$.

Morishima obtains an expression for the rate of exploitation. This formula has already been anticipated in our equation (5) and the expression derived by Bortkiewicz in equation (28) above. Morishima, like Bortkiewicz, takes the proportions of various goods by the worker with his real wage as given and then compares the value embodied in that composite basket with the required amount of labour performed to earn the real wage. He also shows the equivalence of our equations (4a) and (4b). There are, however, no new concepts involved here, though Morishima proves the equivalence in a general model.

The important contribution of Okishio in proving the Fundamental Marxian Theorem is then surveyed by Morishima. We have also encountered this above, so our expositions here can be short. The condition of profitability says as in (58)

$$q_i > ac_i = \Sigma\alpha_{ij}q_j + Wl\alpha_{Oi}$$

Take industry 1 in Samuelson's example

$$q_1 > ac_1 = \alpha_{11}q_1 + W\alpha_{01} \tag{58a}$$

Now we know already that productiveness requires $(1 - \alpha_{11}) > 0$. The question, then, is how low must wage be to allow profit. We have then

$$q_1 > \frac{'\alpha_{01}}{(1 - \alpha_{11})}\,W \tag{60}$$

In terms of value, since $l_1 = \alpha_{01}/(1 - \alpha_{11})$ and $q_1 = p_1 l_1$, this says $W < p_1$ is the condition. Thus the average for an hour's work cannot buy back what the labourer has contributed to the product. We have also seen in (55) above that $W < p_2$. Thus profitability is generated by and requires a positive rate of exploitation.

Like Bortkiewicz, Morishima and Okishio consider the level of real wage and its implication in terms of a positive rate of exploitation as the bridge between the value and the price system. Morishima does, however, bring out the importance of the length of the working day in determining r.

So the problem of determining the rate of exploitation is reduced to the problem of determining the length of the working day. When the worker's position is very weak, the working day will be prolonged as much as possible and the rate of exploitation will be maximised at $\bar{e}$ the rate corresponding to $\omega = 1/\bar{T}$ (ω is the real wage rate per hour of a working day T hours in length, $\bar{T}$ being the maximum length in Morishima's notation) [Morishima (1973) p. 55].

We should add that the fundamental expression for the rate of profit obtained by Bortkiewicz, equation (48) above, gives a succinct summary of the Okishio theorem. It shows that if $r = 0$, $\rho = 0$ and $\rho > 0$ if and only if $r > 0$. If no capital goods are used in the production of wage goods directly or indirectly, then $\delta = 1$ in equation (48) and $r = \rho$. In all other cases $\rho < r$ except when both are zero.

Morishima also examines the question as of the conditions under which $\rho = \pi$. He finds four alternate sets of conditions under which $\rho = \pi$ but only deems the last one satisfactory. These are

(a) $r = 0$ and therefore $\pi = \rho = 0$

(b) All the industries have identical organic composition of capital $g_i = g$. We know then that all $p_i = 1$. This gives identical production periods in all industries. Then $d_i = d = \delta$ in Bortkiewicz's notation (see equations 45 and 48).

(c) A third condition proposed by Samuelson in JEL (1971) is to have the real wage be made up in such a way that $\mu_i \neq o$ for any i as long as the good i is used as an input. Further, every industry uses the material inputs in the same proportion as the aggregate economy. (We shall see how Sraffa uses a similar criterion to arrive at his notion of the Standard Commodity.) For these conditions $\pi = \rho$ but it should be noted that Marx would never have assumed that the real wage consists of use-values which are constant capital as well as those which are consumption goods. (Only corn, in a one-good Ricardian economy is a constant capital as well as the wage-good.) Nor are wage goods direct inputs as we saw from Samuelson's Tableau above. This set of conditions is thus irrelevant.

(d) The last set of conditions is derived by Morishima where aggregate C and V are measured from individual C_i and V_i but the weights used are not actual output proportions, ω^*_2 in *equation (19a), but balanced growth proportion of output along what is called the 'Golden Age' path. This is an optimal growth path where all profits are invested and all wages consumed. We shall return to this in the section on accumulation. Note, however, that Marx's way of calculating profit rate can be 'legitimated' only under very unrealistic conditions. It is better to recognize that price-value divergence being given $\pi \neq \rho$ except by accident.*

SRAFFA

Sraffa does not address his book specifically to questions raised by Marx but the concerns of his short essay are entirely classical. To begin with, he wishes to establish price determination independently of marginalist consideration. Marginalist theory requires changes in demand and/or supply conditions: changes in income or in tastes, in scale or technology, and so on. Sraffa begins by examining an economy that reproduces itself at the same level year after year without any change. No change has occurred or is expected to occur. The notion of a demand schedule is thus irrelevant: nobody has ever encountered a price set other than the prevailing one. Similarly, for supply schedule there is no marginal cost curve, as output has never changed nor is the price ever expected to alter. Thus if one wishes to think in terms of demand supply diagram, we are dealing with a single point in the price-quantity diagram in case of one commodity. In case of two commodities again there is but a point and not a production possibility curve. This is illustrated in Figures 4 and 5.

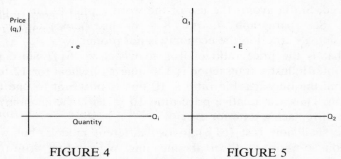

FIGURE 4   FIGURE 5

The Sraffa economy in one and two commodity space

Point e is all we observe. It is *not* the point at which demand and supply curves intersect, as there are no such curves. Point E is similarly the output combination produced with given 'endowments of resources'. There is no other combination.

It is extremely important to understand these notions as Sraffa's argument has frequently been confused by neoclassical economists with irrelevant considerations of constant returns to scale or fixed coefficients – no substitutions, etc. Scale never changes in the economy; hence we do not know whether we have Increasing Constant or Diminishing Returns to scale. 'Factor' prices (or any prices) never change so the question of substitution never arises. We do not know the isoquant but only a point; hence, the slope of the isoquant is a nonexistent category.

The notion of reproduction of the economy used by Marx in his Simple Reproduction Scheme is of course originally Quesnay's. Sraffa first takes up an economy with no surplus. We call this Sraffa Economy with No Surplus (SENS).

We have an economy producing 20 tons of iron and 400 quarts of wheat. The economy is arranged as follows.

$$\left.\begin{array}{c} 280 \text{ quarts of wheat and } 12 \text{ tons of iron produce} \\ 400 \text{ quarts of wheat} \\ 120 \text{ quarts of wheat and } 8 \text{ tons of iron produce} \\ 20 \text{ tons of wheat} \end{array}\right\}(61)$$

This is a productive capital circuit in Marx's terms. Labour is not mentioned as an input to begin with. The economy produces what it consumes as inputs. There is no obvious distinction made at this stage between capital good and consumer good. (Indeed, Sraffa avoids the use of the word capital as far as possible. See paragraph 7, pp. 8–9 in his book.) Thus by Morishima's criterion the economy is not productive.

What is the price ratio of iron to wheat in (61)? Since the only inter-industry transaction is 120 quarts of wheat for 12 tons of iron, the only feasible ratio is 10 quarts of wheat to one ton of iron. Thus at a relative price ratio 10 qr. : 1 t. the economy is in a self-replacing state for ever.

We shall now cast (61) into two different models, but with caution, so as not to distort the meaning. We can first write (61) as an input-output table *but without reducing all entries to pro-*

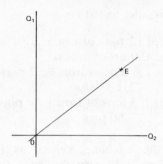

FIGURE 6
The Sraffa Economy: A Wrong Description

portions. That is, we cannot legitimately speak in SENS of α_{ij} but only if Q_{ij}. This sounds trivial, since $\alpha_{ij} = Q_{ij}/Q_j$ and division is 'neutral'. But the neutral mathematical operation changes the economic interpretation by introducing the notion of being able to operate the economy at any scale. What this means is that using α_{ij} rather than Q_{ij} interprets Figure 5 not as a point in the two-commodity space but a *point on a line* connecting E with the origin as in Figure 6. Along the line OE, output proportions are constant but quantities can be anything.

This is not the interpretation of (61) according to Sraffa. With that caution Table 6 renders (61) as an Input Output table. We have zero final demand and total output is total input.

It is easy to check that at price 10 qr. 1 t. there is no profit in the system. Following Bortkiewicz's value equations, we may use wheat values or iron values in (61) or labour values as we shall show later. In all terms the profit rate is zero.

Sraffa generalizes the concept of SENS by giving an example of a 'three-good economy and then giving it a mathematical formulation. The three goods are iron and wheat, as before, and

TABLE 6

Sens as an input output table

	Wheat	Iron	Final Demand	Total Output
Wheat	280	120	0	400
Iron	12	8	0	20

pigs. The tableau parallel to (61) is

$$
\left.
\begin{array}{c}
\text{240 qr. of wheat + 12 tons of iron + 18 pigs produce} \\
\text{450 qr. of wheat} \\
\text{90 qr. of wheat + 6 tons of iron + 12 pigs produce} \\
\text{21t. of iron} \\
\text{120 qr. of wheat + 3 tons of iron + 30 pigs produce} \\
\text{60 pigs}
\end{array}
\right\}
\quad (62)
$$

Sraffa then gives the 'exchange-values' as 10qr. of wheat = 1 ton of iron = 2 pigs. It is easy to check that in any unit of account – wheat, iron or pigs – there are zero profits, that is, no surplus. Then Sraffa's general model for SENS is

$$\sum_j Q_{ji} q_j = Q_i q_i \qquad i = 1, \ldots n \qquad (63)$$

We have further

$$\sum_j Q_{ij} = Q_i \qquad i = 1, \ldots n \qquad (64)$$

Q_{ji} is the amount of j commodity used by industry producing i. q_i are called 'the values of units of commodities ... which if adopted restore the initial position' (p. 4). Then, Sraffa adds, 'one commodity is taken as standard of value and its price made equal to unity'. This is reminiscent of Bortkiewicz's equation (25) or (35). Thus, although Sraffa calls q_i (p_i in his notation) values and prices interchangeably, they are not l_i or p_i but q_i price per unit of a commodity in terms of a chosen numeraire.

Sraffa's concern in his book is to establish the determination of q_i and a profit rate ρ independently of use of aggregating schemes such as labour values (C' – C' circuit) or money prices (M' – M' circuit). This is the classical problem of the invariant measure of value which Adam Smith and Ricardo failed to solve satisfactorily. When Sraffa moves to an economy with surplus (SES), he makes it clear that once surplus emerges the requirement of an equal rate of profit in all industries makes prices and profits interdependent. He does not, however, choose a subsistence wage rate to solve for the profit rate as Bortkiewicz has done. Sraffa establishes the wage profit antagonism *independently* of the assumption of a subsistence real wage.

SRAFFA ECONOMY WITH SURPLUS (SES)

In an economy with surplus a common rate of profit is earned by all activities. Hence we have instead of (63), the following

$$(1 + \rho) \sum Q_{ji}q_j = Q_iq_i \qquad (65)$$

Instead of (64) we have

$$\sum_j Q_{ij} \leq Q_i \qquad (66)$$

An example of SES is given by Sraffa as follows

$$\left.\begin{array}{l} 280 \text{ qr. of wheat} + 12 \text{ tons of iron} \rightarrow 575 \text{ qr. of wheat} \\ 120 \text{ qr. of wheat} + 8 \text{ tons of iron} \rightarrow 20 \text{ t. of iron.} \end{array}\right\} \quad (67)$$

Thus iron is produced in just enough amount of replace inputs but there is 175 qr. of wheat surplus. There is an equilibrium exchange rate of 15 qr. = 1 ton and $\rho = 0.25$. This can be checked by substituting the price in terms of wheat or iron.

Note that, although (67) like (61) and (62) does not mention labour inputs, Sraffa includes them in his general model. Wages are however not advanced and hence profit is earned only on the 'value' of means of production advanced and not on the wage bill as well. [Morishima distinguishes this case as the Walras–von Neumann case, whereas Morishima calls the case we have dealt with up to now the Marx–von Neumann case.] We have thus in place of (65)

$$(1 + \rho) \sum_j Q_{ji}q_j + WL_i = Q_iq_i \qquad (68)$$

$$\sum_i L_i = 1 \qquad (69)$$

and then net national income is also normalized equal to unity

$$\sum_i q_i [Q_i - \sum_j Q_{ij}] = 1. \qquad (70)$$

and of course

$$\sum_i Q_{ij} \leq Q_i \qquad (66)$$

The normalization of labour and of net national income to sum to unity – equation (66) and equation (70) – is of course for convenience.

Sraffa mentions the possibility that once surplus appears wages need not be subsistence but 'may include a share of the surplus product'. It would be better, he says, to split wages into a subsistence portion that would enter the same way as material inputs and earn a profit and a surplus portion that would be variable. He says, however, that he will 'refrain in this book from tampering with the traditional wage concept and shall follow the usual practice of treating the whole of the wage as variable'. One major consequence of this choice is that *wage goods producing industries are then non-basic and their condition of production does not affect the profit rate*. Recall that for Bortkiewicz the relation of the profit rate to the labour content of the real wage was the basic message of Ricardo's theory of profits. In what follows, we shall follow Sraffa's practice.

Sraffa is not concerned with the disposal of the surplus nor with the realization problem. His aim is to discuss the interdependence of the wage rate and the profit rate. Now (68) and (69) can be written as

$$q_i(Q_i - (1 + \rho)Q_{ii}) - (1 + \rho)\sum_{i \neq j} Q_{ij}q_j - WL_i = 0 \qquad (71)$$

Equation (70) and (71) are $(n + 1)$ equations in $(n + 2)$ unknowns q_i, W and ρ. Sraffa then defines the concept of *standard commodity*. His aim is to obtain a measure of the value of means of production which is invariant to the wage-profit division. When the wage rate is unity, all surplus goes to labour; when it is zero it all goes to profit. As the wage rate changes, different prices will change according to the intensity of labour use relative to means of production. It is then utopian to obtain a 'capital-labour ratio' measure independent of prices and wages.

Now rather than measure means of production–labour ratio, Sraffa says one can either have a common measure in terms of labour input or in terms of value of net product to means of production. Now this is again a measure that is a function of prices and hence may differ across industries. But when wages are zero, the common rate of profit in all industries – the maximum rate of profit $\hat{\rho}$ – is also the ratio of value of net product to means of production in all industries. Every industry and all its inputs have the same ratio – it recurs in all industries. This is the balancing ratio which if an industry or a complex of industries use, their prices are invariant to wage changes. Note that $\hat{\rho}$ is the same whatever the actual wage rate and however it changes.

Such a balanced commodity with the balanced ratio of net product to means of production is called the standard commodity. We can only briefly describe it here. The standard composite commodity consists of a combination of all the basic industries in such a way that the ratio of outputs of all individual commodities comprising the standard is the same as the ratio in which they are used in the aggregate as inputs. Thus for basic commodities i = 1, . . . m, we have

$$\frac{Q_i}{\sum\limits_{j=1}^{m} Q_{ij}} = \frac{Q_\kappa}{\sum\limits_{j} Q_{kj}} \quad \text{for all i k } \epsilon \text{ m} \qquad (72)$$

It is best to look at the example Sraffa provides of a Standard System. The actual System consists of three commodities all of which are basic produced in the following amounts

$$
\left.
\begin{array}{l}
90 \text{ t. iron} + 120 \text{ t. coal} + \ 60 \text{ qr. wheat} + 3/16 \text{ labour} \rightarrow 180 \text{ t. iron} \\
50 \text{ t. ,, } + 125 \text{ t. ,, } + 150 \text{ qr. ,, } + 5/16 \text{ ,, } \rightarrow 450 \text{ t. coal} \\
40 \text{ t. ,, } + \ 40 \text{ t. ,, } + 200 \text{ qr. ,, } + 8/16 \text{ ,, } \rightarrow 480 \text{ qr. wheat}
\end{array}
\right\} \quad (73)
$$

Total 180 t.   285 t.   410 qr.   1

Note that in (73), unlike (61), (62) and (67), the wheat input is not the wage fund but material input. There is surplus in the system of 165 t. of coal and 70 gr. of wheat which by definition (70) will form national income. Now Sraffa reduces (73) to a Standard System as follows

$$
\left.
\begin{array}{l}
90 \text{ t. iron} + 120 \text{ t. coal} + \ 60 \text{ qr. wheat} + \ 3/16 \text{ labour} \rightarrow 180 \text{ t. iron} \\
30 \text{ t. ,, } + \ 75 \text{ t. ,, } + \ 90 \text{ qr. ,, } + \ 3/16 \text{ ,, } \rightarrow 270 \text{ t. coal} \\
30 \text{ t. ,, } + \ 30 \text{ t. ,, } + 150 \text{ qr. ,, } + \ 6/16 \text{ ,, } \rightarrow 360 \text{ qr. wheat}
\end{array}
\right\} \quad (74)
$$

150 t.   225 t.   300 qr.   12/16

The proportion of outputs (180:270:360) is the same as that in which they are used as inputs in the aggregate (150:225:300) or 2:3:4. If the whole labour force is to be employed we can scale the system up 4/3 and we shall be left with national income of 40 t. of iron, 60 t. of coal and 80 qr. of wheat. This will be standard national income or standard net product. (Note that components are not weighted by prices to get a scaler measure of net product; it is a vector.)

The profit rate in (74) is 20 per cent, for we can arrange the system by row or columns. This ratio of net product to means of production is then the standard ratio. Sraffa adds,

> *The possibility of speaking of a ratio between two collections of miscellaneous commodities without need of reducing them to the common measure of price arises from the circumstance that both collections are made up in the same proportions – from their being in fact quantities of the same composite commodity (p. 21).*

Now since the standard net product is invariant to price variation, its division between wages and profit is also independent of price variation. Each share must, however, consist of the standard commodity. [This is similar to Samuelson's condition for establishing $\pi = \rho$ that we discussed in context of Morishima's four sets of conditions under which $\pi = \rho$ see above p. 106.] If $\hat{\rho}$ was 20 per cent but the share of wages in the standard commodity 75 per cent then $\rho = 5$ per cent. We get therefore the wage–profit relations

$$\rho = \hat{\rho}(1 - \overline{W}) \tag{75}$$

$\overline{W}$ is the share of wages in the standard product, ρ the actual rate profit and $\hat{\rho}$ the maximum rate of profit. The wage–profit relation is linear.

The wage and its share are *estimated* in the standard commodity but need not be actually *paid* in it. This does not affect (75). Since the standard commodity is a difficult concept to grasp, let us construct an example from (67) above, which consists of only two commodities.

All inputs are material inputs. We already know that $\rho = 0.25$ per cent, and since wages do not figure in (67) $\hat{\rho} = 0.25$ per cent. This gives us the clue for constructing a standard system:

since iron output is 20, we should like total input of iron to be 16, leaving net product of 25 per cent. This is done by multiplying the iron equation by 1 and the wheat equation by 2/3. We then get

$$\left.\begin{array}{l} 8\text{ t. iron } + 120\text{ qr. wheat } \rightarrow \ \ 20\text{ t. iron} \\ 8\text{ t. iron } + 184\text{ qr. wheat } \rightarrow 380\text{ qr. wheat} \end{array}\right\} \qquad (76)$$

$$\overline{16\text{ t.}\qquad\qquad 304\text{ qr.}}$$

The numbers have again been rounded for ease of calculation. Now suppose the share of wages is 60 per cent; hence we expect $\rho = 10$ per cent. The wage can be estimated as 60 per cent of the standard commodity. But in actually paying the wage, the workers need not receive tons of iron. Thus after wage payment what is left would not be in the same proportion as the standard commodity. But the *value* of what is left will be 10 per cent of the total *value* of means of production, the values being calculated using equilibrium prices. For actual payment we go back to (67). The surplus is 175 qr. of wheat, and 60 per cent of that is 105 qr. Profits are 70 qr. Now prices must be such that 70 qr. should be 10 per cent of the value of the means of production. Now Sraffa found equilibrium prices for (67) to 15 qr. = 1 t. It is easy to check that the means of production in (67), 20 t. and 400 qr., equal 700 qr. at that price ratio.

Thus contrary to Samuelson's condition for $\rho = \pi$, the wage is calculated in the standard commodity but can be paid in any commodity that is in actual surplus. The purpose of calculating share in standard commodity is to be able to use the relationship (75), which derives the relation between profit *rate* and wage *share*. [A relationship between profit rate and wage share has also been derived by R.M. Goodwin (1967).]

Sraffa's concern is then to define the rate of profit in such a way that it is independent of wages and prices. The maximum rate of profit has such a property, which then leads through the concept of the standard commodity to the very powerful relationship in (75). Sraffa is not primarily concerned with the *origin* of profits, but the antagonistic relationship between the profit rate and the wage share makes it abundantly clear that in his view, profit rate is a deduction from the wage share. The wage rate or share is not, however, decided within the system. This becomes an exogenous variable given from outside the production system such as (67). Thus wage rate is not tied to subsistence and put into the production system. It is left to be decided by social forces. This last statement, one must add, is the extension of the logic implicit in Sraffa's model. Sraffa himself does not say anything about the matter except that wages are paid from surplus.

The Sraffa system is then very close to the classical system. It is also quite a modern treatment of it. Thus the standard commodity obviates the need for a single invariant measure of value. But surplus is defined in modern terms of national income, that is, output less material inputs. Since the wage is outside the material production system, concepts such as variable capital and rate of surplus value are totally avoided. The production system generates a surplus whose maximum value is calculated by setting $W = 0$ in pricing equation (71). The productivity of the system is thus due to technology (on the interpretation of wage rate adopted). Once the maximum surplus is obtained, then a struggle for shares between labour and capital can be read into the Sraffa model as determining the actual profit rate. The actual profit rate is not therefore determined by productivity (marginal or otherwise) of capital: only the maximum profit rate is conditioned by technology.

MARX, BORTKIEWICZ AND SRAFFA

There has been much controversy surrounding neo-Ricardian and Marxian theories in recent years. The controversy has often been couched in terms of political strategy for working class movements as is suitable in debates about Marxian economics. We shall try, however, to delimit our discussion to developing the common ground and isolating the difference where it is crucial.

Let us first take Sraffa and Bortkiewicz. Bortkiewicz derives equation (48), which he sees as a Basic Ricardian Theorem and a statement of the exploitation theory of wages. We recall the equations (48) and (70):

$$\rho = r/\delta \qquad (48)$$

$$\rho = \hat{\rho}(1 - \overline{W}) \qquad (70)$$

δ relates to conditions of production in the wage goods industries: it is the weighted period of production in those industries which directly or indirectly contribute to the production of wage goods. Thus an improvement in productivity in wage-goods industry or in those machine-goods which contribute inputs will lead to a decline in δ and rise in ρ, *for given r*.

Now Sraffa's equation involves neither r nor δ. This is however entirely due to the definition of wage adopted by Sraffa. As we noted, Sraffa does not take wage to be subsistence plus a variable depending on share of surplus. In a way he sets subsistence to be zero. (This is what defines $\hat{\rho}$.) Thus wage-goods become non-basic. Once subsistence wage is put at zero, one cannot use the real wage as a link to bridge the rate of surplus value and the rate of profit as Bortkiewicz and Morishima do. Such a link is totally snapped by Sraffa's choice of the wage concept (as he himself makes clear. See op. cit. para 8 pp. 9–10). As we have said above, Sraffa's concept is in line with current material income accounting practice and avoids a subsistence wage concept.

In Marxian terms we are dealing here with the circuit of productive capital $P - Q - P$ and eventually money capital when q_i are calculated. But the problem of $(n + 2)$ unknowns in $(n + 1)$ equations (70) and (71) leaves one degree of freedom: either ρ or $\overline{W}$ must come from outside. Sraffa defines $\hat{\rho}$ in terms of standard commodity invariant to all sets of solutions of q_i and then takes $\overline{W}$ as exogenous.

Now it is not too difficult to show that if we reinterpret Sraffa's $\overline{W}$ as the surplus above subsistence, and consider subsistence wage to be part of the input in the productive system, we get answers very similar to Bortkiewicz's. The remaining difference then between Marx and Sraffa will be that between Marx and Bortkiewicz in terms of whether non-basic industries contribute to the formulation of the profit rate ρ or not. In what follows we shall demonstrate this contention. We shall recast Sraffa's example into Marxian value circuit. We shall have for this reason to make some assumption as to what part of material input is wages and we need further a subsistence wage level to make numbers manageable. But any non-zero subsistence wage would give similar results.

(a) SENS: We can start by noticing in (61) that it is

reasonable to take it that wheat is not a material input into making of iron; it then must be the wage fund. In the wheat industry itself we take it that out of 280 qr. of wheat input 40 are used as seed (constant capital) and 240 as wage fund. Assume, then, a wage rate of 6 qr. We then get Table 7. Note that 20 workers produce a net output of 12 tons of iron, which gives $l_1 = 1.66$. Using this, we can calculate that 40 work years of direct labour plus 20 contained in 12 tons of iron input give 360 qr. of wheat. Thus $l_2 = 0.166$. This then enables us to calculate the value circuit. Note that constant capital used up exceeds output of iron industry because wheat functions as its own constant capital as well as the wage good. There is no surplus and hence no surplus value $r = 0$ and $\rho = 0$.

(b) SES: Let us now take system (67). Once again assume that the subsistence wage rate is 6 qr. Since material inputs are unchanged between (61) and (67), we take the same labour force as in Table 7. We then get Table 8.

Given the same input configuration we see that the value of wheat has fallen. We have already seen that in Sraffa's system wheat price declined from 10 qr. to 15 qr. per ton of iron. Now Table 8 shows surplus and Table 7 does not. While they are not meant to be pictures of the same economy before and after emergence of surplus, let us use them as such for pedagogic purposes.

The subsistence wage rate has not changed in physical quantity, but has fallen in value from 0.160 to 0.1125 2/3rd of its former value. Given the value l_2 in SENS, it took a full working year to produce the subsistence wage of 6 qr. $(6 \times 0.166 = 1)$. Now it takes one $67\frac{1}{2}$ per cent of the working year to produce the wage. Thus $32\frac{1}{2}$ per cent is surplus value in the working day. This is reflected in the value magnitudes. There is now a rate of surplus value of 48 per cent.

The increasing productivity in the wage good industry, which has somehow occurred, is not passed on to the workers if wage remains at subsistence. We can, however, immediately define the maximum wage rate which will give wage share $\overline{W} = 1$ and $\rho = 0$ in Sraffa's equation (70). This is given by the reciprocal of l_2W or about 9 qr. (8.9 exactly). Thus as the wage goes from 6 to 9 or as the surplus component of wage goes from 0 to 3, ρ goes from $\hat{\rho}$ ($= 0.25$) to zero.

The reinterpretation of the wage concept can thus narrow the

TABLE 7

SENS as Circuits of Productive and Commodity Capital

	Iron	Wheat	Final demand	Total output	l_i	C_i	V_i	Y_i
Iron	12	8	0	20	1.66	13.3	20	33.3
Wheat	0	40	360	400	0.166	26.6	40	66.6
Labour	20	40	—					
Σ						39.9	60	99.9

TABLE 8

SES as Circuits of Productive and Commodity Capital

	Iron	Wheat	Final	Total	l_i	C_i	V_i	S_i	Y_i
Iron	12	8	0	20	1.66	13.33	13.45	6.55	33.3
Wheat	0	40	535	575	0.1121	24.48	26.90	13.08	64.46
Labour	20	40							
						37.81	40.35	19.63	97.79

differences between the interpretations. In Bortkiewicz's terms, in equations (31) or (32) the wage bill has fallen, since q_2 is now lower. This can be also checked in equation (36) since with one wage good the price of 6 qr. of wheat is the money wage. We can then say that Bortkiewicz's equation (48) is really in terms of $\hat{\rho}$ in Sraffa's terms. It tells us what the relationship between $\hat{\rho}$, r and δ is when a subsistence wage enters into the costs in the same way that material costs do. Sraffa's equation (70) then takes the story a step further and relates ρ to $\hat{\rho}$. We must therefore interpret the Marx–Bortkiewicz system as defining subsistence wage equal to exchange value of labour power and deriving the consequent $\hat{\rho}$ and the associated p_i and q_i. Sraffa's system then gives us a relation between ρ and $\hat{\rho}$ as a function of how far above exchange value of labour power actual wages have gone or how high the share of wage in surplus is.

There are various problems still left. As we said above, we do not nowadays separate wage bill into subsistence and surplus. To make such a distinction, one will have to calculate l_i from the physical data. What is more, some part of the worker's actual consumption will have to be thought of as subsistence and another as surplus. We shall look at the empirical problem of doing so in a later section. Notice, however, that national income statisticians are always calculating such a 'subsistence basket'. The whole concept of the cost of living index is based on a basket of goods, periodically updated as any subsistence concept should be. We therefore have readily available an approximation of the split between subsistence and surplus in actual wages.

Notice also that as accumulation takes place and if technical change occurs, $\hat{\rho}$ will change. A falling rate of profit, as we shall see below, relates to $\hat{\rho}$ and not so much to ρ. (Of course, if ρ is falling due to a rising share of workers, a high $\hat{\rho}$ is no consolation to the capitalists!) What is more, for a given $\hat{\rho}$, as wage share changes and ρ declines, capitalists may react to such changes. Certain processes will become less profitable than others, and this in turn will lead to a change in the production system change. The problem of choice of process and that of fixed capital or joint production is especially difficult, as we shall see in the next chapter.

XIII

THE PROBLEM OF JOINT PRODUCTION

A very basic criticism of Marx's formulation of the Labour Theory of Value has been levelled in recent years. Such criticism has come from Steedman and from Morishima. Though they both point to problems with value calculations, there are substantial differences in the content of their attacks. The discussion of this topic cannot avoid mathematics, but we shall use as simple a formulation as possible. Those who have the necessary mathematical equipment are referred to the original sources in Steedman (1975) (1976), Wolfstetter (1973) (1976), and Morishima (1974) (1976).

We have already referred in the previous chapter to the concept of *Joint Production*. This concept can be explained in two related ways. First, suppose there is no fixed capital. All constant capital is fully used up within the production period. In such a setup, we may have production processes that produce two commodities jointly. Well-known examples, such as mutton and wool, and beef and hide, can be given here. Second, but much more general, is the case where fixed capital is used in production, along with circulating capital (fuel, raw material) and labour. At the end of the production period, the fuel and the raw material have been combined with hours of labour input to produce output – the particular commodity (use value) that the process produces. But at the same time, only the wear and tear of the fixed capital has entered the value of the commodity. We are left with the fixed capital, slightly worn and one period older.

Now, von Neumann in formulating his model proposed the brilliant device of treating the process as having two outputs – the use value commonly thought of as output and the older fixed capital. Thus in virtually every production process that uses durable capital goods, there is joint production of goods and capital goods, of new goods and old goods.

The case of joint production with fixed capital is formally identical to the case without fixed capital. We shall use the words joint products and joint production for both these cases. Joint production has several important consequences for traditional input/output analysis as well as for Marx's formulation. First notice that once durable capital is used every producer has a choice of using old or new durable capital in producing output. Imagine that there is a machine with a maximum length of life of ten years. Then different producers will have a choice of producing the commodity with the help of labour and a new machine, or with a one-year-old machine or a two-year-old machine, and so on. Thus for producing each commodity there will be many *processes* available. In general, therefore, the number of processes will exceed the number of products. Of course, if there are joint products then some products are produced by a small number of processes. For example two products, like wool and mutton, may be produced by one process.

At any point of time not all processes will be in use. Thus a maximum length of life of a ten-year-old machine is a *technical*, not an *economic*, datum. Only those techniques which make at least the going rate of profit will be used. Many will be less efficient; then their price will cover less than costs plus profit at the going rate.

The superior productivity of some processes and, by implication, the inferior profitability of the other processes are expressed in terms of *inequalities* rather than in equations. In equations analogous to equations (52), (57) or (63) we now introduce inequalities. Recall, for example, inequalities (58) or (60). In *equilibrium*, the processes actually employed will be those which exactly yield the going rate of profit or exactly yield a certain rate of physical surplus over inputs.

Last, joint production raises a minor difficulty in that now industries cannot be simply grouped into consumer goods industries and capital good ones. Every industry will produce new goods and old goods. Old goods are most likely to be capital goods. New goods can be either consumer goods or capital goods. We now distinguish between commodities and industries. A commodity can be produced by many industries and an industry may produce many commodities.

Joint production in terms of survival of old units of capital was obvious to Marx, who lived in the factory stage of production and observed the economic reality around him. The middle third of *Capital* Vol. II is given up to the problem of turnover of capital, and the issue crops up in TSV as well. It is one thing, however, to notice that a part of the fixed capital is passed on in the final output and a larger part survives. Such an observation does not constitute a *theory* of joint production. Marx was concerned with the problem caused in the $M - C - C' - M'$ circuit by the presence of fixed capital. Thus if a part of M was spent buying a piece of durable machinery, the output of use value C′ will include only a part of M and selling it will give $M' < M$, since the producer still has the machinery left. If he were to sell the old machinery along with C′, and add the money to sales revenue from selling C′, then M′ may recover M plus profit. *Conceptually*, the same result would be achieved if he were to rent the machinery and M included only the rental. Selling C′ plus the old machinery or renting the machinery will *in equilibrium* lead to identical results. When, however, the capitalist cannot sell C′ or cannot sell his old machinery at its present value (in the accounting sense), or if he wishes to switch to making a different use value and needs to dispose of old machinery suddenly, or, again, when there is a technical development devaluing the old machinery, that is, out of equilibrium, such neat symmetry breaks down. The renting calculus is the Fisherian neoclassical theory of investment and the selling of old machine is the von Neumann theory. Neither of these tells us much about an economy out of equilibrium.

Morishima has taken the view that while Marx chose the neoclassical accounting method whereby M included the rental on machinery, he should have chosen the von Neumann accounting. For the purposes of equilibrium configurations such as the schemes of simple and extended reproduction or in the solution of the transformation problem, we believe the choice does not much matter. But this is a contentious matter which we must look at again.

NEGATIVE AND POSITIVE VALUES

With joint production, we are in the circuit of production capital $P - Q - P$, where we consider physical outputs and inputs. The transformation from physical quantities to labour values is then made analogous to the way in which we demonstrated with the Samuelson and Sraffa models in the previous chapter. However, we have to be careful in this case, because some processes may not be feasible: they may be of such low productivity that they are unlikely to be in actual economic use. This is the role of the inequalities: they tell us at a given set of prices (themselves solved within the system) which processes would be profitable and which not. In his definition of labour values, Marx's use of the concept of socially necessary labour requires that we consider only the most efficient techniques.

In a way the profitability rule (or the requirement that only a socially necessary amount of labour should be used) gives us a criterion for what processes do not survive – that is, for determining the economic life of old capital. Frequently, however, models in which the techniques in use or the oldest capital goods surviving are taken as data are constructed. Such is the case in Sraffa's treatment of joint production. In such cases, curious and anomalous results can easily be produced.

One such case is that of negative values. This anomaly for the case of joint products was noticed at the outset when the theory of linear economic activities was constructed in the 1940s. This is a case where, given a certain set of input coefficients, only negative values are feasible for certain goods.

Let us treat joint production formally now so that we can illustrate such anomalies as well as introduce the reader to the general idea. To repeat, only a sketch of the joint production theory is given here and the mathematics are kept simple. We shall assume that the concepts of matrix and vector are known.

We label outputs as Q and price per unit of physical output as q. Q and q will be vectors. The vector of net outputs or final demand will comprise the same physical commodities as Q but we label them F. Each process of production will be represented by x_i and the vector x will stand for processes or activities using one unit of labour. A process will describe the outputs of each commodity produced and inputs used using one unit of labour.

This will then be called the unit intensity of the process. The process can be used at any intensity (zero or positive) and constant returns to scale are assumed so that any multiple of x_i will produce the same multiple of outputs using the same multiple of inputs.

In input/output analysis of the type we discussed in the previous chapter, each commodity is produced by only one process (industry). Hence the number of commodities Q and number of processes X are identical and output coefficient of each process (industry) is assumed to be unity. Thus the output matrix is the unit matrix I. In joint production, this is no longer the case. Not only is Q number of commodities different from the number of processes, but the output coefficients are non-zero for more than one commodity. Thus the output matrix B is usually a rectangular matrix, as is the input matrix A. This is so because every process has more than one output. The best way to begin a formal presentation of joint production is to take the case where there is no joint production. Each good is produced by one industry and one process. We have already seen in the previous chapter an example of the input/output matrix in Table 5 and the subsequent discussion. This two-Department example can be generalized as follows:

$$\begin{bmatrix} I_1 & 0 \\ 0 & I_2 \end{bmatrix} \begin{pmatrix} Q_1 \\ Q_2 \end{pmatrix} = \begin{pmatrix} A_1 & A_2 \\ 0 & 0 \end{pmatrix} \begin{pmatrix} Q_1 \\ Q_2 \end{pmatrix} + \begin{pmatrix} F_1 \\ F_2 \end{pmatrix} \qquad (77)$$

Q_1 are Department 1 goods and Q_2 are Department 2 goods. Q_i are vectors. I_1 and I_2 are unit matrices with 1 on the diagonal and zero elsewhere. If there are N_1 goods in Q_1 and N_2 goods in Q_2, I_1 is $N_1 \times N_1$ and I_2 is $N_2 \times N_2$. A_i are the input coefficient matrices. Notice that, as in Table 5, Q_2 goods are not direct inputs. F_1 and F_2 are vectors of final demand; they have the same physical form as Q_1 and Q_2. Typically F_1 may be a zero vector.

From the point of view of inputs, we can present an analogue of Table 7 but transposed so as to present material and labour inputs.

$$\begin{pmatrix} Q_1 \\ Q_2 \end{pmatrix} \begin{bmatrix} I_1 & 0 \\ 0 & I_2 \end{bmatrix} = \begin{pmatrix} A_1 & 0 \\ A_2 & 0 \end{pmatrix} \begin{pmatrix} Q_1 \\ Q_2 \end{pmatrix} + \begin{pmatrix} L_1 \\ L_2 \end{pmatrix} \qquad (78)$$

Now Morishima's formula for labour values presented in equation (56) can be written as

$$\begin{pmatrix} l_1 \\ l_2 \end{pmatrix} = \begin{bmatrix} A_1 & 0 \\ A_2 & 0 \end{bmatrix} \begin{pmatrix} l_1 \\ l_2 \end{pmatrix} + \begin{pmatrix} L_1 \\ L_2 \end{pmatrix} \tag{79}$$

l_i are vectors of labour values, each $n_i \times 1$. A_1 and A_2 are as before. Equation (79) enables us to solve for labour values l_1 and l_2 as we did in the case of Samuelson's example in equations (54a) and (54b). The answer for (79) is

$$l_1 = L_1(I - A_1)^{-1} \tag{80a}$$

$$l_2 = L_1(I - A_1)^{-1}A_2 + L_2 \tag{80b}$$

Equations (80a) and (80b) are then general expressions for many goods, whereas (54a) and (54b) are for one good each. Also analogous to (58) and (58a), we can develop price inequalities

$$p_1 > p_1 A_1 + w L_1 \tag{81a}$$

$$p_2 > p_1 A_2 + w L_2 \tag{81b}$$

In joint production, we get quantity inequalities and price inequalities. Although it is difficult to maintain the distinction between Department 1 goods and Department 2 goods, it may be useful to do so. Typically, we think of consumer goods industries as producing old capital goods as byproducts but not vice versa. We write

$$\begin{bmatrix} B_{11} & B_{12} \\ 0 & B_{22} \end{bmatrix} x \geqslant \begin{bmatrix} A_1 & A_2 \\ 0 & 0 \end{bmatrix} x + \begin{pmatrix} F_1 \\ F_2 \end{pmatrix} \tag{82}$$

B_{11} is the output coefficient matrix of capital goods produced by capital goods producing processes x using inputs A_1x. B_{12} is the output matrix of capital goods produced by consumer goods producing processes and B_{22} is the output matrix for consumer goods produced by consumer goods producing processes.

The presentation in (82) is not fully rigorous but is given to provide a parallel to (77). B_{ij} matrix will typically have one on the diagonal but the off diagonal elements will not be zero. There may be only n goods but many more processes. Hence B would be not a square matrix but a rectangular matrix.

Total inputs into the system is Ax (all capital good inputs). Total output of capital goods is a combination of B_{11} and B_{12} producing processes. Hence we can call it B_1x. A concise representation of (82) is

$$B_1x \geqslant Ax + F_1 \tag{83a}$$

$$B_2x \geqslant F_2 \tag{83b}$$

We have to add that processes can be either inactive ($x_i = 0$) or actively in use ($x_i > 0$). Thus we add

$$x_i \geqslant 0 \tag{83c}$$

Values can be measured in joint production by the appropriate dual inequalities

$$B'1 \leqslant A'1 + L \tag{84}$$

where 1 is a vector of values, L is a vector of labour inputs and the prime denotes transpose.

In input/output analysis, once we are given the final demand vector F_1 we can use (77) to compute what outputs will be produced. In joint production, we need a criterion to weed out inefficient processes. In equilibrium only those processes will be used which maximize profits or minimize labour input for a given vector of final demand or maximize the value of output. Thus the objective function may be that for a given vector (F_1, F_2) we minimize total labour input. The labour assigned to each process x_i we denote L_i. This will determine the intensity of the process, the scale at which it is used. We have then

$$\text{Minimize } Lx \text{ subject to (83a), (83b) and (83c)} \tag{85}$$

Alternatively we may say

$$\left.\begin{array}{c} \text{Maximize } F'1 \\[6pt] \text{subject to (84) and } 1 \geqslant 0. \end{array}\right\} \tag{86}$$

The inequalities $x \geqslant 0$ and $1 \geqslant 0$ match. Thus only those processes will be used which produce positive values.

We can now illustrate joint production with two numerical examples. We take a case of two goods and two processes so our B matrix will be square, though it need not be so. We shall show how if inequalities such as (83a) and (83b) or (84) are treated as equations or if the inequality (83c) is neglected, peculiar results may emerge. We shall therefore implicitly assume that both goods are direct inputs in both processes.

The first example is then as follows. The first process x_1 takes one unit each of Q_1, Q_2 and labour to produce 1.8 units of Q_1 and 0.6 units of Q_2. Thus the *net* output of Q_1 is 0.8 and *net* input of Q_2 is 0.4. The second process x_2 uses the same inputs but produces 0.6 of Q_1 and 1.3 of Q_2. Thus we have for values similar to (84)

$$\begin{bmatrix} 1.8 & 0.6 \\ 0.6 & 1.3 \end{bmatrix} \begin{pmatrix} l_1 \\ l_2 \end{pmatrix} \leqslant \begin{bmatrix} 1 & 1 \\ 1 & 1 \end{bmatrix} \begin{pmatrix} l_1 \\ l_2 \end{pmatrix} + \begin{pmatrix} 1 \\ 1 \end{pmatrix} \tag{87}$$

For the second example, we retain the same input coefficients but alter the output coefficients for x_1. Now x_1 produces 1.5 Q_1 and 0.4 of Q_2 and x_2 produces 0.6 of Q_1 and 1.3 of Q_2 as before. We have for the value inequalities

$$\begin{bmatrix} 1.5 & 0.4 \\ 0.6 & 1.3 \end{bmatrix} \begin{pmatrix} l_1 \\ l_2 \end{pmatrix} \leqslant \begin{bmatrix} 1 & 1 \\ 1 & 1 \end{bmatrix} \begin{pmatrix} l_1 \\ l_2 \end{pmatrix} + \begin{pmatrix} 1 \\ 1 \end{pmatrix} \tag{88}$$

Now we ignore the inequalities and assume that both processes are used at hint intensity. The equations (87) will give

$$\left.\begin{array}{c} 0.8\ \lambda_1 = 0.4\ \lambda_2 + 1 \\[6pt] 0.3\ \lambda_2 = 0.4\ \lambda_1 + 1 \end{array}\right\} \tag{87a}$$

We can then see that the solution of (87a) is $\lambda_1 = 8.75$, $\lambda_x = 15.0$.
Both values are positive. But (88) gives

$$\left.\begin{array}{l} 0.5\ \lambda_1 = 0.6\ \lambda_2 + 1 \\[2mm] 0.3\ \lambda_2 = 0.4\ \lambda_1 + 1 \end{array}\right\} \qquad\qquad (88a)$$

This set of equations gives $\lambda_1 = -10$, $\lambda_2 = -10$.

But how can values be negative? Does it mean that in the system (88) if we work negative hours, positive outputs will come? Does it mean that labour creates no value? Such is, of course, not the meaning of (88). We have in (88) an example where the two processes consume more inputs than they produce as outputs. The net output of the two processes taken is negative, just as in the Sraffa example with no surplus the net output of the system was zero.

Such processes which yield negative net outputs will be excluded from any actual economy. They violate the condition of productiveness that we illustrated (see pp. 104–105 above). The only processes worth considering from an economic viewpoint are those that yield net surplus. This is not peculiar to Marxian economic theory but is common to the notion of production as such. It is similar to the case in Walrasian general equilibrium theory in which we exclude the possibility of negative prices. If there are commodities whose demand and supply curves intersect only at negative prices we say that such commodities are in excess supply and have zero prices. We similarly exclude processes with negative net outputs.

The analogy with demand/supply analysis is made clearer in Figure 7 a/b where we draw the solutions to Set 1 and Set 2. For Set 1, the two processes intersect in the positive orthant and in Set 2 in the negative orthant.

The intersection e in each case yields the mutually consistent set of outputs when each process is run at unit intensity. We can see that in Set 2 there is no intersection for l_1, l_2 positive.

With this background we can now go on to discuss the paradox of negative values and positive profits put forward by Steedman.

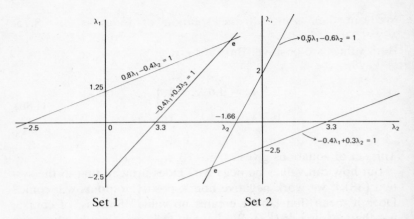

Set 1   Set 2

FIGURE 7   Positive and negative values illustrated (not drawn to scale)

NEGATIVE VALUES AND JOINT PRODUCTS

Let us now look at the joint products case. Steedman has argued that, contrary to the demonstration by Okishio, Morishima and Bortkiewicz, as we saw, positive profits do not require positive rate of exploitation. He put forward a numerical example in which negative values were produced but profits were positive. Steedman's critique of Marx's value theory has proved to be controversial; hence it is important to look at it.

Steedman's article was written in response to an article in which Wolfstetter had quite rigourously established various propositions concerning Marx's value theory. Wolfstetter maintained the distinction between the price system (money capital circuit in our terms), the quantity system (productive capital circuit) and the value system (commodity capital circuit) very carefully. He then established several propositions, including the necessity and sufficiency of positive rate of exploitation for positive profits. We shall not look here at Wolfstetter's article in detail because it is mathematically demanding. But our previous development of Marxian value theory is in sympathy with Wolfstetter's views.

Steedman gave an example of joint production which can be summarized as follows. The first process takes 5 units of commodity Q_1 and 1 unit of labour to produce 6 units of Q_1 and 1 of Q_2. The second process takes 10 units of Q_2 and 1 of labour to produce 3 of Q_1 and 12 of Q_2. The he further assumes that 6 units of labour are employed, 5 on process 1 ($x_1 = 5$) and 1 on process 2 ($x_2 = 1$). Process 1 thus takes 25 Q_1 and 5 labour to yield 30 Q_1 and 5 Q_2. Process 2 takes 10 Q_2 and 1 labour to produce 3 Q_1 and 12 Q_2. Thus 6 units of labour produce net outputs of 8 Q_1 and 7 Q_2.

To apply the method we used in our two examples, we get

$$\left.\begin{array}{c} \lambda_1 = -\lambda_2 + 1 \\ 2\lambda_2 = -3\lambda_1 + 1 \end{array}\right\} \tag{89}$$

This yields the solution $\lambda_2 = 2$ and $\lambda_1 = -1$. Thus Q_2 has positive 'values' and Q_1 has negative value. Figure 8 illustrates this example and we see that the intersection of the two processes is in the Southeast quadrant with λ_2 positive and λ_1 negative.

Steedman demonstrates that despite the negative value of x_1 both processes make positive profits and both commodities command positive prices. The price calculation is done in the physical quantity space rather than value space but that is of no consequence. Steedman defines the wage bill of 6 units of labour as 3 Q_1 and 5 Q_2. Thus both the commodities partake of the character of constant capital as well as variable capital. In his price equations, Steedman follows Sraffa's practice and applies profit mark up to material costs but not to labour costs.

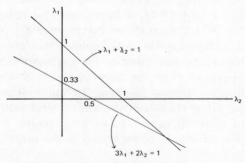

FIGURE 8   Steedman's example

132 *The problem of joint production*

This yields him three equations:

$$6q_1 + q_2 = (1 + \rho)\, q_1 + 1$$
$$3q_1 + 12q_2 = (1 + \rho)\, 10\, q_2 + 1$$
$$\text{and} \quad 3q_1 + 5q_2 = 6 \tag{90}$$

Thus the money wage is the numeraire. The wage bill of 6 units of labour is 6 units of money wage which equals the money equivalent of 3 Q_1 and 5 Q_2. The price per unit of Q_1 is q_1, q_2 the price per unit of Q_2 and ρ as usual is the (money) profit rate.

Steedman obtains two solutions of the price equations (90). The first set he adopts gives $\rho = 0.20$, $q_1 = 1/3$ and $q_2 = 1$. He also cites an alternative solution which gives $\rho = 0.016$, $q_1 = -12/19$ $q_2 = 30/19$. He adds, however, that 'the negative price . . . makes this solution economically insignificant' (op. cit. footnote 1, p. 115). Let us note in passing that while he excludes negative prices as economically insignificant, Steedman does not exclude processes with negative values on the same grounds.

But it is on Steedman's preferred solution that we must concentrate. Note that taking $\lambda_1 = -1$, $\lambda_2 = 2$, one can calculate variable capital, surplus value and so on. Since 6 units of labour command 3 Q_1 and 5 Q_2 and the value of this wage bill comes to 7 units, Steedman finds that as total labour (V + S) is 6 and V is 7, surplus value is negative. Notice also that 25 Q_1 and 10 Q_2 are used as material inputs. The value of constant capital is also negative in the aggregate being −5. The value of gross output of 33 Q_1 and 17 Q_2 is barely positive being equal to 1. Thus C + V + S = Y identity at the aggregate is trivially satisfied. Both constant capital and surplus value are negative, the positive values being generated by the necessary labour.

Thus we have an economy here that pays a wage bundle so high that surplus value is negative. Its material inputs are also unproductive, since their contribution to total value is negative. The ratio of constant capital to variable capital is negative for prices and for the whole economy, as is the (value) rate of profit.

Steedman attributes the occurrence of negative values to the joint production aspect. As he says,

one reason for finding 'negative value' rather odd, is that one is used to thinking of the Marxian value of a commodity as the labour required to produce a net output consisting of that commodity alone. Reflection will show, however, that with joint production, it is, in general, not possible to produce only one commodity, this being so even if all values are positive (op. cit. p. 118).

He prefers the interpretation of values in terms of employment multipliers.

The more appropriate way to conceive of value is as the change in employment *resulting from a change in net output from* (y_1, y_2) *to* $(y_1 + 1, y_2)$ *or* $(y_1, y_2 + 1)$ *where each output can be produced by some meaningful, positive allocation of labour between the processes (op. cit. p. 119).*

Thus the negative value of x_1 means that the more x_1 and the same amount of x_2 can be produced with fewer labour units.

Steedman demonstrates this by considering two economies. The first is the economy we have considered above, which pays a real wage bundle of 3 Q_1 + 5 Q_2 to 6 units of labour and produces a net output 8 Q_1 and 7 Q_2. He compares it to another economy with a different real wage bundle, 6 Q_1 + 3 Q_2 for 5 units of labour, and which produces from the same process 9 Q_1 + 7 Q_2.

Thus by comparison with our first economy the second has the same net output of commodity 2, yet produces one more *unit of commodity 1 even though employment is one unit* smaller. *This is the meaning of the result that commodity 1 has a value of* −1.

A curious feature of Steedman's economy that was brought out in the discussion by Morishima is that of the two processes. Process one is absolutely inferior to Process 2. Thus while Steedman assumed that both processes were in use and that the inefficient process absorbed the bulk of the labour, it may be possible to produce a larger net surplus by discarding process 1 altogether ($x_1 = 0$). Consider two alternatives: giving all 6 units of labour to process 1 ($x_1 = 6$) or all six to process 2 ($x_2 = 6$). Since the jointness is in output rather than inputs, both are perfectly feasible alternatives. Thus process 1 will use 30 Q_1 and 6 labour to produce 36 Q_1 and 6 Q_2 or a net output (6.6). Process 2 will use 60 Q_2 and 6 labour to produce 18 Q_1 and 72 Q_2 or a net output of (18,12). Thus Process 2 gives higher net outputs than Process 1 does. There is nothing that makes Process 1 necessary. Indeed its inefficiency (its production of negative net output) is shown by the fact that it is dominated entirely by Process 2. Why should any economy operate both processes when one would do?

Morishima demonstrates that by showing that Steedman's input/output coefficients are, analogously to (82) above,

$$\begin{bmatrix} 6 & 3 \\ 1 & 12 \end{bmatrix} \begin{pmatrix} x_1 \\ x_2 \end{pmatrix} = \begin{bmatrix} 5 & 0 \\ 0 & 10 \end{bmatrix} \begin{pmatrix} x_1 \\ x_2 \end{pmatrix} + \begin{pmatrix} 8 \\ 7 \end{pmatrix} \qquad (91)$$

This is the primal problem corresponding to equation (85) (on p. 127) and the vector of net outputs 8 Q_1 and 7 Q_2 is written in. Thus Steedman ignores inequalities and arbitrarily takes $x_1 = 5$ and $x_2 = 1$. But treating the problem as one of inequalities, one could ask what is the minimum labour time in which the vector of final demands 8 Q_1 and 7 Q_2 be produced. Let us say as in (85)

Minimize Lx

Bx $\geq$ Ax + F

where B, A and F are as already defined and the numerical values given above. Morishima then shows that putting $x_1 = 0$ and $x_2 = 3.5$, i.e. discarding process 1 altogether and using 3.5 units of labour on the second process, produces 10.5 Q_1 and 7 Q_2 i.e. a surplus of 2.5 Q_1 and 2.5 labour. Process 1 is inefficient and hence redundant.

It should be added that Steedman was aware of this possible objection. He dealt with this in his original article. His justification of the assumption that both processes must be used in equilibrium needs to be examined carefully. Steedman sets forth the profit inequality for each process if each is to operate with all 6 units of labour.

He gets

$$30\, q_1\, (1 + \rho) + 3\, q_1 + 5\, q_2 \geqslant 36\, q_1 + 6\, q_2 \qquad (92)$$

$$\text{or} \quad 30\, q_1\, \rho \geqslant 3\, q_1 + q_2 \qquad (92a)$$

for the first process. Similarly,

$$60\, q_2\, (1 + \rho) + 3\, q_1 + 5\, q_2 \geqslant 18\, q_1 + 72\, q_2 \qquad (93)$$

$$60\, q_2\, \rho \geqslant \equiv 15\, q_1 + 7\, q_2. \qquad (93a)$$

These two equations say that profits must not exceed ρ times material costs in each process, or equivalently, costs plus mark-up plus wages must be greater than or equal to total revenue. These are the inequalities on the price side that we referred to above. They correspond (are dual) to the inequalities on the quantity side that Morishima in his comment says Steedman neglects to specify.

Steedman now argues that '(I)n a competitive equilibrium both (prices) must be positive and therefore excess demand for each commodity must be exactly zero. ... Hence if a competitive equilibrium exists, it *must* invoke the operation of both processes'. This is quite obviously wrong because, as we said above, in competitive equilibrium prices need to be non-negative; that is, they can be zero or positive. Nothing prevents the equilibrium from existing with $q_1 = 0$ and $q_2 > 0$. This is clearly so because Q_1 is not needed as a material input in the second process. Given the arbitrary composition of the real wage bundle, Q_1 is consumed by workers but even here operating the second process with 6 units of labour will more than meet the real wage demand for Q_1. Thus Q_1 is in excess supply and hence in competitive equilibrium its price must be zero. Thus we have

$$60\, q_2\, \rho = 7\, q_2$$

and from the wage equation, given $q_1 = 0$

$$5\, q_2 = 6$$

Hence $q_2 = 1.2$ and $\rho = 7/60$ or 11.66 per cent. Now of course we know that one unit of labour produces a net output of 2 Q_2 and 3 Q_1. Since Q_1 is in excess supply, it is a commodity not needed. Marx states quite clearly at the very outset of his definition of value that a commodity that is not required by anyone has no value. Hence the value of Q_1 is zero. Each unit of labour produces 2 Q_2 hence Q_2 has a $\frac{1}{2}$ as its 'labour value'. This then implies that 6 units of labour have variable capital equivalent to $2\frac{1}{2}$ units and the rate of exploitation is 140 per cent. The value of output 72 Q_2 and 18 Q_1 is 36 and the value of constant capital of 60 Q_2 is 30. Thus once we set the price of the commodity in excess supply equal to zero (and its value also correspondingly to zero), we have positive rate of exploitation and positive profits.

Thus Steedman's criticism of labour theory of value and his claim to have demonstrated that negative values coexist with positive prices can be seen to depend upon a particular arithmetical anomaly. Once the underlying economic logic is clarified, the paradox dissolves. It is because he insists that inefficient processes continue to be used and that a commodity in excess supply have positive price that we get the curiosum of negative value and positive profits.

Morishima in his comment on Steedman brings out that posing the quantity side of the problem in terms of equalities rather than inequalities is a fundamental error on Steedman's part. As Morishima remarks,

As far as his example is concerned, these Steedman values have nothing to do with the labour values of commodities, nor with Marxian values, because the latter should be non-negative by definition, while the former contain negative ones.

He adds in a footnote:

As we all know, the value of a commodity is defined as the total amount of human labour power expended directly or indirectly for its production. It should be non-negative. How can we exert, or expend, a negative amount of labour? Whatever can be meant by a negative amount of labour?

Morishima also does not accept the interpretation of values as employment multipliers that Steedman advances. This is because such an interpretation is valid only under certain restrictive conditions. As Morishima says,

He (Steedman) identifies these negative and positive multipliers with labour values, by the help of the Sraffa-Morishima equivalence theorem between values and employment multipliers. But in his argument he makes no reference to various conditions such as no joint production which must be fulfilled in order that the employment multipliers obtained by solving input-output equations should give true Marxian values.

A second purpose of Steedman's paper was to demonstrate that using Sraffa's notion of Standard commodity does not run into any of the problems that Marxian value notions encounters. We shall not go into that topic here but refer the reader to Wolfstetter's comment on Steedman's paper. Wolfstetter shows

that the possibility of negative labour values and the more extreme possibility of a negative surplus value coexisting with positive prices and profits indicate a fundamental weakness in Sraffa's theory of joint production which deprives that theory of valid economic meaning (op. cit. p. 864).

Wolfstetter's demonstration is a rigourous mathematical analysis of the joint production problem as posed by Steedman.

MORISHIMA'S CRITICISM OF MARX'S VALUE THEORY

Morishima's criticism of Marx's value theory is a sympathetic one, as we said above. In extending Marx's value notion to the Joint Production case, Morishima wishes to preserve as far as possible the notion of value as minimum labour time expended in production and to retain the Fundamental Marxian Theorem of Okishio–Morishima that a positive rate of exploitation is necessary and sufficient for a positive rate of profit. His argument against Marx's definition of values is that such a definition is inappropriate for joint production. To analyse the actual techniques in use, as Marx had done, gives actual values. Now for the case of joint production, Morishima shows that Marx's method of calculation does not apply and that values may be non-additive. He first advances the idea that values should be thought of in terms of optimal allocation of labour to different activities so as to produce a given bundle of goods with minimum expenditure of labour (true values) or alternatively to maximize the total labour value of a vector of goods subject to the available labour supply and given technology (optimum values).

The notion of optimum values corresponds to a planning regime rather than to a capitalist regime. It says that the objective function of a society should be to minimize labour time required to produce a given bundle of goods or to maximize aggregate value produced. This is not the objective in a capitalist economy where profit maximization by each entrepreneur is the rule. But even ignoring that, as Morishima himself acknowledges, optimum values are not unique *and* they will depend on the bundle of goods chosen to be produced. Non-uniqueness is often a mathematical problem but its other aspect is an economic one. The bundle of goods produced in a capitalist economy at any time depends on demand and hence on the given distribution of income and wealth. It is 'optimal' only relative to that distribution. Wasteful or luxury goods are produced. Once we accept that they should be produced then we can compute the socially necessary labour time required to produce them. This may not be the best way to allocate society's labour resources.

Thus optimum values obtained by minimizing labour time for a given bundle of goods will not correspond to what actually happens in a capitalist economy except in the ideal textbook world of perfect competition with no market failure, no externalities, no public goods, no uncertainty and so on. They will not correspond to profit maximizing values in general.

But in the case of joint production, since a process produces more than one commodity and a commodity is produced by more than one process, the concept of the value of a commodity as the sum of the value of constant and variable capital used in its production and surplus value is hard to maintain. Thus Morishima shows in his comment on Steedman that the notion of 'true value' applies in the aggregate rather than to individual commodities. These various propositions need to be spelt out mathematically.

The input/output matrix can be stated as before

$$Bx \geqslant Ax + F \qquad (82a)$$

since not all processes are always used, $x \gtreqqless 0$ (83c)

Optimum values are defined by solving the dual problem as in (86)

$$\left. \begin{array}{c} \text{Maximize } F'1 \text{ subject to} \\ B'1 \leqslant A'1 + L \text{ and } 1 \geqslant 0 \end{array} \right\} \qquad (86)$$

Thus we maximize the aggregate value of goods produced subject to the input/output constraints stated in value terms rather than in physical quantities. The solution to this programming problem gives 1^0 – the vector of optimum values. The individual elements of 1^0 individual optimum values are not uniquely defined. (It will take too much detail to demonstrate this. See the original source for a proof.)

True values are defined by solving the primial problem which we saw above in (85).

$$\left. \begin{array}{c} \text{Minimize } Lx \\ \text{subject to} \qquad Bx \geqslant Ax + F \\ x \geqslant 0 \end{array} \right\} \qquad (85)$$

The true value of the composite bundle F is then $1^*{}_F = Lx^*$ where x^* is the solution to the problem above. x^* will indicate which processes are efficient and will be used ($x_i > 0$) and which not ($x_i = 0$). Now replace F by a column, where F_i is one and all other F_j are zero; that is, let us try to compute the optimum process (or combination of processes) required to produce one unit of ith commodity alone. The solution to that problem will define the true value of 1_i of ith commodity. Thus now 1_i are uniquely defined for each commodity.

Morishima then establishes the following propositions

1. $1^*{}_F = 1^0{}_F$

This only states the obvious result that the solution to the primial and dual correspond to each other.

2. $l^*_F = \Sigma \, l^*_i \, F_i$

This is the sum of true values of individual commodities where the amount of each commodity is the same as in the general problem but the individual true values are determined separately.

Thus the true value of a composite bundle of goods F does not equal the sum of true values of individual commodities. Thus the true values are not additive once joint production is allowed.

Having developed the notion of value corresponding to the solution of a programming problem, Morishima points out that

The actual values of commodities are not necessarily equal to their true values unless a number of conditions, such as no joint-production, no alternative methods of production and so on, are satisfied. If some of them are violated, the conventional value equations and input/output equations are no longer useful for determining values.

Morishima has therefore established the various conditions under which one can define the minimum labour time necessary to produce a given bundle of commodities. This notion of value assigns to it the role of allocating labour efficiently in an economy. Now it is quite true that while the old notion of additive value is inappropriate for joint production, we still need a notion of value for joint production where the decision as to which commodity to produce and which process to use is taken on profit maximizing grounds by individual capitalists rather than in a planning context. This is not only because Marx was interested in actual values, but also, as we have said in the introduction, the purpose of value theory for Marx is to seek the origins of profit and explain it in terms of the class relations in a capitalist society.

The purpose of value theory for Marx is not to explain price formation nor to explain the allocation of scarce resources among alternative ends. Since it relates to actual production and has to relate to prices to 'unmask hidden relations', these appear among its concerns. But the central purpose of political economy and of value theory is to explain how capitalism produces and reproduces class relations and how profits arise from the surplus value created by labour. Many think that Marx was wrong, prejudiced or irrational in seeking to do this. There is no doubt, however, that he wished to do this. Thus, while joint production poses technical problems for value calculus, one ought to get back to the appropriate value notion for doing what Marx wanted to do.

Wolfstetter (1973) has argued that the use of value calculus for Marx is *ex post* analysis of power relationship rather than *ex ante* prediction of consequences of changes in technology, tastes and so on. Marx's interest was of course also in *ex ante* prediction of the dynamics of capitalism. But in terms of the Transformation Problem, Wolfstetter is quite correct. We observe an economy in which certain goods are produced with certain processes. We observe prices, wages, profits. The choice of processes has been made by the profit maximizing capitalist. Can we then explain the origin of profits in any way that relates to the class structure of the society? Do profits arise because the concentration of ownership of means of production in hands of one class? Does the creation, distribution and disposal of profits perpetuate (reproduce) the class system and if so, precisely how?

These are the concerns of Marx's value theory. It is not to be a diehard dogmatist to say that these concerns are the same with joint production as without. The modifications required by joint production should lead us to define more rigorously the notions of value, without at the same time abandoning the central concerns of value theory.

Morishima's other objection to value calculus concerns the problem of heterogeneity of labour. In any economy, we have labours of various skills and training being used as inputs. These various skill categories earn different wages. In order to reduce all skilled labour to abstract indifferentiated labour we need to deal with the production of skilled labour as extra activities which use consumer goods and capital goods as well as other labour as inputs. One of the inputs is of course the simple unskilled labour time of the worker undergoing the training. This will enable us to define an hour of skilled labour as equivalent to so many units of unskilled labour (Morishima 1973).

Let θ_i be the ratio of an hour of ith skilled labour to unskilled labour. Thus, for example, a doctor may have θ of fifty. One hour of a doctor's labour may be worth fifty hours of unskilled labour. We add on the θ unknowns to the value equations

$$1 = Al + R\theta + L \qquad\qquad (94a)$$

$$\theta = T_1l + T_2\theta + M \qquad\qquad (94b)$$

R is the input matrix of skilled labour into goods. T_1 is the input matrix of goods into production of skills and T_2 is the input matrix of other skills (teachers to impart skills) into production of skills. L and M are inputs of homogeneous unskilled labour.

These equations have straightforward solutions as long as the system is productive. But Morishima raises the objection that in such a case it will be impossible to satisfy the requirement that every category of labour has the same rate of exploitation. But real wage differentials are not always equiproportionate to skill differentials. Different groups of workers may be exploited at different rates. Morishima therefore feels that a scheme such as (94a) and (94b) cannot be used to reduce skilled labour to abstract labour. For the purpose of converting skilled labour to abstract labour, actual money wages paid should be used. When skill differences are approximated by market prices, values are no longer independent of market conditions and may also fluctuate as demand/supply conditions change.

Morishima considers this to be a very weighty objection. He says 'we conclude by suggesting to Marxian economists that they ought radically to change their attitude towards the labour theory of value'. However, we would question, however, the requirement, that of a uniform rate of exploitation, as a basic tenet.

We must here distinguish equilibrium characterization from day to day historical course. For Marx, the rate of exploitation, the money wage and the length of working day are determined by the course of the class struggle. Thus in the historical course of an economy, differential rates of exploitation will exist due to unequal spread of capitalist relations in different parts of the

Invisible Value Domain	*Visible Price or Exchange Domain*
Social relations between men	Relations between things
Class division between capitalist as owner of means of production and means of subsistence and worker as free labourer	Equal relation of exchange between buyer and seller
Value of labour power equal to the socially necessary labour time required for production and reproduction of the labourer equal to paid labour which is less than total labour expended	The wage form Wages are paid for a full day's work
Rate of surplus value equals $$\frac{\text{unpaid labour}}{\text{paid labour}}$$	$$\text{Rate of profit} = \frac{\text{Profits}}{\text{Stock of fixed capital} + \text{advanced circulating capital}}$$
Total value = Surplus value + variable capital + constant capital = (1 + rate of surplus value) × variable capital + constant capital, where constant capital has its full value transferred to the final product but creates no surplus value	Total profits = Total revenue minus total cost = Selling price minus cost price, where cost price equals cost of labour (wage bill) plus cost of materials and wear and tear of fixed capital

FIGURE 9

economy, uneven growth of trade unionism in different trades and industries, the strength and recent history of workers' struggles expressed via strikes and so on. Marxists have themselves studied the difficulties of combining working the class into a single force for struggle due to existence of aristocracy of labour or relations of dominance between town and country or between metropolis and periphery.

When looking at static equilibrium characterization, we may be tempted to posit a tendency towards equal rates of exploitation. We have, however, repeatedly made clear that value categories are not behavioural. Workers do not respond to changes in differential rates of exploitation, but to the visible correlates of it, such as length and intensity of work, money wage and so on. The assumption of equal rates of exploitation is made in order to make the task of translating price relations into value relations easier and is an approximation.

We have already seen this in our discussion of Bortkiewicz' solution in the general case (Chapter XI). There in the value domain we had $(n + 2)$ unknowns e_i, r and $\overline{w}$ [see equations (24)–(26)]. For the same n commodities we also had $(n + 2)$ unknowns q_i, ρ and W [equations (31) to (36)]. Now if we have n goods and m types of labour, we have $(n + m + 1)$ unknowns in the price domain q_i, ρ, W_j. What, then, are the corresponding unknowns in the value domain? They can be e_i, r_j and $\overline{w}$. Morishima chooses them to e_i, r and $\overline{w}_j$ and then says $W_j/\overline{w}_j$ is not constant across different labour types j.

There is no mechanism, however, to equalize $W_j/\overline{w}_j$, the ratio of money wage of ith category of skilled labour to the value of its labour power. As we have seen for all commodities, prices diverge from values systematically. Thus the ratios $W_j/\overline{w}_j$ will differ from one skill category to another.

This does not imply that the problem of heterogeneity of labour is unimportant. Historically it has been very important in creating problems for any workers' movement which hoped to combine all sections of the working class. Analytically it complicates further the price-value transformation. More needs to be done on this topic.

PART THREE

Accumulation and the Rate of Profit

XIV

EXTENDED REPRODUCTION: INTRODUCTION

At many points in all the three volumes of *Capital*, Marx emphasizes that a revolution in value takes place continuously within the productivity process under capitalism {34} {47} {68}. Changing technology as well as improvements in methods of utilizing given inputs, revolution in methods of circulation (packaging, transport, credit, marketing) are all occurring all the time. Along with growth and as a necessary part of it are crises – business cycles that force change upon individual capitalists {75}. In addition to these is the course of the class struggle – strikes, trade union growth, growth of new forms of capitalist associations (for example multinational firms) changes in form of governments (for example, growth of the welfare state) and so on. Beyond mentioning these changes, we can do little more because these have not been treated in analytical detail to any great extent. Historians have charted many of these changes with great success but economists have failed to incorporate them in their formal schemes.

In Marx's own discussions, there is a contrast between his arithmetical examples of expanded reproduction and his many discussions in the 'literary' parts. The arithmetical example – the 'model' of extended reproduction – is constructed so as to show a *balanced* and continuous growth of the two Departments under fairly restrictive assumptions. It is when we come to look at the logic behind such balanced growth that several contradictions emerge. Once again the unsolved problems are those of prices and of the money circuit. But let us first set out Marx's model.

Chapter XXI of Vol. II of *Capital* is devoted to

'Accumulation and Reproduction on an Extended Scale.' Marx's examples are constructed with a two-Department scheme as in our equations (1) under Simple Reproduction. Marx further imposes two assumptions that are in no way a necessary part of his theory, but convenient for arithmetical calculations.[1] These are (1) identical rates of exploitation in the two Departments ($r_i = r$), which also remain *constant* throughout accumulation ($r_{it} = r_i = r$); and (2) given values of organic compositions for the two Departments which also remain *constant* throughout accumulation. The rate of exploitation was assumed to be 100 per cent. In Department I, the organic composition was 4/5 and in Department II 2/3. All the discussion is throughout carried out in terms of values rather than (that is, proportional to) prices. (It was not until Vol. III that Marx came to the value-price transformation problem).

Marx further assumed that one half of surplus value of Department I – the machine goods producing Department – is reinvested or readvanced as capital and the remainder is spent on wage goods. This makes the activities of the capitalists of Department II completely dependent on what Department I does and on the balancing equations required to ensure that all the assumptions are fulfilled. (This has often led to a general policy of the 'primacy' of Department I in Soviet Union and Eastern European countries. It is necessary, therefore, to emphasize that this assumption is for *arithmetical* convenience and not required for the general model).

Marx's table for expanded reproduction is given in Table 9. We see that r = 100 per cent and $g_1 = 4/5$, $g_2 = 2/3$. Total output of Department I is 6,000, whereas the total demand for C_i as input is only 5,500. Thus $Y_1 > C_1$. By analogy we have V + S = 3,500, whereas the output of Department II is only 3,000. Remember that since we do not have Department III, surplus value must be spent either on Department I or Department II, unlike in the three-Department representation of simple reproduction. The discrepancy between Y_1 and C and Y_2 and S + V clearly indicates that the system is not in simple reproduction. The capitalists do not spend all their surplus value as revenue but advance it as capital. The simple rule is that ½ of S_1 – surplus value in Department I – is accumulated as capital. In order to preserve the organic composition g_1 at 4/5, only 4/5

TABLE 9

Numerical Examples of Extended Reproduction

Year		C_i	V_i	S_i	Y_i	
1	Dept. I	4000	1000	1000	6000	Initial Scheme for Year 1 Ex ante
	Dept. II	1500	750	750	3000	
		5500	1750	1750	9000	
		C_i	V_i	CF_i	Y_i	
2	Dept. I	4400	1100	500	6000	'Arrangement changed for the purposes of accumulation' Ex Post Scheme for Year 2
	Dept. II	1600	800	600	3000	
		6000	1900	1100	9000	
		C_i	V_i	S_i	Y_i	
	Dept. I	4400	1100	1100	6600	Initial Scheme for Year 2
	Dept. II	1600	800	800	3200	
		6000	1900	1900	9800	
		C_i	V_i	CF_i	Y_i	
	Dept. I	4840	1210	550	6600	Ex Post Scheme for Year 2
	Dept. II	1760	880	560	3200	
		6600	2090	1110	9800	

of $\frac{1}{2}$ of S_1 is advanced as constant capital. Thus out of S_1 of 1,000, 400 is advanced as constant capital, 100 as variable capital and 500 as spent as revenue on goods of Department II.

This arbitrary rule for Department I capitalists completely closes the system, since we then impose the balancing identities that ex post $Y_1 = C$ and $Y_2 = CF + V$. The ex post C, V, CF are different from the initial or ex ante categories. They are what would appear as final expenditure (in value terms). Thus CF in the ex post scheme is not total surplus value but the value of capitalists' purchase of wage goods (consumption fund). In price terms or in value terms, the ex post CF is not identifiable with surplus value nor useful as a measure of exploitation.

Given Department I's decision and the identities, Department II makes up the gap in this scheme. Let us denote the ex ante categories by asterisks, remembering as always that they are not directly observable. Then the ex post $C_1 = C_1^* + \frac{1}{2} g_1 S_1^*$ and $C_2 = Y_1 - C_1$. Thus though $Y_1^* > C^*$, $Y_1 = C$. Given C_2 it is easy to see that Y_2 is determined by g_2 – the organic composition has to be maintained at 2/3. Thus we get $C_2 - C_2^*$ and $V_2 - V_2^*$ as the net accumulation out of S_2^* by Department II, the remainder being spent as revenue on wage goods.

The decision to accumulate has its own consequences, however. Now the capitalists of Department I have advanced 4400 C_1 and 1100 V_1, which when put into production as productive capital generate surplus value of 1100 and at the end of the productive process given total value of 6600. Similarly, Department II has total output of 3200 since the advanced capital is 1600 + 800. Thus whereas the ex post expenditures in Year 1 add up to – absorb – total value produced, this implies a similar ex ante imbalance for Year 2. Once again $Y_1^* > C^*$ and $Y_2^* < (V^* + S^*)$. Once again the decision by Department I capitalists to accumulate $\frac{1}{2}$ of S_1^* will yield numbers which ex post will satisfy the balancing equations.

Before we look critically at the process by which ex post harmony is established from ex ante conditions of disequilibrium, let us examine the quantitative dimensions of the solution (Table 4). The total value output goes up from 6000 to 14,348 by the sixth year. This involves, apart from the first year when the growth rate is nine per cent, a steady growth rate of ten per cent per year. The value of machine goods output grows steadily at ten per cent per annum. The value rate of profit ($\bar{p}$ in our notation) is constant at twenty four per cent. Given the equal rate of exploitation and the unequal organic composition of capital, the value rate of profit in one Department is different from that in the other. The expenditure of Department I capitalists on wage goods goes up every year by ten per cent (in value terms). We see in Table 4 that the expenditure which changes from goods for Department II capitalists goes from 600, 560, 616, 678, 745. . . It is only after the second year that it grows at ten per cent; for the first year it goes down by about six per cent.

While not much emphasis should be put on actual magnitude in this example, it raises very important questions. We have in this example a capitalist economy capable of growing at ten per cent for ever and ever, with the value rate of profit constant and no upward tendency in the overall organic composition of capital. Is this example to illustrate the possibility of a crisis free growth of capitalism or is it designed to show how unlikely it is that so many balancing conditions will be simultaneously satisfied? What is the mechanism that ensures that these conditions will be fulfilled year after year?

The arbitrariness of the rule by which Department I capitalists invest half their surplus value has already been mentioned. Notice also that they reinvest only within their industry; all investment is internally financed. What guides them to decide on these matters? Is it the desire to maintain a certain money rate of profit or to bring the gap between the money rate of profit in the two sectors? We need to know the prices corresponding to the values and the money rate of profit each year to be able to know the process by which profits are equalized and prices set. It may be that at the level of prices, the equilibrium growth pattern of value sums is disturbed. Marx clearly has failed to pose the problem of expanded reproduction in the

TABLE 10

Expanded Reproduction: A Summary View

Total Value of output	Change in value of output	Value of machine goods output	Change in value of output	Value profit of profit	Capitalist spending on wage goods	
$Y_1 + Y_2$	$\Delta(Y_1 + Y_2)$	Y_1	ΔY_1	$S^*/C^* + V^*$	Dept. I	Dept. II
9000		6000			500	600
9800	800(9%)	6600	600(10%)	$1750/7250 = 24$	605	560
10780	980(10%)	7260	660(10%)	$1900/7900 = 24$	605	616
11858	1078(10%)	7986	726(10%)	$2090/8690 = 24$	666	678
13043	1185(10%)	8784	798(10%)	$2299/9559 = 24$	732	745
14348	1304(10%)	9662	878(10%)	$2529/10514 = 24$		

price domain. He also does not explicitly solve the problem of expanded reproduction in the M – M' circuit. His attempts to introduce monetary circulation in this scheme are incomplete and unsatisfactory.

Marx's decision to pose the problem of accumulation in the commodity circuit of capital rather than integrating it with the money capital circuit and the productive capital circuit leaves the scheme of Expanded Reproduction (SER) as a conundrum. Indeed it has been the subject of an intense debate among Marxists ever since the publication of Volume II. Many have taken it as a picture of the possibility of sustained growth in capitalism. Others have tried to find a flaw in the logic of the scheme which will modify its equilibrium character and generate a picture of cyclical growth. The contrast between the dynamic implied in the Falling Rate of Profit and in the SER is a blatant one. How is one to interpret the SER, and much more difficult, how is one to integrate it back into the general Marxian model of disequilibrium dynamics in a monetary capitalist economy?

One view is that the SER is unsuited to analysis of capitalist dynamics even in a relatively abstract setting of a two Department model. This view, recently expressed by Mandel, says that the SER like the Scheme of Simple Reproduction (SSR) is designed to demonstrate the *possibility* of equilibrium and nothing more. Marx came to set up the schemes in his attempt to explain Adam Smith's notion of national income. He wanted to reconcile the notion of national income as the sum total of value added (in modern income accounting sense) with the notion of gross revenue of an enterprise. He was particularly concerned to account for depreciation or consumption of constant capital in such a scheme with or without net accumulation taking place. Thus he wanted to show that interindustrial flow of intermediate products had an important part to play in sustaining economic activity.

This interpretation has some basis in Marx's writings. It matches with Marx's early attempts in TSV part I to puzzle through Adam Smith's definition of national income as the sum of wage rent and profit in different firms. In *Capital* Vol. II as well, the discussion of the schemes is preceded by a historical excursion into Adam Smith's views.

It would seem then on this view that the SER is meant to show the working of the Invisible Hand. As Mandel puts it,

Marx's reproduction schemes play a closely defined and specific role in his analysis of capitalism and they are designed to solve a single problem and no other. Their function is to explain why and how an economic system based on 'pure' market anarchy in which economic life seems to be determined by millions of unrelated decisions to buy and sell does not lead to continuous chaos and constant interruptions of the social and economic process of reproduction, but instead on the whole functions 'normally' – that is with a big crash in the form of an economic crisis breaking out (in Marx's time) once every seven or ten years [*Roman added; Mandel (1975) p. 25*].

The problems with the Invisible Hand interpretation are made clear in the romanized part of the quotation. Marx's schemes can perhaps be thought to establish the existence of general equilibrium of a market economy. This would make the SER similar to Walras's attempts. What the SER does not do is say anything about a 'big crash' every seven or ten years. The last part of Mandel's statement is a paraphrase of Marx's views of how the actual economy functioned – cyclically and not in terms of general equilibrium. It is because SER does not admit economic crises that authors like Rosa Luxemburg, Hilferding *et al.* have been unhappy about the SER.

The SER as it exists is a strongly equilibrium oriented model. We shall however show that if we understand its structure correctly it can be generalized using other parts of Marx's work. Let us first however look at Rosa Luxemburg's critique of Marx's schemes as she raises most of the conceptual problems with the SER. After that we shall construct a general model of expanded reproduction and isolate the crucial element in SER which yields the balanced growth result.

XV

ROSA LUXEMBURG ON ACCUMULATION

Rosa Luxemburg starts with the question of the incentive in the system to expand at 10 per cent per annum. Why should Department I expand at 10 per cent? Why should the capitalists decide to accumulate? The question of technical change – revolution in methods of production continuously changing' values forcing capitalists to accumulate in order to keep up with competitors – has been ignored by Marx in this discussion. The value sums grow at given rates due to accumulation of surplus value rather than due to technical change. What is the driving force then for accumulation?

We begin with the initial situation where we have already left simple reproduction behind. There is clearly excess value of machine goods output being produced in relation to its rate of use. Where will the extra demand come from for 500 value units of machine goods? According to Marx, the capitalists of Department I decide to demand 400 units for themselves. They decide for some reason to expand. Being rational, they must do this with some expectations of rising demand for their product in the future although at the moment they face a demand gap. If we grant that they invest 400 they still need to spend 100 on variable capital. They cannot, however, pay their workers – both old and new – in machine goods. They must sell their entire output 6000 (or of 1600 deducting 4400 for their own use), convert it into money and then go out into the market for more workers. In terms of the three circuits of capital, they have to go through the $C' - M' \rightarrow C$ circuit. They can sell their output and convert it into money and advance 100 additional value units as variable capital and spend 500 units on wage goods only if there is a market for them. This market in the arithmetical scheme is provided by Department II. Quite arbitrarily, Department II decides to mop up all the excess supply of machine goods 1500 + 100 so that Department I can grow at 10 per cent. In the process they, too, have to sell their entire output of 3000. *Ex ante* if the capitalists of Department I do not take into their heads to accumulate as much as $\frac{1}{2}$ of their surplus value, Department II as well faces a situation of excess supply (in value terms) for their product. They can only sell 1750 units of Y_2 as replacement capital. The demand for Y_2 for capitalists' consumption depends on the realization of surplus value. Marx's accumulation scheme requires them to spend 2400 units ($1600C_2 + 800V_2$) so they must sell their product before they can buy 100 additional value units of machine goods from Department I. What guarantees the mutual sale? Where does Department I get *the money* to buy 100 units of constant capital?

A hoard of money from previous years was tentatively suggested by Marx as the answer. This hoard of money may consist of accumulated unspent parts of m, for example in depreciation reserve. The problem is, however, not of some past hoard but of expected future demand. Why does Department I want to expand at all, even if it could find the money to finance purchase of 100 units of variable capital? It cannot be for the capitalists' consumption since their consumption could be as high without growth; in any case, the driving force of capitalism for Marx is not capitalists' consumption but profits. It cannot be that it is the workers' growing demand which drives accumulation; workers can have no demand for wage goods unless they are employed and their continued employment depends on accumulation and not vice versa.

This means that the starting point of capitalist production is not a given number of workers and their demands, but that these factors themselves are constantly fluctuating; dependent variables of the capitalists' expectations of profit.[1]

Growing population either of the capitalists or of the workers, by the same logic, cannot provide an explanation for growth. The existence of a 'middle class' of rentiers, clergy, government officials, teachers is rejected by Marx as a possible source for demand since these derive their income from surplus value and cannot have demand over and above what is already present in capitalist spending on wage goods. (The 'third' class or the third Department is, however, an important escape hatch in recent debates among Marxists about the remarkable capacity of capitalism to survive and expand. We shall discuss this later.) Marx also rejects the idea of foreign trade – dumping surplus output in other capitalist countries. This can have relevance only for a country but, taking the capitalist system as a whole, the problem remains.[2] (It should be added, however, that despite this rejection the importance of international trade for capitalists of one country as a solution for their own crises is quite obvious. Many of the post-Second World War crises in the sphere of international trade and payments arise out of the successful attempts of some countries to solve their accumulation problem in foreign trade as against their less successful rivals.)

The puzzle therefore remains. In the scheme for expanded re-production, capitalists of both Departments miraculously seem to be able to realize surplus and total value by selling to each other for ever and ever. There is no realization problem, no monetary crisis, no brake on accumulation. This contradicts Marx's own emphasis on the inherent contradictions of capitalism. It is this contradiction between the picture of capitalism ridden by crises and faced with a long run tendency of the rate of profit to fall in Vol. III. and the smooth expansion of Volume II which is *the central unsolved problem of Marxian dynamics*. It is of much greater importance than the value-price contradiction of Vol. I and Vol. III – the Transformation Problem which has been much discussed by economists from Bohm Bawerk onwards.

There was an intense debate among Russian Marxists during the 1890s regarding this problem. A large section of Rosa Luxemburg's work is devoted to this debate in which Tugan-Baranowsky, Lenin and many of the leading Russian Narodniks and legal Marxists participated. They did not, however, advance the problem beyond where Marx had left it. Rosa Luxemburg in the last section of her book advances her own solution to this problem. We shall devote the next section to her solution and then return to take another look at why the problem arises.

ROSA LUXEMBURG'S SOLUTION

Rosa Luxemburg's solution is to place capitalist expansion in a realistic social context, where it is surrounded by non-capitalist (pre-capitalist) modes of production. Instead of assuming, as Marx did, for the theoretical model, that the capitalist mode was universally prevalent, she argues that a capitalist mode emerges from a pre-capitalist setting at home and has access to pre-capitalist countries abroad as well. Nineteenth-century trade and imperialism are the more realistic setting for the expansion of capitalism in the nineteenth century and she incorporates these into the model of expanded reproduction.

Her analysis, though not formal, is quite detailed. She cites the sale of British cotton textiles (Department II) to foreign markets such as India and the export of British railroad equipment (Department I) to European countries and USA as examples whereby international trade within the capitalist world, but especially with the outside non-capitalist world, helps realize value, particularly surplus value. The access to increasing raw materials as constant capital for expanding reproduction is provided by increasing productivity in the use of existing materials from Nature and from the non-capitalist countries themselves. Many consumer goods and means of production are also produced outside the capitalist system – import of corn into Britain from Russia. International trade thus helps to realize surplus value, and acquiring raw materials from abroad, to generate further surplus value.

Where does the labour power necessary for expanded reproduction come from? The amount of variable capital goes on expanding each year in line with expansion of capital but this requires additional labour power to be on hand. Here again, Rosa Luxemburg mentions the decay of pre-capitalist sectors – artisans, agricultural labourers, international migration from non-capitalist countries (Irish migration to the US). This shows the dependence of the capitalist sector on the non-capitalist. By access to non-capitalist markets and sources of supply, Rosa Luxemburg sees capitalism as transforming the non-capitalist world in its own image. Commodity exchange is introduced, with private property in land and natural resources and conditions of wage labour in the non-capitalist world. So contradictions are present even in the search for an escape from contradictions.

With respect to trade with other capitalist countries, especially those struggling to emerge into capitalist status, Rosa Luxemburg emphasizes the role of international loans – private capital flows abroad. These help finance the purchase of the surplus product of the lending country and retain its influence on these newly emerging countries. The *surplus value is then realized* from the peasants and proletariat of the borrowing country, be it pre-capitalist or newly capitalist. The smooth expansion of the old country is financed, then, partly from a tax on the peasants of the new country.

Lastly, Rosa Luxemburg mentions militarism as a factor. Here she introduces a third Department which makes armaments. As a starting point 100 units of variable capital are diverted away from the workers by providing them fewer means of subsistence, for example forced saving by inflation. This leads to a diminution of the aggregate social product (output of Departments I and II) but this diminution need not diminish the total surplus value according to her model. The diminution in the aggregate social product can come out of diminution of constant capital and a decline in the variable capital. The formal details of this three Department model are worth setting out.

Taking as her example a different illustration of expanded reproduction than the one we have discussed above (also taken from Vol. II of *Capital*), the model is as follows:

	C_i	V_i	S_i		
I	5000	1000	1000	7000	Initial Scheme
II	1430	285	285	2000	
	6430	1285	1285	9000	

Now suppose that workers receive only 1185 units of value in means of subsistence and the 100 is diverted to armaments. The armaments industry has the same organic composition as the two Departments 5/6 and 100 per cent rate of exploitation. Thus we have in this Department III

$$71.5 + 14.25 + 14.25 = 100$$

But this reduction of 100 in demand for means of subsistence alters all the amounts in Departments I and II. We get finally

	C_i	V_i	S_i	
I	4949	989.75	989.75	6928.5
II	1358.5	270.75	270.75	1900
	6307.5	1260.50	1260.50	8828.5

There is no reason, however, for the decline in surplus value since only the upkeep of the workers has reduced in value. The entire drop in the aggregate social product equal to the 171.5 drop in aggregate social product must come off the variable capital if possible rather than from surplus value. A drop of 171.5 in aggregate variable capital could lead finally to the following composition for the aggregate product

$$6430C + 1113.5V + 1285S = 8828.5$$

If the adjustment were to come from constant capital instead of variable capital, we could get

$$6307.5C + 1236V + 1285S = 8828.5$$

The effect of an armaments cut, then, is to reduce aggregate social product, but while the value of armaments output does not enter the aggregate social product as Marx defines it, it still represents a market for selling of output of Departments I and II. From the point of view of the *individual* capitalists, there is no change, since the market for 100 means of subsistence is replaced by that of 100 armaments. Armaments do not need to be sold on the market since they are paid for by taxation, but the armaments sector purchases inputs from the other Departments.

If the drop in variable capital has been financed by inflation, then prices of all goods would be higher, though not by the same proportion as a result of this diversion. Adding the 100 units of armaments to 8828.5 (as in the current practice in national income accounting) we get 8928.5 value units of national income. We still have to derive money value of output, since we *may* get a higher money value of output as a result.

This point has a bearing on the question of fiscal policy multipliers. The multiplier of 100 units of armaments financed by 100 taxation may be greater than one if we follow the modern rather than the Marxian national income accounting. We shall take up this problem when discussing the impact of Keynes in modern Marxian economics. This does, however, point to a major flaw in Marx's and Rosa Luxemburg's analysis of the problem of expanded reproduction. This is their failure to check the price consequences of expanded reproduction. By posing the problem in value terms alone, they fail to explore fully the process by which realization problems are met under commodity exchange. This is not an easy problem to solve but we shall indicate in the next chapter the direction in which the answer may be found.

XVI

MARX'S MODEL OF ACCUMULATION

Let us in this chapter explore the structure's of Marx's schema. In his book, Morishima has formulated Marx's model generally and explained the strongly stable character of Marx's model. He has also attempted to generate cyclical growth from Marx's model by changing the investment function. We use a slightly different approach. [Morishima (1973). This chapter derives from Desai (1977), Desai and Skott (1978).]

To begin with, we can cast SER in a time dated framework. Each Department purchases commodity capital input C_{it} and V_{it} at the end of a production period t. This is put into production and output emerges at the end measured as $Y_{i, t+1}$. Thus we have in the circuit of commodity capital

	Buying and	
Production	Selling	Production

$$C_t \Longrightarrow C'_{t+1} \Longrightarrow C_{t+1} \Longrightarrow C'_{t+2} \ldots$$

At the end of the period, the problem of disposing of output of realizing value and surplus value arises. Let us further simplify matters by assuming that all sales and purchase takes place at the end of the period in course of a 'single market day'. Once purchases have been made production can resume.
Thus output is

$$Y_{i, t+1} = C_{it} + V_{it} + S_{i, t+1} \qquad (77)$$

Surplus value emerges *during* the production period so ideally it should be labelled neither $S_{i,t}$ nor $S_{i,t+1}$ but $S_i(t)$. For simplicity, we can say that surplus value is dated the same as output.

Now the increase in output depends on the proportion of surplus value accumulated. Out of $S_{i,t+1}$, a_{it} is accumulated and divided in proportion g_i and $(1 - g_i)$ between constant and variable capital. Writing (77) in first difference form

$$Y_{i,t+1} - Y_{it} = \Delta Y_{it} = \Delta C_{i,t-1} + \Delta V_{i,t-1} + \Delta S_{i,t}$$

Let $S_{it}/V_{i,t-1} = r_{i,t}$ and $C_{it}/(C_{it} + V_{it}) = g_{it}$

$$\Delta Y_{it} = [g_{it-1} + (1 + r_{it})(1 - g_{it-1})]a_{it}S_{it} \qquad (78)$$

Notice the time subscripts in equation (78). We have allowed for g_i and to be variables over time. This is to enable us to appreciate the force of each of Marx's simplifying assumptions.

Since we are in time dated world, rate of profit is defined as

$$\Pi_{it} = S_{it}/(C_{it-1} + V_{i,t-1}) = r_{i,t}(1 - g_{i,t-1})$$

Now dividing (78) by Y_{it} we get an expression for growth rate in ith Department.

$$\mu_{it} = \Delta Y_{it}/Y_{it} = [g_{i,t-1} + (1 + r_{it})(1 - g_{i,t-1})]a_{it}(S_{it}/Y_{it})$$

$$= [1 + r_{it}(1 - g_{i,t-1})]a_{it}\left\{\frac{\pi_{it}}{(1 + \pi_{it})}\right\} \qquad (79)$$

$$\mu_{it} = a_{it}\pi_{it}$$

Growth rate of total value output in each Department is a product of the rate of profit and the proportion accumulated. This is by no means a novel relationship in economics but we have spent some time in deriving it to make the steps clear.

Marx's SER is much more restricted than the model outlined above. Due to constancy of r and g_i, $\pi_{it} = \pi_i$. The variation in growth rates of Departments is caused by fluctuations in a_{it}. Now since Marx arbitrarily assumed that $a_{1t} = \bar{a}_1$, growth rate in

Department II becomes a constant. The bar over a_1 denotes that it is a matter of choice.

$$\mu_{1t} = \pi_1 \bar{a}_1$$

Given the accumulation decision of Department I, Department II mops up all the surplus Department I goods available for accumulation. Each Department replaces used up capital: there is no decumulation. Thus $a_i \geqslant 0$. How much can a_{2t} be? This depends on total output of Y_1, and the replacement requirement of each Department and $\bar{a}_1$. Let us ask what is the *maximum* proportion Department I can accumulate ignoring Department II altogether. [In the numerical example of Table 10 this is, for example, equivalent to buying all the surplus 500 units of constant capital for itself plus a matching 125 of variable capital i.e. 625 out of 1,000 surplus value]. Thus the maximum units of constant capital Department I can buy $(\hat{a}_{1t} g_1 S_{1t})$ is given by available output after replacement requirements have been met.

$$\hat{a}_{1t} g_1 S_{1t} = \left(Y_{1t} - \frac{g_1}{k_1} Y_{1t} - \frac{g_2}{k_2} Y_{2t} \right)$$

$k_i = (1 + \pi_i)$. Subscripts on g_i and k_i are dropped because they are constant. g_i/k_i is the replacement requirement for constant capital per unit of output. Dividing by Y_{1t}, and labelling $(Y_{1t}/Y_{2t}) = y_t$, we get

$$\hat{a}_{1t} = \frac{[1 - g_1/k_1 - (g_2/k_2)y^{-1}_t]}{g_1 \pi^*_1}$$

$\pi^*_1 = (\pi_1/1 + \pi_1)$. Since g_i, k_i are constant we have

$$\hat{a}_{1t} = \alpha_1 - \beta_1 y_t^{-1} \quad \alpha_1 > 0, \beta_1 > 0 \tag{80}$$

The maximum rate at which Department I can accumulate is determined by the proportion of output in the two Departments

Now Department II will buy whatever Department I does not take

$$a_2 g_2 S_{2t} = (\hat{a}_{1t} - \bar{a}_1) g_1 S_{1t}$$

The left hand side gives the number of additional units of constant capital bought by Department II and the right hand side expresses the availability after Department I has made its decision. Of course Department I cannot choose any rate of accumulation, since $a_1 \leq \hat{a}_{1t}$ for all t. Since Departments do not borrow from each other, a_i can also not exceed unity. Dividing across by Y_{1t} and manipulating, we get

$$a_{2t} = \frac{(\hat{a}_{1t} - \bar{a}_1)g_1\pi_1^*}{g_2\pi^*} \, y_t \qquad (81)$$

The accumulation rate of Department II is determined by the maximum permissible rate of accumulation of Department I, the actual rate of accumulation chosen by Department I and the proportion of output in the two Departments.

Now we can substitute (80) into (81) and get

$$a_{2t} = \frac{g_1\pi_1^*}{g_2\pi_2^*} \{[\alpha_1 - \beta_1 y_t^{-1}] - \bar{a}_1\}y_t$$

where

$$= \lambda \, [(\alpha_1 - \bar{a}_1)y_t - \beta_1]\} \qquad (82)$$

$$\lambda = \frac{g_1\pi_1^*}{g_2\pi_2^*}$$

So far we have assumed no specific numerical values for g_i or a_i. We have adopted Marx's assumptions constancy of g_i, r, and of the way Department I fixes on a constant proportion $\bar{a}_1$ and the way Department II mops up the remaining constant capital.

We can now model the course of events in SER. Note that the difference in the growth rate of the two Departments is approximately the growth rate of the proportion of the two Departments output

$$\mu_{1t} - \mu_{2t} \approx \Delta \log y_t = \pi_1\bar{a}_1 - \pi_2 a_{2t}$$

$$= \pi_1\bar{a}_1 - \pi_2\lambda[(\alpha_1 - \bar{a}_1)y_t - \beta_1]$$

$$\Delta \log y_t = (\pi_2\lambda\beta_1 + \pi_1\bar{a}_1) - \pi_2\lambda(\alpha_1 - \bar{a}_1)y_t \qquad (83)$$

or

$$\Delta \log y_t = b_o - b_1 y_t \qquad (83a)$$

Equation (83) can be called a fundamental equation of Marx's model of expanded reproduction. It summarizes all the relevant details of the SER. The difference in growth rates of the two Departments or the growth rate of the output proportion depends only on two elements $\bar{a}_1$ to be chosen by Department I capitalists and the existing proportion of output y_t. The remaining terms are constants by assumption about g_i and r.

One way of looking at equation (83) is to ask what value of y is the balanced growth value. For this we set the left hand side of (83) equal to zero and get

$$y^* = \frac{\pi_{2}\lambda\beta_1 + \pi_1\bar{a}_1}{\pi_{2\lambda}(\alpha_i - \bar{a}_1)} = \frac{b_0}{b_1} \qquad (84)$$

Note that y^* is an increasing function of $\bar{a}_1$. Thus

$dy^*/d\bar{a}_1 = (b_1\pi_1 + \pi_2\lambda b_0)/b_1^2 > 0$. It is also easy to check that $d^2y^*/d\bar{a}_1 > 0$.

An alternate question to ask is the following. Given an initial value of y_t (y_o) what value of $\bar{a}_1$ will achieve balanced growth? This only involves rearranging (83) and again settling $\Delta \log y = 0$

$$\bar{a}_1^* = \frac{\pi_2\lambda(\alpha_1 y_o - \beta_1)}{\pi_1 + \pi_2\lambda y_o} = \frac{\pi_2\lambda\hat{a}_{10}y_o}{(\pi_1 + \pi_2\lambda y_o)} \qquad (85)$$

$\hat{a}_{10}$ is the maximum investment possible by Department I given initial output proportion. We see then that $\bar{a}_1^*$ is also positive but diminishing function of y_o $d\bar{a}_1/dy_o > 0$ $d\bar{a}_1^2/dy_o^2 < 0$.

Equation (84) says that once a value of $\bar{a}_1$ is chosen, corresponding to that value a balanced growth proportion always exists. Thus if $\bar{a}_1 = 0$ then $y^* = \beta_1/\alpha_1$. Now β_1/α_1 also happens to be the value of y_t for which $\hat{a}_{1t} = 0$. Thus when income proportion is β_1/α_1, Department I is so small that no net accumulation is possible. The economy constantly replaces itself

rather like the Sraffa Economy with No Surplus. As $\bar{a}_1$
increases the value of y^* increases. In the initial period 0, $\bar{a}_1$ of
course cannot exceed $\hat{a}_{10}$. Within the range $\hat{a}_1$ and $\bar{a}_1 = 0$, y^*
will take various values. Similarly equation (85) says that for a
given initial proportion of output in the two Departments there
exists a value of $\bar{a}_1$ which if selected will guarantee balanced
growth.

Marx's model however not only relates to the question of
existence of balanced growth. It contains a much more powerful
result. This is that starting from *any* initial value and *any* chosen
value of $\bar{a}_1$, an economy will attain balanced growth in *one
year*. As Morishima has said, Marx constructed a two-sector
growth model with the shortest lag before covergence to
balanced growth. Except for the obvious constraint that
$\hat{a}_{1t} \geqslant \bar{a}_1 \geqslant 0$, and $1 \geqslant \bar{a}_1 \geqslant 0$, there is no other qualification to
that statement. Indeed (85) illustrates a slightly stronger result
than that. This is that *any given value of y_o is a balanced growth
value provided an appropriate $\bar{a}_1$ is chosen*. Equation (84) on
the other hand says that once you have chosen $\bar{a}_1$ y^* is defined
though it is not guaranteed that it will be y_o. It will definitely be
y_1.

There is thus no conceivable possiblity of finding unbalanced
or disproportional growth in the SER. Once its structure is
given, its conclusions follow with an iron necessity. The result is
totally independent of the values of g_i, r or y_o chosen by Marx.

Why is this so? Morishima proves this by showing that once
$a_{1t} = \bar{a}_1$, $\mu_{1t} = \mu_1$ and then $\mu_{2t+1} = \mu_{1t} = \mu_1$. We can illustrate
this by using equation (83). A change in $\bar{a}_1$ given y_o changes
both the slope and the intercept of the equation. The point at
which the line cuts the x axis in Fig. 10 is y^*. The slope gives
the speed of convergence. The simultaneous change in slope and
intercept reduces the problem to one of quick convergence.
Four values of $\bar{a}_1$ are shown. b_{oo} is the intercept for $\bar{a}_1 = 0$.
For this value $y^* = \beta_1/\alpha_1$ b_{o3} corresponds to $\hat{a}_1$ b_{o1} is a value of
$\bar{a}_1 > 0$, and b_{o2} is a higher value of $\bar{a}_1$. For each value of a_1 we
get an increasing value of y^*.

We consider only economies for which $\bar{a}_1 \geqslant 0$ i.e. value of
$y \geqslant y^*_1$. An economy at y_o, can end up at A, B or C. If it
chooses the relatively lower value of a_1, it will be at A, if not at

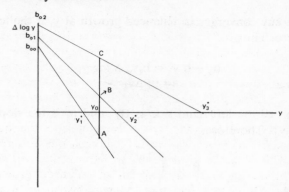

FIGURE 10
Changing Values of Balanced Growth Output as $\bar{a}_1$ Changes

B. Now the height $y_o A$ shows the difference between the rate of growth of Department I and of Department II. Since μ_1 is given the height of $y_o A$ shows how a choice of $\bar{a}_1$ determines the growth rate of Department II. At B μ_{2t} it is lower than at A. Thus C corresponds to $\bar{a}_1 = \hat{a}_{1o}$ the maximum rate of accumulation and at C, $\mu_2 = 0$.

Once a value of $\bar{a}_1$ is chosen, however, the next period's growth rate is affected too. The higher the difference in growth rate this period the higher y_1 relative to y_o. But by equation (80), we see that this raises $\hat{a}_{11}$. Since Department I has fixed demands for accumulation, the higher $\hat{a}_{11}$ the more investible constant capital remains for Department II. Thus the low growth rate for Department II at $t = 0$ is compensated by high growth rate in year 1. So the higher $\Delta \log y_t$ in $t = 0$, the lower it will be in $t = 1$. Indeed in $t = 1$, $\Delta \log y_t = 0$.

What we need to prove is that the economy will reach balanced growth in exactly one year or immediately. In terms of Figure 10 what we need do show is that at y_o the growth rate By_o takes the economy to $y_1 = y^*_2$. In other words, we show that $y_1 - y_0 = y_o y^*_2$. By equation (83)

$$\Delta \log y_1 = b_o - b_1 y_1$$
$$= b_o - b_1 y_o (1 + \Delta \log y_o)$$

The economy converges to balanced growth at y_1 if the left hand side is zero. Thus

$$b_o - b_1 y_o = b_1 y_o \, \Delta \log y_o$$
$$= b_1 \, \Delta y_o$$

By Figure 10 the left hand side is By_0 and b_1 is the slope given by $By_o/y_o y_2^*$. Therefore,

$$By_o = \left| \left(\frac{By_o}{y_o y_2^*} \right) \right| \Delta \, y_o$$

Thus $y_o y_2^* = \Delta \, y_o.$

The economy moves from y_0 to y_2^* in one year. The same proof can be used for Ay_0 and a_{10} and the move from y_0 to y_1^* and y_3^*. [See Desai and Skott (1978) for a more rigorous proof.]

Thus starting from any $y_0 > y_1^* = \beta_1/\alpha_1$, that is, as long as $\hat{a}_1 \geq 0$, the economy will converge to balanced growth in one year. The precise value of a_1 e.g. $\frac{1}{2}$ as taken by Marx does not matter. The form of the investment function – choice of $a_{1t} = \overline{a}_1$ and a_{2t} adaptive to the gap between $\hat{a}_1$ and $\overline{a}_1$ – is the most important. We can now go on to prove that *for every y_0 there is an a_1 such that* $y_o = y^*$. Thus every economy is in balanced growth if the capitalists of Department I choose the correct rate of accumulation. This is already implicit in equation (85). There we see that a given y_0 will yield a_1^* such that $\Delta \log y_0 = 0$. The only constraint is $0 < a_1^* < \hat{a}_{10}$. Another way to look at it is to draw (83) differently. Figure 11 does this. Now we draw $\Delta \log y_0$ against a_1 for each value of y_0. We write

$$\Delta \log y_0 = \pi_2 \lambda \, (\beta_1 - \alpha_1 y_t) + (\pi_1 + \pi_2 \lambda y_t) \overline{a}_1 \qquad (83c)$$

$$= \gamma_0 + \gamma_1 \overline{a}_1 \qquad (83d)$$

$\beta_1 < \alpha_1 y_t$ by the fact that $\hat{a}_1 \geq 0$. Thus the intercept y_0 is negative. The slope is positive and increasing with y_0, y_{00} and y_{01} are two intercepts with $y = y_{00}$ and y_{01} where $y_{01} > y_{00}$. Each line will cross the x axis as long as $y_0 < 0$. The value of a_1^* is

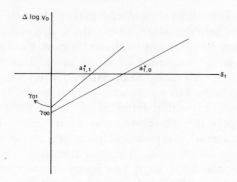

FIGURE 11   The relation between $\bar{a}_1$ and Growth Rate

given by the point at which the equation for $\Delta \log \dot{y}_0$ crosses the x axis. For each value of y_0 the appropriate a_1^* will yield an investment programme that will keep $y_0 = y^*$.

While none of these results depend on the numerical values chosen by Marx, the numbers in Table 10 can be used to check our calculations. We have $\pi_1 = 1/5$, $\pi_2 = 1/3$, $g_1 = 4/5$, $g_2 = 2/3$, $k_1 = 6/5$, $k_2 = 4/3$, $\pi_1^* = 1/6$, $\pi_1^* = 1/4$. These values give $\alpha_1 = 2.50$, $\beta_1 = 3.75$, $\lambda = 0.8$, $b_0 = (1.0 + \pi_1\bar{a}_1)$, $b_1 = 0.267 (2.5 - \bar{a}_1)$. Equation (83) can be then written alternatively for (83a) and (83d) as

$$\Delta \log y_t = (1 + 0.2\ \bar{a}_1) - 0.267\ (2.5 - \bar{a}_1)y_t \qquad (86a)$$

$$\Delta \log y_t = (1 - 0.66\ y_t) + (0.2 + 0.267\ y_t)\bar{a}_1 \qquad (86b)$$

ing $\bar{a}_1 = 1/2$ in (86a) we see that $y^* = 1.1/0.534 = 2.0625$. This is the ratio of outputs in Table 10 after the initial year. The initial value of y = is 2.0. The initial value of $\bar{a}_1^* = 0.32/0.734 = 0.436$.

Thus given the parameters Marx's choice of $a_1 = 0.5$ gives a value of $y^* = 2.0625$ not far away from $y_0 = 2.0$. Alternately, had Marx chosen $a_1 = 0.436$, the initial proportion would have been confirmed as balanced growth. At this value both Departments will have grown at 8.7 per cent. The value of $\hat{a}_{10}$ is 0.625 as can be checked. [Readers can experiment with alternate values of the parameters to check these results.]

This discussion of Marx's model makes clear the very powerful conceptual scheme Marx invented for discussion of accumulation. He may have meant to illustrate how the Invisible Hand
works, that is the existence of equilibrium. But this could be
done by SSR as well as by SER. He ended up with not only an
equilibrium scheme but a balanced growth model to which every
economy converges either immediately or at most in one year.
One can appreciate, therefore, why many critics found it difficult to understand the powerful tendency towards equilibrium
growth or to generate cycles from the model.

Brilliant as the SER is, it has many shortcomings. Thus all
outputs are measured in labour values and hence the SER is
entirely confined to the circuit of commodity capital. Each
Department earns a different (value) rate of profit and no
attempt is made to link accumulation to formation of prices or
of money profits. The organic composition of capital stays constant as does the rate of exploitation. We do not even know if
value per unit of physical quantity is declining, that is if a larger
mass of use values is produced during the course of growth.
There is no constraint due to shortage of labour; each year the
economy is able to grow at ten per cent at fixed organic compositions of capital.

More than all these assumptions what strains credulity is the investment behaviour of the capitalists. Why should Department I
capitalists invest a fixed proportion of their surplus value, beg-
ging for the time being the question of the form in which they
hold their surplus value? There is no threat of technical change
or constant revolution in values (that Marx mentions in other
parts of his work) in this economy. Even if there were such constant revolution in values, a two-Department framework is
inadequate to deal with it. There is no threat to the (value) rate
of profit. We do not know what may be happening to the
money rate of profit since prices are not formed. It is true that
it is the capitalists' nature to accumulate, but such an 'explanation' is not enough to account for the constancy of accumulation.

The behaviour of Department II capitalists is equally puzzling.
They look not to their own future demand or profit rate. They
exist to solve the realization problem of Department I capitalists and little else. They invest 20 per cent of surplus value in

the first year and 30 per cent in the second year and ever after. They too invest only within their Department like the Department I capitalists.

One way to understand the investment behaviour is not in terms of a capitalist economy with decentralized decision making and profit motive but in terms of a planned economy. Thus a planner chooses a_i in such a way that each Department can sell all its output, so as to alleviate all realization problems. The planner can compute the balanced growth requirements of the economy. It is this interpretation we explore in the next chapter.

We also need to explore further the underlying reasons for Marx's result. We have already seen that the numerical values chosen do not matter for the balanced growth conclusion nor do they affect the speed of convergence. We locate the crux of the matter in the investment function. We explore how important the primacy of Department I, that is, $a_{1t} = \bar{a}_1$ assumption is in Marx's scheme.

XVII

THE SCHEME OF EXPANDED REPRODUCTION AS A PLANNING MODEL

An interpretation of SER as a planning model is not too far fetched. The first attempts at planning in the USSR in 1920s made extensive use of the SER as a starting point for the plan formulation. Feldman in his famous planning model relied heavily on SER and in Indian planning Mahalanobis also arrived at a Marx Feldman model quite independently. Indeed, while in terms of a model of capitalist growth the SER is inadequate and has been the subject of controversy, in planning it has proved very fruitful [Domar (1957)].

The constancy of $\tilde{a}_1$ and the adaptive course of a_2 makes little sense in a capitalist economy, but is eminently sensible in a planned economy. One can think of a capitalist economy in which the state plays a commanding role (say as in war-time planning) or of a socialist economy in which the state owns all means of production. Such economies may be constrained in their accumulation by shortage of capital goods. So it is the planner's task to allocate capital goods so as to maximize growth. (In the SER Marx considers constant capital which is used up in every period, that is he neglects fixed capital. This somewhat limits its applicability to actual economies).

The overall growth rate of the economy (μ) is a weighted sum of growth rates of the two Departments, the weights being their share in total output, that is $\omega^*_{it} = Y_{it}/Y_t$

$$
\begin{aligned}
\mu_t &= \omega^*_{1t}\mu_{1t} + (1 - \omega^*_{1t})\mu_{2t} \\
&= \omega^*_{1t}\pi_1 a_{1t} + (1 - \omega^*_{1t})\pi_2 a_{2t}
\end{aligned}
\tag{87}
$$

The planner maximizes this subject to the constraint

$$a_1 g_1 S_1 + a_2 g_2 S_{2t} = \hat{a}_{1t} g_1 S_{1t} \qquad (88)$$

The constraint states that accumulation by the two Departments cannot exceed the total available supply of capital goods. Now (87) can be written as

$$\mu = \left(\frac{y_t}{1 + y_t} \right) \pi_1 a_{1t} + \left(\frac{1}{1 + y_t} \right) \pi_2 a_{2t} \qquad (87a)$$

Equation (88) can be rearranged using $\lambda = g_1 \pi^*_1 / g_2 \pi^*_2$,

$$a_{1t} + \frac{1}{\lambda y_t} a_{2t} = \hat{a}_{1t} \qquad (88a)$$

In addition we can express the balanced growth proportion of investment ratios. Balanced growth requires $\mu_{1t} = \mu_{2t}$. Hence

$$\frac{a_{1t}}{a_{2t}} = \frac{\pi_2}{\pi_1} \qquad (89)$$

The problem is illustrated in Figure 12. This is a linear programming problem. Equation (88a) will describe the constraint set and the objective function will be a series of straight lines representing different levels of μ with slope $\pi_2 / \pi_1 y_t$ for each time period t. The planner will choose the highest value of μ within the constraint set.

Each year the constraint set will move outwards, as with increasing output $\hat{a}_{1t}$ will increase. The slope of the constraint line will change as y_t changes and will be unchanged only in balanced growth. As a planning model this is a one period ahead 'myopic' exercise. The planner will be able to settle on a balanced growth path quite soon.

In Fig. 12, $\hat{a}_{2t}$ represents the value of a_2 when $a_1 = 0$. Now e is the point of intersection of the balanced growth proportion and the constraint set. For year 0 in Marx's example, we have worked out that at e, $\bar{a}^*_1 = 0.436$. Thus a growth line passing through e in the initial period is not growth maximizing. At e with $\bar{a}_1 = 0.436$, each sector grows at 8.7 per cent and hence

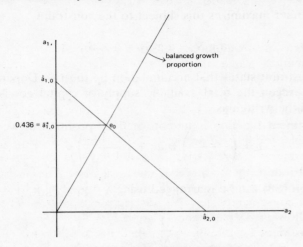

FIGURE 12 SER as a Planning Model

$\mu = 8.7$ per cent. Marx's choice of $\bar{a}_1 = 0.5$ locates a higher growth line since actual growth rate in the first year is $800/900 \approx 8.88$ per cent.

This is illustrated in Figure 13. Marx's $\bar{a}_1$ is above the value given by e_0. In the next period $\bar{a}_1$ cuts the balanced growth line at e_1 which satisfies the constraint on $\hat{a}_1$. At e_1 the economy is in balanced growth and grows at 10 per cent annum. When $\bar{a}_1 = \hat{a}_{10}$ we have a maximal growth rate.

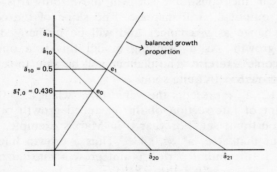

FIGURE 13 Marx's Solution as a Planning Model

ASYMMETRY IN SER

Though his method of work consisted of interminable arithmetical calculations, Marx arrived at an accumulation scheme which has strong balanced growth properties and is amenable to a planning interpretation. We must, however, understand its generality further. Thus granting that the investment function is unmotivated by profits, can we preserve the balanced growth property if we reverse the priority between Department I and Department II? Is Marx's balanced growth result independent of who chooses a_i first? The answer, as we shall see, is no. Given every other assumption in Marx's model about constancy of g_i, r, we only change the nature of the result by allowing Department II capitalists to fix $a_{2t} = \bar{a}_2$ and let Department I capitalists mop up their unsold output of constant capital. This is neither more nor less realistic that Marx's own assumption. There is no inherent logic in the primacy of Department I.

Assume, then that Department II capitalists choose $a_{2t} = \bar{a}_2$ and Department I capitalists mop up the rest. We can define $\hat{a}_{2t}$ as before,

$$g_2 S_{2t} \hat{a}_{2t} = (1 - g_1/k_1)Y_{1t} - (g_2/k_2)Y_{2t}$$

$$\hat{a}_{2t} = \frac{(1 - g_1/k_1)}{g_2 \Pi^*_2} y_t - (g_2/k_2)$$

or

$$\hat{a}_{2t} = \alpha_2 y_t - \beta_2 \qquad \alpha_2 > 0, \beta_2 > 0 \qquad (90)$$

Equation (90) is derived the same way as equation (80) and is symmetrical to it. Then

$$g_1 S_{1t} a_{1t} = (\hat{a}_{2t} - \bar{a}_2)g_2 S_{2t}$$

$$a_{1t} = (\hat{a}_{2t} - \bar{a}_2)\left(\frac{g_2 \pi^*_2}{g_1 \pi^*_1}\right)\bigg| y_t^{-1}$$

This can be simplified as before

$$a_{1t} = \lambda^{-1}(a_{2t} - \bar{a}_2)y_t^{-1} \tag{91}$$

Again (91) is symmetrical to (81). Then substituting (90) into (91)

$$a_{1t} = \lambda^{-1}\{\alpha_2 y_t - \bar{a}_2 - \beta_2\}y_t^{-1}$$

$$= \lambda^{-1}\{\alpha_2 - (\bar{a}_2 + \beta_2)y_t^{-1}\}. \tag{92}$$

By the same calculations as before, we derive the differential growth rate

$$\Delta \log y_t = \pi_1 a_{1t} - \pi_2 \bar{a}_2$$

$$= \lambda^{-1}\pi_1\{\alpha_2 - (\bar{a}_2 + \beta_2)y_t^{-1}\} - \pi_2 \bar{a}_2$$

$$\Delta \log y_t = (\lambda^{-1}\pi_1\alpha_2 - \pi_2\bar{a}_2) - \lambda^{-1}\pi_1(\bar{a}_2 + \beta_2)y_t^{-1} \tag{93}$$

$$= \delta_0 - \delta_1 y_t^{-1} \tag{93a}$$

Equation (93) is the other fundamental expression for Marx's model giving priority this time to Department II rather than Department I. Notice, however, that (93) is a curve rather than a straight line. As $y \to 0$, $\Delta \log y_t \to -\infty$ and as $y \to \infty$ $\Delta \log y_t \to \delta_0$. Figure 14 illustrates equation (93). The point at which the curve cuts the x-axis is of course the balanced growth proportion.

$$y^* = \delta_1/\delta_0 = \frac{\lambda^{-1}\pi_1(\bar{a}_2 + \beta_2)}{\lambda^{-1}\pi_1\alpha_2 - \pi_2 a_2} \tag{94}$$

where $dy^*/d\bar{a}_2 > 0$ and $d^2 y^*/d\bar{a}_2^2 > 0$

The non-linearity of equation (93) means we cannot employ the same technique of proof as before. We can show very simply the impossibility of balanced growth in this version of the SER. Except by accident – if $y_0 = y^*$ — balanced growth will not be approached. Take the point y_0 in Figure 14. This gives Ay_0 for a given value of $\bar{a}_2$. Now $y_0 > y^*$ but a positive value of $\Delta \log y_0$

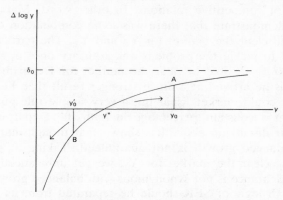

FIGURE 14   SER with $a_{2t} = \bar{a}_2$: Unbalanced Growth.

means that in the next period $y_1 > y_0$. Already Department I will be larger than its equilibrium proportion, but the choice of $\bar{a}_2$ implies that this disproportionality increases. Similarly y'_0 will give By'_0 and Department II will grow more rapidly than Department I, but Department I is already smaller than its equilibrium value. The equilibrium point y^* is, in technical terms, *a saddle point*.

The prospect of unbalanced growth or increasing disproportionality is indicated by the arrows indicating divergence of y_t away from y^*. We see than that the balanced growth result in Marx's SER is due to the primacy of Department I. Reverse the primacy and the balanced growth result is not symmetrical. Disproportionality can be obtained in Marx's model as easily as balanced growth. Thus Marx's *model* is more general than the SER. The model need not involve $a_{1t} = \bar{a}_1$ but the scheme does.

Note that the discussion above does not establish a possibility of *cycles*. It says only that if investment behaviour is as Marx modelled in SER with only a symmetric change from $\bar{a}_1$ to $\bar{a}_2$, disproportional or unbalanced growth can occur. Once, however, SER has been opened up in this way, one can further generalize the model positing different investment behaviour.

Let us once again take up the interpretation of SER. As we said above, it is argued by Mandel among others that SER only demonstrates the possibility that markets can clear even in the anarchy of competitive relations. In other words Marx wanted only to demonstrate that there was *some* combination of a_{1t}, a_{2t} which will clear the market for Y_{1t} and Y_{2t}. The particular way he chose to tackle the problem was arbitrary once $a_1 = \bar{a}_1$ then a_{2t} had to be flexible to clear the market for Department I. In doing this he arrived at a much stronger result than he needed. Not only could markets clear but a very simple rule guaranteed growth at a constant percentage in both the Departments for ever. Our discussion above has shown that though markets can clear, balanced growth is not guaranteed. Taking $a_{2t} = \bar{a}_2$ and letting a_{1t} clear the market for Y_1, we get unbalanced growth. Market clearance is not synonymous with balanced growth. Thus the growth logic of SER should be separated from its Invisible Hand logic. SER can be used to explore unbalanced growth and cycles once its underlying logic has been clarified.

XVIII

EXPECTATIONS AND ACCUMULATION

From our discussion of the SER so far we see that in the course of analysing the concept of national income for a growing economy, Marx arrived at a powerful two-sector growth model. Not only was this the first effort at formalizing a two-sector growth model, but by making balanced growth so easily attainable, it also complicated considerably the task of reconciling the vision of capitalism as riddled with crises in Vol. I of *Capital* with SER. Of the various authors who subsequently tried to tackle this task, we have concentrated especially on Rosa Luxemburg's work. This is not because she provided the correct answer but because she asked the searching questions.

We have looked earlier at the usefulness of keeping accounts in monetary, physical and value units. This matches the three circuits of capital, which is an infrequently used but very helpful device. In terms of the three circuits, we can see that SER concentrates exclusively on the value calculus. It is in the circuit of commodity capital $C - C - C$ that SER operates. The connection of SER with the money circuit and the physical circuit remains to be made.

This missing connection becomes apparent at various stages. Thus excess output of Department I of 500 units of value will take the form of extra machines. These are also not fixed capital but circulating capital as the durability of past investments is kept out of account. Being nondurable, they have to be used up in the current period. If they are not sold, they are use-less – their value cannot be realized. This is why it is important that the accumulation process clears the market for Department I output. The *physical form* of the 500 units of excess output is important here, since excess output of wage goods can always be 'eaten' by the capitalists themselves.

But market clearance is not the motive force in capitalism. The capitalist advances money capital and wishes to recover his capital in money form. His ability to recover his money capital as well as to realize a profit depends, however, on his willingness and other capitalists' willingness to accumulate. If the capitalists do not decide to accumulate they will not realize their profits. The converse is more often asserted: if the capitalists do not realize profits they cannot invest.

The monetary dimension of accumulation is completely ignored in SER and this is one of the questions raised by Rosa Luxemburg. She asks how Department I capitalists can accumulate one half of their surplus value before they have realised it. Where does the money to buy the inputs come from?

This question is easily answered in the commodity circuit context. Thus if we conceive of each Department as being run by a single capitalist, then we see that Department I needs only to have 100 extra units to buy *additional* variable capital. Having sold 1500 units of constant capital for replacement to Department II, Department I buys only 1100 units of Y_2 even after accumulation. It has 400 units 'trade surplus' which can be spent on capitalists consumption. The financing problem is therefore of Department II if anyone's.

The important question is not how accumulation is financed but why it occurs at all. Why should Department I accumulate faced with potential excess supply of its output? Given the parameters of the problem, the (value) rate of profit and the organic composition of capital remain constant. Thus there is no pressure on the rate of profit to cause capitalists to accumulate. No increase in the organic composition is required to stave off the fall in the rate of profit. No technical change seems to be occurring. Why should accumulation take place?

A trivial answer is that capitalists accumulate because they have always done so. That is their role in life. Not for profit, or to survive competitive pressure, but because of (say) their Calvinist upbringing. Even if this were granted, why should they accumulate a constant proportion of the (still unrealized) surplus value as Department I capitalists seem to?

Another answer could be that accumulation takes place to

solve the realization problem. But we have to be careful not to muddle up the logical sequence here. No capitalist faced with excess supply will desire to accumulate just to solve the realization problem. Indeed, if the only purpose of the system was to avoid realization problems, each Department could go on buying its own output up and never sell any output. The absurdity of such a notion is apparent on several grounds. Each Department has to buy some inputs from the other Department, and in order to buy, it has to sell to convert some of its output into money. If it is to accumulate, it has to sell increasing amounts of its own output to finance increasing input requirements from the other Department.

It is much more plausible to argue that accumulation takes place and the realization problem gets solved, sometimes, without any *intended* link between the two. Accumulation depends, as we have learned from economists such as Wicksell and Keynes, on basis of *expectations* concerning future profits which may accrue.

Capitalists have to base their accumulation plans on their vision of an uncertain future. They may base their expectations regarding future profitability on current profitability, among other factors. While each pursues his plan, clearance of markets may be an actual outcome. (But of course balanced growth need not come about, as we saw in the previous chapter).

Accumulation *plans* based on expectations must be distinguished, therefore, from accumulation *outcomes*. In the process of transition from plans to outcomes, prices may change or stay stable, sales may exceed or fall short of expectations and so on. Not only must such factors be included in any theory of accumulation, but we must also firmly situate it in the context of a money circuit.

Economic theory has seen many attempts to build a fully dynamic theory of capital accumulation and by no means has a satisfactory answer been reached. Economists such as Tugan-Baranovski, Schumpeter and Kalecki derived their clue from Marx. Others, such as Wicksell, Myrdal, Hayek, Irving Fisher and Keynes, have pursued other solutions. We cannot hope to settle the problem at the present but we may suggest some possible lines of attack.

To keep the problem in perspective, let us take up Marx's

SER example. To begin with we must add a money dimension. Each Department must have advanced $M_{i,t}$ of money capital to buy inputs. Thus for each Department we get

$$\left. \begin{array}{l} M_{1t} = p_{1t} (4000) + p_{2t} (1500) \\ M_{2t} = P_{1t} (1500) + p_{2t} (750) \end{array} \right\} \quad (95)$$

Now the amount of money capital each Department can recover from its output depends on how much it can sell and the price it can sell at. Let Z_i be the amount actually sold by the ith Department and $\tilde{Z}_i$ the amount it expects to sell and similarly for M_i' and $\bar{M}_i'$.

$$\left. \begin{array}{ll} \bar{M}'_{i,t+1} = p_{i,t+1} Z_{i,t+1} & i = 1, 2 \\ \bar{M}_{i,t+1} = p_{i,t+1} \tilde{Z}_{i,t+1} & i = 1, 2 \end{array} \right\} \quad (96)$$

If $\bar{M}_{i,t+1}$ is less than $M_{i,t}$ then the ith Department will be expecting to make a loss and hence would not *plan* any accumulation. How then is expected revenue determined? This depends on expected sales $\tilde{Z}_i$ and expected price $\bar{p}_i$.

The expected sales of each Department will depend on sales for replacement purposes, plus any sales from expected accumulation from itself and from the other Department. We derived the expression for replacement demands in our equations of $\hat{a}_i$ above. Thus

$$\tilde{Z}_1 = \frac{g_1}{k_1} Y_1 + \frac{g_2}{k_2} Y_2 + \Delta\tilde{C}_{1,1} + \Delta\tilde{C}_{2,1} \quad (97)$$

$$\tilde{Z}_2 = \frac{(1-g_1)}{k_1} Y_1 + \frac{(1-g_2)}{k_2} Y_2 + \Delta\bar{V}_{1,2} + \Delta\bar{V}_{2,2} \quad (98)$$

We have deleted the time subscripts since both sides refer to the same time period. $\Delta\tilde{C}_{ji}$, $\Delta\bar{V}_{ji}$ refer to the accumulation of constant and variable capital by the jth Department as expected by the ith Department. This additional complication has to be introduced because expected sales $\bar{Z}_i$ are what the ith Department expects of its own sales.

In (98) we have not included capitalists' consumption as anticipated by Department II. There are two broad views possible here. We may take a view that capitalists' consumption function is stable. Thus they may save a stable proportion of their income (expected and actual). If we assume this, then a_i for each Department becomes constant and $(1 - a_i)$ is the proportion of surplus value consumed.[1]

An alternative view would be that capitalists consumption is a residual based on what remains of profits after accumulation. The accumulation decision depends on many unforeseeable events and hence the constancy of a_{it} is unlikely.

Whether in a commodity circuit or in a money circuit, the crucial question still remains about accumulation plans. Take Department I first. It expects to sell 5500 units for replacement purposes out of 6000. Thus if it expects no accumulation by either Department then it will expect to sell 91.67% of its output. Thus let $\bar{x}_i = (\bar{Z}_i/Y_i)$ and hence $\bar{x}_1 = 0.92$ if $\Delta \bar{C}_{ji} = 0$ for both j. Expecting excess supplies, Department I will have no reason to plan accumulation since accumulation will only increase future output and exacerbate excess supplies. If anything, Department I should plan to cut its future output if it firmly expects no accumulation.

Department I may not accumulate itself, but it may expect Department II to do so. Such an expectation may be based on the previous accumulation behaviour of Department II. For each level of expected accumulation by Department II, $\bar{Z}_1$ will be higher and so will $\bar{x}_1$. One can thus derive a schedule of expected sales for each level of $\Delta \bar{C}_{2,1}$.

Each level of $\Delta \bar{C}_{2,1}$ represents a growth rate of capital stock and of output. Since the growth rate of output μ_i is proportional to the proportion of surplus value accumulated, it also represents a_i. We can express expected sales proportion $\bar{x}_1$ in terms of $\bar{\mu}_i$ or $\bar{a}_i$. Thus equation (97) can be recast as

$$\bar{Z}_1 = Z_{1,-1} + \Delta \bar{C}_{1,1} + \Delta \bar{C}_{2,1} \qquad (97a)$$

The replacement sales of this year of Department I products equals actual sales of last year. Dividing across by Y_1 and rearranging, we get

$$\tilde{x}_1 = \frac{x_{1,-1}}{(1 + \mu_{1,-1})} + \bar{\mu}_{1,1}\frac{g_1}{k_1} + \bar{\mu}_{2,1}\frac{g_2}{k_2} \tag{97b}$$

Here the subscript -1 represents last year's value. Thus $Z_{1,-1}/Y_1 = (Z_{1,-1}/Y_{1,-1})(Y_{1,-1}/Y_1)$. The second term represents the reciprocal of the actual growth factor between last year and this. We can put the first term as a known constant. The expression $\bar{\mu}_i g_i = (\Delta C_{it}/C_{it-1})(C_{it-1}/Y_{it})$. We can simplify (97b) as

$$\tilde{x}_1 = \alpha_0 + g_1 \pi_1^* \bar{a}_{1,1} + g_2 \pi_2^* \bar{a}_{2,1} y^{-1} \tag{97c}$$

Equation (97c) is similar to earlier equations (88) and (88a). In SER, Marx did not consider expectations, but derived those a_1, a_2 combinations which would give $x_1 = 1$.

We can derive a similar expression for x_2, except that we must take some account of the expectations of Department II capitalists concerning the capitalists' consumption demand for their output. Capitalists' demand for consumption is a residual after allowing for accumulation. We can therefore add to equation (98) the expected demand of capitalists for consumption. For each Department this also depends on the expected growth rate of capital stock. We have

$$\tilde{Z}_2 = Z_{2,-1} - \{(1 - a_{1,-1})S_{1,-1} + (1 - a_{2,-1})S_{2,-1}\}$$
$$+ \Delta\hat{V}_{1,2} + \Delta\tilde{V}_{2,2} + \{(1 - \bar{a}_{1,2})\tilde{S}_{1,2} + (1 - \bar{a}_{2,2})\tilde{S}_{2,2}\} \tag{98a}$$

The replacement demand for variable capital in the current year equals total sales less capitalists consumption last year. To this we have added this year's consumption demand $(1 - \bar{a}_{j,i})\tilde{S}_j$. Notice that expected demand for consumer goods depends on expectation concerning proportion of surplus value accumulated and concerning the amount of surplus value realized. Dividing across by Y_2 and rearranging, we get

$$x_2 = \frac{[1 - (1 - a_{2,-1})\pi_2^*]x_{2,-1}}{(1 + \mu_{2,-1})} - \frac{(1 - a_{1,-1})\pi_1^*}{(1 + \mu_{1,-1})} y$$

$$+ (1 - g_1)\pi_1^* \tilde{a}_{1,2} y + (1 - g_2)\pi_2^* \tilde{a}_{2,2} + (1 - \hat{a}_{1,2})\hat{\pi}_1^* \bar{x}_1 y$$

$$+ (1 - \hat{a}_{2,2})\hat{\pi}_2^* \bar{x}_2 \qquad (98b)$$

Equation (98b) looks somewhat formidable, but its structure is similar to (97b). The first two terms on the right hand side come from last period's actual sales and consumption demand of Department II capitalists last year. The third term is Department I capitalists' consumption demand last year; notice that it involves the current output proportion y_t as a variable. The next two terms are parallel with equation (97b), representing accumulation demand. The last two terms concern expected consumption demand this year. We have expressed $\tilde{S}_{1,2}/Y_2$ as $(\tilde{S}_{12}/\tilde{Z}_1)(\tilde{z}_1/Y_1)(Y_1/Y_2)$.

The complications in (98b) arise because we show expectations concerning unknown variables explicitly. If we take expectations of capitalists' consumption this year to be the same in amount as last year, then in equation (98a) the expressions in the two curly brackets cancel out: We then get

$$x_2 = \frac{x_{2,-1}}{(1 + \mu_{2,-1})^i} + (1 - g_1)\pi_1^* \tilde{a}_{12} y + (1 - g_2)\pi_2^* \tilde{a}_{2,2} \qquad (98c)$$

To keep the exposition simple we shall work with (97c) and (98c). This says that Department II capitalists have static expectations concerning consumption demand by capitalists. Of course this implies that expectations concerning consumption and accumulation need not add up to total actual output; a shortfall in effective demand is one of the possibilities envisaged by capitalists.

We can now put together our exploratory analysis so as to extend SER to take account of uncertainty and expectations. Thus we have in (97c) and (98c) two equations each of which gives an isosales line for a level of $\bar{x}_i$ for combinations of $\tilde{a}_{ij}$. The question we ask is whether these expectations will be compatible so as to clear both markets. If this is so, then we have a warranted growth path in SER. We want to see if (97c) and (98c) intersect for values of $\bar{x}_1 = \bar{x}_2 = 1$ at compatible values of growth rates.

The two equations can be compactly written as

$$\bar{x}_1 = \alpha_0 + \alpha_1 \bar{a}_{1,1} + \alpha_2 \bar{a}_{2,1} \tag{97d}$$

$$\bar{x}_2 = \beta_0 + \beta_1 \bar{a}_{1,2} + \beta_2 \bar{a}_{2,2} \tag{98d}$$

Setting $\bar{x}_1 = 1$, we get

$$\bar{a}_{1,1} = \left(\frac{1 - \alpha_0}{\alpha_1} \right) - \frac{\alpha_2}{\alpha_1} \, \bar{a}_{2,1} \tag{99a}$$

$$\bar{a}_{1,2} = \frac{(1 - \beta_0)}{\beta_1} - \frac{\beta_2}{\beta_1} \, \bar{a}_{2,2} \tag{99b}$$

Equation (99a) is what Department I thinks will clear markets for its output in terms of investment plans. Similarly (99b) looks at the problem from the point of view of Department II. Each equation has a positive intercept and a negative slope. Examining the slopes we see that

$$\frac{\alpha_2}{\alpha_1} = \left(\frac{g_2 \pi_2^*}{g_1 \pi_1^*} \right) y^{-1} \qquad\qquad \frac{\beta_2}{\beta_1} = \frac{(1 - g_2) \pi_2^*}{(1 - g_1) \pi_1^*} \, y^{-1}$$

Only if $g_i = g$ for both Departments will the slopes be identical. We can exclude that possibility. We will otherwise get an equilibrium solution for the warranted growth path.

We have thus expanded the SER to include expectations regarding sales and shown that mutually compatible plans can exist. Whether actual growth rate will equal such a warranted growth rate is a separate question. It depends on how accumulation plans are actually formed by each Department. This will involve assuming a specific accumulation equation, for example an accelerator relationship. We leave this question aside.

We have only made a very small beginning to bridging the gap between SER and the specification of a dynamic Marxian model of cycles in a monetary economy. We said earlier on that to integrate SER with the three circuits of capital is a vital part of such a task. Our modification of SER has allowed for the realization problem to enter explicitly into the scheme but there are many aspects of a monetary economy we have still left out.

We shall only mention such aspects as much work needs to be done here. Thus we said in equation (96) that expectations concerning prices as well as concerning sales are important. In subsequent discussion we have assumed away price expectations. The formation of price expectations are important. Secondly, once we are in a monetary context, we must allow for consumption as well as hoarding out of profits. The possibility of borrowing and lending to bridge the gap between available resources and required uses comes up in a monetary economy. We may also extend the SER to a three-Department model where taxation, credit creation and surplus absorption can be the tasks of the third – state-sector. This can form the rudiments of a financial model to be integrated with the model of accumulation. Lastly, we have to explore alternative assumptions concerning investment behaviour, allowing for influence of the rate of profit, technical change, capacity utilization and so on.

The schemes for expanded reproduction are an abstract framework but by no means therefore useless or a hindrance to further research. Many gaps have to be filled so that we can interpret data from contemporary economy in light of Marxian categories. Only when such gaps have been filled shall we be able to cast the data in a form in which we can 'test' Marxian hypotheses. At present we have no theoretical scheme that will enable us to address the empirical information available. Testing of Marx's predictions is therefore a hazardous undertaking. In the next chapter, one such attempt will be examined.

XIX

THE FALLING RATE OF PROFIT

The long standing neglect of Marx in traditional economic theory (and in the wider intellectual context) has been based on two main criticisms. Firstly, following Bohm-Bawerk, Wicksteed and others, it is claimed that the labour theory of value is erroneous and unnecessary as an explanation of relative prices. Marx's failure 'to prove' that prices are proportional to labour content in Vol. III, as against his assertion of such proportionality in Vol. I, is thought to have settled the matter. The labour theory of value is assigned then to the status of theories which have been superseded by better ones – we could call this 'the labour theory as flat earth view'. This view also implies that empirically it is obvious that prices are not proportional to labour content anyway – that the earth is round. Thus both logically and empirically the labour theory of value according to this view is superseded and its continuing defence is dogmatic.

This argument, in our view, has missed the main purpose of labour theory of value in Marx. Once his arithmetical errors have been corrected (as by Bortkiewicz) prices are derivable from (though not proportional to) value categories. We should add, however, that both logically and empirically the translation of values into prices (and vice versa), while important in order to bring out the social dynamics, is a much more complex task than either critics or defenders of Marx have ever previously allowed for.

The second criticism is that Marx's prophecies have been contradicted by the course of capitalist society. The working class is not immiserized either relatively or absolutely: socialist revolutions have failed to occur in mature capitalist countries; full employment rather than the reserve army of unemployed is the order of the day and the rate of profit has not fallen as Marx predicted it would.

It would be fruitless to deny that twentieth century-capitalism, especially post-1945 post-Keynesian capitalism, contradicts many of the gloomy prophecies. Many defenders of Marx have tried to redefine and rationalize the predictions in such a way that they come out to be valid or at least not contradicted. Thus the less developed third world is seen to be the reserve army of unemployed; their people are the increasingly immiserized proletariat. There were even attempts, happily forgotten now, to prove that the increasing productivity of the modern worker meant increasing relative rate of exploitation and hence increasing misery in psychological terms. We do not wish to take up such a last ditch defence position. We shall concern ourselves with the question of testing Marx's predictions, especially the prediction about the falling rate of profit.

In the following pages we look at Marx's statement of the problem and at least one detailed attempt (by Gillman) to test the prediction. We examine the problem of testing the prediction, particularly in the light of our discussions about the value-price transformation problem. Once again, it emerges that Marx's predictions are testable (that is, they are falsifiable) but that the test is complex and may be very difficult to carry out. Such tests as have been rigourously performed or casually carried out up to now make crucial assumptions about value-price proportionality which render them invalid. Marx's discussion of the law of the falling rate of profit or the law of the tendency of the rate of profit to fall is stated in terms of a one good model. The relevant rate of profit here is what we have called the value rate of profit. Readers will recall that in his erroneous solution of the Transformation problem, Marx required each industry to earn an average (value) rate of profit equal to $\bar{p}$ where $\bar{p} = S/C + V$. In Part III of *Capital* Vol. III, Marx discussed the conditions for the law to hold.

To begin with, *assuming a given wage and a given length of working day*, Marx is able to express variable capital as an index number of labourers (note the assumptions carefully). Now if a given number of workers is presented with an increasing *quantity* of material means of production, this is also likely to mean a growing *value* (not necessarily equiproportionate) of constant capital accompanying the given amount of value of variable capital. Now a constant rate of surplus value under these assumptions tautologically indicates a falling rate of profit since, as we have seen before,

$$\pi = r \left[1 - \left(\frac{C}{C + V} \right) \right] = r(1 - g)$$

The question of the general validity of any law therefore does not depend on the formula above but in the assumptions made about the behaviour of the components r, C and V.

We have here two measures being employed simultaneously. First is the ratio of labourers (working a given number of hours at a given wage) to the quantity of raw materials and the quantity of machinery and fixed capital. This is the physical input ratio (which raises many complex problems of measuring the *quantity* of machines independent of the profit and price information). Then we have the total value of constant capital and variable capital and the corresponding expression of the organic composition of capital. Similarly, the output of all this activity can be measured in physical units ('the real mass of use-values') or in value terms. By assuming a given rate of surplus value, we are saying that surplus value is the same amount as variable capital but we are not saying anything about the ratio of physical units of output per worker or per hour worked. Thus requires further information about productivity and so on.

There is a third measure that is directly observable in terms of prices. These are the recorded figures of wages, costs, profits, prices and so on. In testing the Marxian prediction, we have to use data on money value of profits (strictly all non-wage income) and compare it with an appropriate measure of constant and variable capital in price terms. We have already seen that even in simple reproduction with given constant magnitudes of r and g_i, prices are not proportional to values. With extended reproduction, changing magnitudes of g_i (and also r) as well as increasing physical productivity and decreasing length of working day, the price-value translation is even more difficult. Any casual empiricism about the rate of profit derived from the published national income and wealth statistics is not much help here.

Now during the process of growth, the physical productivity of labour power in both the Departments goes up; hence the same value amounts represent progressively higher physical quantities of machines and wage goods. Growth of productivity in wage goods industry can reduce the value of labour power since it will take less time to reproduce itself; the effect of such productivity on wages is not easy to predict, since it will depend on the strength of the working class and the historical course of the class struggle. Only in a mechanical ahistorical model of Marxian economic theory does the real wage rate always equal the subsistence level and hence the value of labour power. Such a model allows no scope for changing class relations, and by divorcing the model from social relations reduces a Marxian model to a Ricardian model of labour theory of value.

Changing the ratio of value to physical units would slow down the tendency of the rate of profit to fall since the physical ratios can go up much faster than value ratios. A change in the ratio can occur not only due to growing productivity but also as a result of foreign trade. If we treat all developed capitalist countries as a system, then such trade must be with the non-capitalist and pre-capitalist countries. This point has already been mentioned in connection with Rosa Luxemburg's solution of the problem of extended reproduction and will not therefore be further elaborated here. We need to add, however, that if such trade is reinforced by the unequal status involved in a colonial relationship, the price-value ratio may also be favourable to the developed metropolitan country in addition to the lowering of value due to trade.

The law relates to the (value) rate of profit and does not make predictions about the amount of total surplus value, or the amount of money profits, though in general the amount of profit (the mass of profits) may go up, since as the total amount of capital goes up, a tendency for surplus value (or surplus) to rise is not necessarily in contradiction with the falling rate of profit. Nor is there any clear-cut prediction here about the share of profits or wages in income. Since the problem has never been analytically formulated in a way that will allow for all the dynamic elements mentioned previously, the prediction in Marx's theory regarding the share of profits is ambiguous. Marxist economists in recent years have tried to develop models of contemporary capitalism dealing with each of these two aspects – rising amount of surplus and rising share of wages in income – but it must be said that these models stand in no clear relation to the law of the falling rate of profit.

The notion of constant capital is taken in the sense of the amount used up during the production period. This is a flow concept corresponding to physical depreciation plus user cost in the Keynesian sense. This, however, adds the additional complication that the rate of use of capital (the period of turnover) may also change due to technology and also as a corrective response to the falling rate of profit on the part of the capitalists. This makes the measurement of the rate of profit all the harder because depreciation is also influenced by accounting conventions, tax laws and fiscal policies designed especially to boost investment.

Mention must be made at this stage of the possible counteracting forces noted by Marx. We have already discussed the possible cheapening of elements of capital and foreign trade. There is also the additional possibility of increasing the rate of surplus value. This can be done absolutely by increasing the length of the working day, though this does not imply that at any point of time the country with a longer working day has the higher rate of surplus value. Alternatively, the intensity of work and the productivity of the worker may increase the rate of exploitation relatively. Growth of concentration of capital and monopolistic tendencies have also been mentioned, but given the aggregate notion of the rate of profit, it is difficult to relate these factors analytically to the general proposition.

It is well known that a law of falling rate of profit is a recurring theme in classical political economy. Adam Smith, Ricardo and John Stuart Mill each enunciated such a law. The stationary state corresponding to the zero rate of profit also meant different things to these economists. John Stuart Mill contemplated the stationary state with pleasurable anticipation. In Marx, the role of the falling rate of profit is different. The tendency of the rate of profit to fall illustrated the second contradiction of capitalism. The first contradiction is the emergence of free labour and the class monopoly of means of production. The second contradiction is the growing disparity between the productive capacity of the system – the productive potential and the actual output as dictated by the profit motive. Reproduction in a capitalist system for Marx is not the production of use values – not production for the sake of eventual consumption. Production is the production of capital in such a way that expansion of capital occurs – production for profit and for increased accumulation. The falling rate of profit comes about because of the tendency of the system to concentrate on surplus value and to replace variable capital by constant capital. The capacity of the productive system to produce use values is continually increasing, but the falling rate of profit prevents it from fully realizing this potential capacity. It is in order to illustrate this contradiction that the tendency of falling rate of profit is crucial to Marxian economic theory.

GILLMAN'S TEST OF THE FALLING RATE OF PROFIT

Joseph Gillman, in his book *The Falling Rate of Profit*, has subjected the law to a series of tests using US data for the period 1849–1952. As far as I know, no attempt has been made to bring these calculations up to date. Gillman in using published data identifies the value categories directly with the price categories. Thus variable capital is measured in his calculations by the wage bill for production workers; constant capital by the cost of materials (and where available) the amount set aside as depreciation, depletion and amortization. He has carried out these calculations for all manufacturing industries. We summarize all his calculations in Table 11 at the end of the chapter. They are as follows:

(1) Using Census of Manufacturing data decennially for 1849–1899, quinquennially for 1899–1919 and bienially for 1919–1939. Since census data did not publish depreciation, the cost of materials was taken to measure constant capital (C) and wages of production workers to measure variable capital (V). Surplus value was measured as value of product minus ($C + V$), or equivalently as value added less V. As we can see in columns 1a–1c, the organic composition of capital (defined as C/V) goes up from 2.3 in 1849 to 3.8 in 1919 but remains more or less constant around a lower figure of 3.5 thereafter. The rate of surplus value goes up from 1849–1919, and after a drop in 1921, goes up until 1929, but is cyclical with a slight downward

TABLE 11[1]

Gillman's calculations of the rate of profit

	1a	1b	1c	2a	2b	2c	3a	3b	3c	4a	4b
	g	r(%)	p	g	r(%)	p	g	r	p	$\bar{p}_1$	$\bar{p}_2$
1849	2.3	96	29								
1859	2.7	125	34								
1869	3.2	125	30								
1879	3.6	108	24				0.8	102	122		
1889	2.7	123	33				1.1	114	102		
1899[1]	3.2	144	35				1.7	132	79		
1899[2]	3.4	145	33								
1904	3.4	147	34								
1909	3.7	155	33								
1914[3]	3.7	148	32				2.3	137	61		
1919	3.8	147	31	3.9	135	27.6	3.2	125	40	15.4	12.0
1920				3.4	111	25.2	3.1			9.2	8.0
1921	3.3	132	31	3.5	116	26.0	4.1	103	25	2.0	2.1
1922				3.5	124	27.2	3.5			10.6	9.8
1923	3.3	142	33	3.5	128	28.6	3.0	121	41	12.2	9.8
1924				3.6	131	28.9	3.2			10.2	8.3
1925	3.5	157	35	3.7	142	30.3	3.1	136	44	11.4	8.8
1926				3.6	140	30.4	3.0			11.8	9.4
1927	3.4	161	37	3.6	144	31.6	3.1	139	45	10.0	8.0
1928				3.7	159	34.1	3.2			11.9	9.3
1929	3.4	181	41	3.6	164	35.4	3.1	159	51	12.5	9.6
1930				3.6	161	35.0	3.7			5.7	4.9
1931	3.2	178	43	3.5	154	34.4	4.4	147	33	1.3	1.2
1932				3.6	145	31.5	5.6			–	–
1933	3.4	184	42	3.7	154	32.9	4.9	150	31	3.4	3.8
1934				3.6	137	29.6	4.0			5.8	5.6
1935	3.6	154	33	3.8	136	28.2	3.4	130	38	8.9	7.2
1936				4.0	150	30.2	3.0			11.9	8.6
1937	3.5	149	33	3.7	134	28.6	2.7	130	48	11.0	7.9
1938				3.9	149	30.6	3.5			5.9	4.7
1939	3.5	172	38	3.7	149	32.0	3.0	151	50	11.1	8.2
1940							2.8				
1941							2.2				
1942							1.8				
1943							1.5				
1944							1.5				
1945							1.9				
1946							2.3				

TABLE 11 (*continued*)

	1a g	1b r(%)	1c p	2a g	2b r(%)	2c	3a g	3b r	3c p	4a $\bar{p}_1$	4b $\bar{p}_2$
1947							2.4	129	54		
1948							2.5				
1949							2.8	129	46		
1950							2.7	141	53		
1951							2.6	133	52		
1952							2.6	132	51		

trend afterwards. The rate of profit in column 1c shows no trend that can be discerned but more a tendency to cyclical fluctuations. These calculations therefore show that up to 1919 the rise in C/V was compensated by a rise in r to yield no trend in p. After 1919, the cycles in p are pronounced but still there is no downward trend; if anything the trend is upward.

(2) Combining the biennial census data with annual data from the Bureau of Internal Revenue, Gillman produces an annual series on $\bar{p}$ for 1919–1939, after some adjustments (for example, splicing) have been made. These figures include depreciation as published by the Bureau of Internal Revenue. These data are in columns 2a–2c. Here again there is no clear upward or downward trend in any of the three ratios. There is some case for arguing in favour of an upward trend in r and $\bar{p}$ for 1919–1939 and a downward trend or constancy afterwards. In genral, p shows no downward trend by this calculation.

(3) Since the ratio of depreciation (and user cost) to stock of capital could be varying, Gillman computed the rate of profit on stock of capital. The stock of fixed capital was measured as 'the values of plant and equipment taken at their reproduction costs at current prices net of depreciation.' These differ from book values since these are often in historical value. Using these figures, there is a decline in the rate of profit for 1880–1919 but no trend from 1919–1952. These are listed in columns 3a–3c. Including the stock of fixed capital and circulating capital – inventories – similar results are obtained as in columns 3a–3c. These do not add anything of substance.

(4) Gillman does a further calculation by deducting from his measure of surplus value a measure of unproductive expenditure. These would comprise selling costs, employment of non-production workers and so on. This item is measured as the gap between surplus value and net profits plus rent and interest paid. He calculates $p_1 = S - u/C$ on a stock measure of C and $p_2 = S - u/C + V + u$ as a flow measure on the argument that being costs of realizing surplus value, u should be added to total capital used up in producing surplus value. $\bar{p}_1$ figures for 1919, 1929 and 1939 are 15.4 per cent, 12.5 per cent and 11.1 per cent respectively. $\bar{p}_2$ figures for the same three years are 12.0 per cent, 9.6 per cent and 8.2 per cent. If government activity is regarded as an alternative measure of unproductive expenditure, then we can also net out total tax collections from profits. For 1929, 1939 and 1949, Gillman deducts federal and state corporation income and excess profits taxes from surplus value and gets a measure of rate of profit for these years as 24.2 per cent, 21.7 per cent and 17.0 per cent respectively. Data for $\bar{p}_1$ and $\bar{p}_2$ are given in columns 4a–4b.

On balance, one can say that the rate of profit as measured by Gillman in flow terms does not decline. When adjustments are made on a stock basis, there is some tendency for a decline in the 1880–1919 period. If we accept unproductive expenditure as a deduction from surplus value then the post-1919 period also shows a decline. It must be said, however, that these tests are not decisive either way. The use of national income statistics and census data involves many measurement problems that complicate testing of hypotheses even in mainstream economic theory. These data involve inaccuracies, measurement errors and index number problems. These are not reflections on the quality of Gillman's workmanship, but complications of testing theories against inadequate real world data. Imperfect as it may be, it was a pioneering effort at empirical work in Marxian economics which unfortunately has not been followed up for other countries or other periods.

The problem is also with Marx's theoretical formulation of the law, as we have repeatedly emphasized. Not only is the law not stated by Marx in terms of the money rate of profit, but even on the value basis there are unspecified assumptions regarding increasing productivity, rate of turnover, changing length of working day and so on. The law needs to be reformulated in so far as it is possible allowing for such complications. Then the problem of transformation needs to be tackled. Only then can we use published data, imperfect as they will surely be, to verify the law.

Gillman's treatment of unproductive expenditure may appear arbitrary, a way of rationalizing the data in favour of Marx. We shall go into this question of unproductive expenditue when we consider recent developments in Marxian economic theory. At present, Gillman's treatment points to the fact that *even as formulated by Marx, the law of the falling rate of profit does not allow for problems of realizing surplus value*. This is because it is cast in a one-good framework using only value categories. Since prices do not systematically enter the law, the problem of realization of surplus value has no obvious place. The situation is similar to Marx's model of extended reproduction, which assumed away crises in constructing the arithmetical examples. Once again the circuit of money capital is ignored in Marx's formulation, whereas in the real world these monetary and financial factors are interwoven into the economic fabric with other factors. In treating selling costs as unproductive expenditure to be netted out of surplus value, Gillman is taking the view that these are costs of realization and a deduction from the amount available for accumulation in the future. A similar argument can be made about the government sector, since by keeping up effective demand, but without generating material output, government expenditure eases the realization problem.

The law of the tendency of the rate of the profit to fall is, in conclusion, neither well specified nor unambiguously seen to be proved or disproved. The difficulty is that both the defenders and detractors of Marx have stayed within the terms defined by Marx. Even when modern mathematical tools have been applied in this respect, they have only tidied up certain inconsistencies and solved old puzzles. The theory has not been further developed in the spirit in which Marx initiated it using his tools. Rosa Luxemburg was of course the singular exception. She asked original critical questions and was not satisfied with accepting the problem as stated and solved by Marx. Mainstream economics has not gone on to develop Marx's model in his terms because it has clearly other tools and other concerns.

The task of developing Marx's model has fallen to Marxist economists.

It is clear that there exists no agreed body of analytical modēls developing further from Marx's theory which either enrich Marx's model or bring it into relation with new developments in capitalism. This is not to say that many have not worked in this area. However, when we look at their contributions we find that for various reasons – some of which have been political or ideological – there is no substantial body of ongoing work in the Marxian paradigm which can be taken with any seriousness. [Shaikh (1978a), which is a considerable advance on the existing literature, came too late to our attention to revise this chapter.]

XX

SOME CONTEMPORARY DEBATES

We have so far addressed questions of an analytical nature with a fairly well defined economic connotation. But even more than that, the previous chapters have concerned themselves with clarifying, explaining and sometimes developing Marx's economic theory. Not surprisingly, the dominant theme is of a competitive capitalism, accumulating and revolutionizing technology without interruption. In this stylized model of nineteenth-century competitive capitalism, the state hardly gets a mention either for its economic or its social and political role. By the same token, the workers enter into a wage contract where wage is fixed prior to and independent of the type of work they perform. Trade union organization, rise of social democratic parties (in the early sense of the word), impact of social reform legislation and the growth of political democracy are all post-Marxian historical phenomena as far as the stylized model is concerned.[1]

In this chapter we shall look at all various problems involved in using the Marxian economic theory to understand contemporary capitalism.[2] This not only raises all the familiar problems of proceeding from an abstract stylized model to a concrete historical situation, but much more, it raises the problem of the extent to which Marx's model should be updated or revised. Once it is updated or revised, the next task is how to make the transition from the theoretical model to contemporary reality.[3]

Updating, revising or discarding Marx has been a persistent activity ever since he died. To begin with, we have already mentioned that in every generation there is someone like

Bohm–Bawerk who claims to have disproved Marx. It is done with greater or lesser degree of praise and charity but it is always being done. Secondly, there is the notion that because time has passed since Marx wrote and things, especially capitalist institutions, have changed, Marx's theory is outmoded. This idea has been advanced by those who reject the revolutionary aspect of Marx and plump for a belief in steady automatic improvement of the lot of the majority as economic expansion takes place. Without sounding too deterministic, one can point to a loose coincidence between the rise of such arguments and an expansionary phase of the world economy. Thus Bernstein, writing during the long phase of expansion which began in the 1890s or Anthony Crossland, writing when full employment and steady growth seemed to have permanently arrived in the 1950s, readily come to mind. These are the times when the glowing, healthy face of capitalism is turned towards the onlooker and, like Dorian Gray, projects eternal youth.

This is not to deny the need for revision or updating of Marx's theory. There has always been disagreement about what essential structure to retain and what to revise. Our perception of the 'essential Marx' has also changed over the years as the political and economic climate has changed. The Stalin purges, the Cold War, McCarthyism, Destalinization, the Hungarian Revolution, Vietnam, the Colonial independence movements, Prague Spring – all these have changed the ways we perceive Marx both as a critic of capitalism and a harbinger of socialism.

Our theme is, however, economic, and it is Marx's economic theory and we shall focus on the need to revise it and the directions in which it may be revised. In the process of doing so, we shall be able to look at some of the recent controversies on the nature of contemporary capitalism.

Before we plunge into newer theories, we should also note that the availability of Marx's earlier works, their translations and interpretation has immensely enriched our understanding of the development of Marx's thought. Not only the *Economic and Philosophical Manuscripts* but also the *Critique of Hegel's Philosophy of Right*, the *Grundrisse*, chapters from earlier editions of *Capital* Vol. I, have all come out in recent years, especially for the English language reader. We now know that

Marx addressed himself to questions that Hegel had taken up and offered an outline of an alternative solution as early as 1845–1846. By 1846 Marx had arrived at the concept of the proletariat (contrasting with Hegel's notion of Bureaucracy) as the universal class. He had come to look upon private property as a fetter rather than a precondition of free development of human potential. He had also seen beyond Hegel's notion of the German State as the epitome of human development to communism as the ideal.[4]

In this context, we must remember that Marx, like Hegel, accepted the separation of Man (*homme*) and citizen (*citoyen*), the division between State and Civil Society as a fact. This was the Rousseau problem. Hegel thought the French Revolution had failed to bridge the gap, while Marx thought that it had only confirmed the gap. Civil society, the domain of contract and private property, of *economic relations*, was seen to be drifting away from political society and the state and to be developing autonomously. This separation of the economic and the political was caused by the breakdown of extra economic coercion in economic life that was part of feudalism. The emergence of free labour, as we saw in Chapter II, was a central event in the development of capitalism.

This separation of the economic and the political, of the state from the civil society, was thus a starting point of Marx's thought. The question of whether such separation was historically a fact in the early nineteenth century even in an advanced capitalist country such as England is an open question. Adam Smith had, however, shown convincingly that the civil society *could* develop without political interference and perhaps *ought* to do so. From this it was a small step to take as a starting point for theoretical analysis that indeed the civil society *did* develop independently of the political.

Starting as a political philosopher and developing his arguments as a critique of Hegel's political philosophy, Marx concentrated his efforts increasingly on the understanding of the economic mechanism of the civil society. One can date this shift in his efforts after the failure of the 1848 revolution in France and the restoration of a Bonaparte. The twenty years between 1851 and 1871 were taken up with economic researches. (After

1871 and the collapse of the Paris Commune Marx took up study of the societies on the 'periphery' of the capitalist mode. He studied anthropology and developed an interest in Russia.) Throughout this period, the separation of state and civil society was maintained in his analysis.

This separation is the starting point of many of the problems we have in updating Marx's analysis. An attitude of absolute reverence to every word he wrote (even when in contradiction with other words he wrote) does not help. But aside from that, the analytical problems are enormous. There is, to begin with, the problem that value categories are not directly perceived. A three-fold account in terms of value, price and quantities or equivalently of the commodity, money and physical circuits of capital has to be given. Any crude matching of price, wage and profit data to value measures only makes analysis difficult. This is so even for the competitive capitalist model that is developed independently of political institutions. But if one had to take historical data from the nineteenth century and interpret them in terms of Marxian categories, there is the further problem that as a historical description, the separation of civil and political society is not accurate. The major role the state played in economic development of Germany, Japan, Italy and Russia in late nineteenth century has been well documented. In France, the state has always played a major role. Only in England, and even there only after 1845 (after the passage of Free Trade legislation and Banking Acts), could one pretend that the state was absent from the civil society. Even in England the state played an active role in maintaining the overseas Empire.

One would need a major theoretical effort at synthesizing the state with Marx's model of competitive capitalism. The role of the state in sponsoring social welfare legislation, due either to the push given by the anti-bourgeois aristocracy, as in Britain, or as a result of calculation, as in the case of Bismark, is already evident in nineteenth century. Do we consider this as an attempt to socialize the cost of reproduction of labour power or as a palliative for the reserve army of unemployed? Such a question cannot be answered until one can redefine concepts such as value of labour power in an abstract model which allows for the role of the state in reproduction of social relations. If the value of labour power is defined in context of a two-class model with wage bargain as between the individual labourer and the capitalist, then all outside influences will seem arbitrary.

This is also reflected in the crude theory that the state is only an agent of the ruling class interests – a committee for the bourgeoisie. Recent works by Marxian political theorists have emphasized the autonomy of the state, its relative independence of the ruling classes.[5] In a two-class model of the civil society where at the beginning the state has been ruled out, one can introduce the state only by arbitrarily relating it to one class or another. Both at the level of abstract analysis and for understanding historical events this is a wrong approach.

Modern approaches to developing Marxian theory are also compunded by another difficulty. This is that following Hilferding and Lenin, it is said that capitalism entered a monopoly phase in the twentieth century. This monopoly phase is to be understood as being in addition to the class monopoly of ownership of means of production. This monopoly phase was described in terms of increase in size and concentration of industries, of the linkage between them provided by finance capital by Hilferding. Lenin used this concept (in conjunction with Bukharin's theory) to understand rivalry among imperialist powers in the First World War as motivated by struggle between national capitals for markets. Thus, in the monopoly phase increasing concentration of capital made it possible for Marxists to speak of national capital and to see the state as an agent of national capital in external relations.

Thus a somewhat simple dichotomy emerged. In the competitive phase, the state played a passive role in Marxian models. In the monopoly phase, the state is interlinked with capitalist society. This simple dichotomy has been a serious obstacle to development of Marxian economic theory. First, because as we said above the separation of the state and the economy in the competitive phase is a simplification which is analytically unsatisfactory and historically inaccurate. On the other hand, it leads to an implicit belief that the competitive phase is the original or natural phase of capitalism. This is reflected in teleological labels such as the highest phase of capitalism, the last phase or the old age (*le troisieme age* in Mandel's words) of capitalism reserved for recent periods. But historically capitalism emerged with mercantilism, where the state played an active role in mobilization of economic surplus from trade and empire. The monopoly phase with active role of the state precedes the competitive phase of capitalism historically.

But we have to deal with the analytical problem most of all. The separation of the state and the civil society in one age and the emergence of monopoly capitalism with state involvement are not subsequent stages in the hierarchy of models. We have an analytical model of competitive capitalism, in isolation from the state, in Marx's work, although it has many missing elements. The next step would be an analytical model of monopoly capital or a fusing of competitive model with the state. But we lack any analytical model of monopoly capitalism. We do not know, in other words, how for example the value-price transformation differs in monopoly capitalism for competitive capitalism. We do not know whether the wage relationship is reproduced differently or how accumulation and realization problems interact.

When discussing monopoly capitalism, one often takes the full competitive model and only adds monopoly as a complicating model (indeed as much neoclassical economic theory does). This is done frequently in measuring rates of exploitation from wage data. Or we get a combination of Marxian labels with mainstream economic analysis. Thus the theory of monopolistic competition of Chamberlin is often taken up along with Kalecki's theory as the Marxian theory of monopoly capital. The connection between value and price is severed and profits are linked not to surplus value but to high mark-up above costs maintained by market power. Such is the theory of Baran and Sweezy in their Monopoly Capital which we have already discussed on an earlier occasion. [Desai (1974) pp. 114–116.]

Mandel in his *Late Capitalism* has put forward a sketch of how monopoly capitalism works. His work covers a broad panorama of developments during the last hundred years but here we shall concentrate on monopoly capitalism. Mandel begins with the idea that the equalization of profit rates across industries is only a long run tendency. Actual economic movement takes place through uneven development and difference in level of profit rates. This is the dynamic disequilibrium path even in the competitive phase. There may be movements of capital in search of high profits tending to even out differences but this is not actually accomplished. But in monopoly capital, there is not even a theoretical tendency for profit rates to equalize. Although monopolies are never absolute and subject to forces of competition, there is a constant reproduction of unequal profit rates.

Through accumulation and technical progress, monopoly seeks to make super profits, higher than average profits. This may come about through differences in organic composition of capital between enterprises in the monopoly sector and out of it, by forcing down the price of labour and of constant capital purchased from outside and by constant improvements in productivity. Mandel argues, 'In all these cases we are dealing with surplus-profits which do *not* enter the process of equalization in the short-term, and so do not lead simply to a growth in the average rate of profit.'

These surplus-profits do not, therefore, go into the pool of profits which are then distributed so as to equalize the rate of profit as in Marx's solution of the value-price transformation. To some extent, surplus-profits of the monopoly sector are due to a diversion of surplus value of the non-monopolized sector. Recall that price-value transformation breaks the link between surplus value produced by an individual firm/industry and its profits. Mandel is extending this idea to model the transfer of surplus value from a non-monopoly sector to a monopoly sector.

Thus one can think of an economy in two sectors – monopolized and competitive. They may produce different commodities but not necessarily so. Mandel's model can then be formulated as saying that there is one profit rate prevailing in the competitive sector and that the monopoly sector has either one or many rates which are all higher than the competitive rate. Monopolies sustain (reproduce) the differential profit rate by using barriers to entry among other weapons. But they face limits to their ability to prevent the equalization of profit rates. Thus, while barriers may be placed against small capitals from within an industry or a country, large capitals from other industries or countries will enter into competition if the differential gets very large. Thus monopoly power is never absolute but always relative. Also it does not always reside in the same firm. A monopolistic firm one day may find itself thrown on the scrap heap of competition by the superior technology of another firm.

Mandel's attempts to provide a numerical scheme to illustrate his thesis (pp. 532–534) are somewhat vitiated by the fact that he adopts both the erroneous price-value transformation method of *Capital* Vol. III as well as an arbitrary accumulation behaviour reminiscent of the Scheme for Extended Reproduction of *Capital* Vol. II. Thus accumulation rates are assumed without any market logic and input values are not but output values are transformed into prices. This aside, Mandel tries to state a law of monopoly capital as follows: '(T)he higher the monopoly profit over the average profit, and the larger the monopolized sector, the faster must the monopoly profit drop to the level of the average social profit operative at the start, or decline together with it' (p. 535).

The only evidence Mandel offers in support of his law is a numerical example, which, as we said above, has many arbitrary features. Still, Mandel's assertion should form the subject of further investigation. Mandel's statements on monopoly capital form part of a wider historical and descriptive investigation. Thus he contrasts phases of long expansion with an undertone of optimism with phases that have an undertone of contraction. These phases are not so regular as to be called cycles and have more than purely economic causes underlying them. Thus the long expansionary phase from the 1940–45 till the end of the 1960s could be traced to the weakened position of the working class at the end of Depression, which led to a reduction in real wage growth, a boost of technological discoveries in the war that brought about the third technological revolution and to an expansion of the market on an international scale. But in these developments, the state played a large role, guaranteeing the tempo of military investments, especially in research and developments, easing the realization problem by fiscal policy and rescuing the loss making enterprises by subsidy or nationalization.

The growth of state expenditure viewed benevolently through the quarter-century following the Second World War is now everywhere being viewed with alarm. Recent experiences of inflation and recession in all the developed capitalist countries have led to divisions among economists and disturbed the confident note of the Sixties. It seemed then that full employment and a more or less steady growth was a permanent feature with inflation and balance of payment disequilibria only niggling worries. The seventies began with the collapse of the Bretton Woods System and witnessed increasing intervention in wage bargains and price setting by governments, the increasing sense of an ecological threat to maintenance of existing life styles, the massive transfer of economic surplus to the OPEC countries and a period of high unemployment that has now lasted nearly five years.

Increased state expenditure has been linked to inflation by Marxists writers much as the monetarists have done, though their reasoning differs.

Marxists economists have emphasized the constraints put by the total mass of surplus value on total realizable profits. They have often emphasized that fiscal expansion can ease the realization problem but not increase the mass of surplus value. This remains a debatable point. As we said above, the concepts are taken from a purely capitalist model and transposed to the mixed economy. Thus the state's ability to raise surplus value depends on whether one considers public sector employees productive or unproductive. The purest definition of productive labour that we mentioned in the first part does not permit any government employee (except perhaps in nationalized manufacturing enterprises) to be labelled as productive. Much debate has been generated on this point but this is an instance in which citing chapter and verse from Marx is no help. One needs to understand what role the notion of productive labour plays in the model of pure capitalism and then seek to define similar concepts for the mixed model. Thus in the pure model exchange value of labour power coincides with the wage costs borne by the employer and the income received (and consumed) by the worker. But in an era of social security taxes, deductions for pensions, social and health care and insurance provided from public funds with free or subsidised educational and vocational facilities, there is a wedge between these two sides. What the employer pays, the worker does not receive, at least immediately. What the worker consumes, what reproduces him is often not paid for by his income. The worker and the employer pay taxes to finance the 'social wage', but just as surplus-value and profits do not coincide for the firm, the payments and receipts do not coincide for the individual worker and often not even for the class. In such a context, it is hard to distinguish who is employed from revenue and who from capital. The complex of taxes and subsidies puts an additional layer of complication to the task of unravelling the price relationships in terms of value categories. What is more, we lack the appropriate value categories to handle the state-economy interaction even in an abstract model.

Much progress is, however, being made on the conceptual and the empirical fronts in this respect. Many economists are coming to grips with the task of unscrambling national income accounts in terms of value categories. On the theoretical side, we should mention James O'Connor's book *The Fiscal Crisis of the State*, which has many points of similarity with Mandel's *Late Capitalism*. O'Connor divides the economy into three sectors, the monopoly sector, the competitive sector and the state sector. The monopoly sector is technologically progressive, with high wages and high relative rate of surplus value where trade unions play an active role in bargaining and where cost plus pricing is the rule. The technologically progressive nature of the monopoly sector means that even in expansionary phases, it expands its employment by small amounts. On average, it sheds labour instead of absorbing it. This labour, along with many less skilled and underprivileged workers (women, immigrants, blacks, youth) form the labour force in the competitive sector. Here the technology is not very progressive and absolute rate of surplus value is the source of profit. Output expands by expanding employment. In this sector unions have to struggle for recognition. It includes the reserve army of unemployed – those who are 'hired last and fired first'. The cost of maintaining the reserve army – unemployment compensation, social security poverty programs and so on is borne by the state sector. The state sector also bears the costs of research and development and the more risky undertakings – costs that are now socialized, though the benefits they generate accrue to the monopoly sector in the form of additional profits that are privately appropriated. The private appropriation of profits and the socialization of costs – costs of maintaining the labour force as well as of education and research and development – represents for O'Connor the major contradiction that leads to increasing fiscal burden.

The monopoly sector needs the competitive sector as a

supplier of reserve labour as well as of raw material and component inputs. The pricing system transfers surplus value from the competitive sector to the monopoly sector. The monopoly sector also needs the state and its attitudes towards state activity are 'progressive' or benevolent. This is because of the willingness of the state to bear the social costs – social wage and research and development. But the unwillingness of either of the two private sectors to bear the costs in terms of taxation leads to continuous deficits. The state has to accommodate the political demands of surplus labour and of capital and herein lies the nub of the fiscal problem.

Mandel and O'Connor reject any crude theory of the state. They recognize that the state has relative autonomy and that its form does not correspond exactly to the production relationships. O'Connor sees the state as performing the twin tasks of accumulation and legitimation. In its accumulation task, the state's expenditure represents social capital. In this *social constant capital* represents expenditure that will increase labour productivity and consequently the rate of profit. Social variable capital concerns the expenditures that lower the (private) reproduction costs of labour and hence raise the rate of profit. On the other hand, *social expenses* are projects required to maintain social harmony – to fulfil the legitimation function.

Obviously each item of expenditure may partake of one or more such features. But the crucial part of O'Connor's thesis has to do with limitations on the growth of employment in the monopoly sector and of productivity in the competitive sector which puts restrictions on the state's capacity to balance its budget. The state has to spend money on social expenses because of the slow growth of employment due to the failure of the monopoly sector to generate full employment. This is in turn due to limitations on the growth of market demand.

The monopoly sector generates surplus labour, that is, productivity grows faster than total demand and employment falls in the long run. The monopoly sector wages are determined by bilateral bargaining and follow productivity and price level increases. But this is a high wage island, entry to which is restricted. Prices in the monopoly sector are on a mark-up basis. But given stagnant or declining employment, and rising prices for its own products, the monopoly sector finds a limited market for its products among its wage earners. The competitive sector is a sea of lower wage, less than fully employed workers. Prices have fallen with productivity increases and profits are being constantly squeezed, while wages are determined by market forces of demand and supply in this sector. But on the whole, the competitive sector does not represent a growing market for the monopoly sector. The terms of trade are going against the competitive sector; hence, its real purchasing power in terms of monopoly sector products is shrinking. Thus the monopoly sector is producing surplus products to be disposed of either by state expenditure providing a market or by exports. Wages in the state sector are linked to the monopoly sector wages but productivity does not grow here. This is one of the causes of the fiscal crisis.

O'Connor's book relates much more to US experience than to European experience, but it represents, along with Mandel's work, some common strands of thinking. Thus they both present a picture of differential profit rates in the monopoly as against the competitive sector. They both explore the dependence of the monopoly sector on the competitive sector as well as the dependence of the monopoly sector on the state sector. But both their theories are dependent on limitations of growth of market of the monopoly sector. This has not been satisfactorily demonstrated in their work.

As we said above, Marxists and monetarists have often sounded alike in their attack on Keynesian remedies and on the growth of state expenditure. The monetarists theorize about the natural rate of unemployment as an insuperable barrier that stands in the way of attempts by governments to reduce unemployment and they are skeptical of wage-price controls as counter-inflationary measures. The orthodox Keynesian answer has been to locate inflation in the wage-price spiral caused by trade union militancy and the tendency for wage increases to be passed onto price increases. Both these approaches appear in their Marxist guise in the form of limitations of market due to slow growth of employment and wages or of the mass of social labour. The wage explosion thesis is turned as an attack on capital by workers, as an example of the political determination of wages in the modern society.

The demand for higher state expenditure has traditionally

come from working class organizations. Full employment policies were adopted not merely as a cunning trick by big capital but after considerable struggle on the part of social democratic parties. It was the mobilization of population for the war effort which led in a number of countries, especially in the UK and USA, to the strengthening of this demand. Capitalist societies were now living in a democratic world, as they had not in the nineteenth century. The promises of the First World War – 'a land fit for heroes' – were not fulfilled, and massive deflation following the full employment and inflationary experience of 1916–1921 led to unemployment and a long depression in the UK. The US Depression came later, but was nonetheless a massive blow to the living standards. A repetition of such experience in the context of democratic politics, especially after 1945, was unthinkable. Even today, we think of high unemployment not as ten per cent or twenty five per cent but as five per cent. While Keynes provided the theory and the policy rules to guide in this task, it was not a demand granted from above but won from below.

This is not just a historical accident. The state has relative autonomy, and this autonomy is strengthened by widely spread franchise and the exercise of political democracy. In societies where either of these conditions are not fulfilled – in nineteenth century or in contemporary 'socialist' countries – the state does become 'the committee of the ruling class'. Indeed, it is because the state is perceived as potentially autonomous – an institution which by political action can be made to realize its potential for autonomy – that over the last century trade unions and social democratic parties have concentrated on the demands that the state play a more active role. Thus in securing health care, unemployment benefits, guaranteed wage, trade union rights, safety at work and so on through government action, the struggle over the past century has quite rightly succeeded. No doubt the capitalist can take advantage of these arrangements and manipulate them for profit, but that is no sign that capital, even big capital, *demanded* full employment and state intervention. The struggle to make these gains more beneficial to the lower paid will continue, but this does not mean that the gains are illusory.

Even inflation must be seen in a class perspective. During the

1950s and 1960s inflation was viewed benevolently as it aided personal and corporate wealth accumulation. But over the period, the share of wages in income was also rising. In the UK, at any rate, serious complaints about inflation began when it started to hurt middle and higher income groups. The wage control policies began to narrow differentials (this again being a necessary price for a political incomes policy in a democratic society).

Thus in judging inflation one has to ask who it benefits and who it hurts. An inflation that eliminates the rentier is different from an inflation that hits the poor and unemployed. Similarly, in countering the growing budget deficit, one has to look for what expenditure cuts will mean in terms of their distributive impact on different classes. In the last three years or so, 'Social Contract' has been accepted without widespread resistance in UK because inflation has been seen as hurting workers. The idea that 'inflation hurts everybody' and especially the workers, has been conveyed by governments, and it is not entirely false consciousness that has led many to accept this idea.

This shift in attitudes towards state expenditure and inflation can be understood only through detailed analytical and statistical study of the various roles played by the state in the modern economy. Ian Gough (1975) has made one such attempt. He begins with a critique of O'Connor while basically accepting the social capital/social expenses division. He rejects functional theories of the state that assign to it the task of ensuring profitability or legitimation. He rightly criticizes the appelation of unproductive labour for all state expenditure. Such a characterization can be made only if the state is viewed as an appendate to the civil society. Such a view gives no role for the class struggle. This is not to say that the state is completely autonomous or neutral, but that it is potentially so. Without the political background of adult franchise and democracy, as we said above, the state cannot be seen as autonomous.

Gough also points out that the growth in state expenditure was financed without a secular increase in borrowing in the 1950s and 1960s. It is only in the 1970s that the fiscal crisis has been serious, and one must not project recent events backward and forward through time. In the trend of expenditure, armaments have had a declining share and social services – the social wage – an increasing one. There has also been a growth in state aid to private industry and on legal and coercive apparatus. Gough also distinguishes between spending and transfers and counters the commonly held notion that the state takes resources away from the private ('productive') sector.

Gough quite rightly places the growth of state expenditure in a historical and international perspective. Though he does not point this out, some of the state aid to private industry in Europe came as a result of rivalry with American multi-nationals. It was to protect national capital, often publicly owned, against inroads by the larger, more efficient multi-nationals. On social expenses, Gough points out that 'the strength of working class pressure can roughly be gauged by the *comprehensiveness* and the *level* of the social benefits' (p. 75).

Any effort to understand contemporary capitalism in a Marxist framework is bound to be fraught with problems. We have concentrated on the need to develop analytical models that can encompass the state and the economy both in the classical competitive and the modern monopolistic competitive forms. But even the model of pure capitalism that Marx left behind was an unfinished one. The uncompleted nature of Marx's work has dictated a number of tasks of clarification and filling in the missing pieces. Thus an integration of money, commodity and physical circuits to provide a theory of crisis and cycles within the assumptions of *Capital* is still an open challenge.[6] We then need to re-examine the separation of state and civil society that Marx took as a starting point, though his plan of work clearly indicates that he intended to return to the state in future volumes of *Capital*. Then we need to look at the models of 'monopoly capital' that have been put forward and subject them to the same scrutiny that the well-worn parts of Marx's work, such as the Transformation Problem, have undergone. At the same time the task of relating the models to historical data will always remain. There is no shortage of issues to consider.

There is, however, much work being done. The last fifteen years have witnessed a growth of a critical attitude towards Marx – critical in the proper and best sense of the word. There is also a tremendous upsurge in the sheer number of people studying various facets of Marxian economics. The emergence of specialized journals, such as the *Radical Review of Political*

Economy and *Capital and Class* (to mention two of the English language journals), the growth of societies such as Union of Radical Political Economy and the Conference of Socialist Economists, the renewed interest in Marxian economics within the mainstream economics profession, the growing awareness of non-Western traditions of Marxian economics, such as the Japanese school, and the urgency provided by contemporary problems of recession and inflation, of underdevelopment and of tensions in the 'Socialist' countries, will all only aid in the future development of this, far from degenerate, 'research programme'.

APPENDIX

QUOTATIONS FROM MARX

In each case the Roman numeral indicates volume, the next set of numbers the chapter and the last the page of the citation. Many of these quotations include superscripts for footnotes but these have been omitted except when Marx is quoting from another source, when this information is included at the end of the quotation. The editions of *Capital* used are as follows:

Capital Vol. I (Translated from the Third German edition by Samuel Moore and Edward Aveling; edited by Friedrich Engels: Encyclopaedia Britannica Inc., Great Books of the Western World, Vol. 50, Chicago and London).

Capital Vol. II (Foreign Languages Publishing House, Moscow, 1957).

Capital Vol. III (Foreign Languages Publishing House, Moscow, 1962).

In a few cases, words are put in {   } to elucidate the meaning. Interpolations in parentheses are in the original.

Quotations from Theories of Surplus Value (TSV) are indicated similarly by citing part, chapter and page. 'Add' refers to Addendum at the back of TSV.

1 *Labour Time*

The labour time socially necessary is that required to produce an article under the normal conditions of production, and with the average degree of skill and intensity prevalent at the time. I/1/15

2 *Things and Commodities*

A thing can be a use-value, without having value. This is the case when its utility to man is not due to labour. Such are air, virgin soil, natural meadows, etc. A thing can be useful, and the product of human labour, without being a commodity. Whoever directly satisfies his wants with the produce of his own labour creates, indeed, use-values, but not commodities. In order to produce the latter, he must not only produce use-values, but use-values for others, social use-values. (And not only just "for others". The medieval peasant produced grain for feudal dues and for the tithe. But this grain did not become a commodity merely because it was produced for others. In order to become a commodity, the product must be transferred *by exchange* to the person whom it will serve as use-value). I/1/16 Interpolation by Engels.

3 *The Commodity Form*

Whence, then arises, the enigmatical character of the product of labour as soon as it assumes the form of commodities? Clearly from this form itself. The equality of all sorts of human labour is expressed objectively by their products all being equally valued; the measure of the expenditure of labour power by the duration of that expenditure takes the form of the quantity of value of the products of labour; and finally, the mutual relations of the producers, within which the social character of their labour affirms itself, take the form of a social relation between the products. I/1/31

4 *Fetishism*

There is a physical relation between physical things. But it is different with commodities. There the existence of the things *qua* commodities, and the value relation between the products of labour which stamps them as commodities, have absolutely no connection with their physical properties and with the material relations arising therefrom. There it is a definite social relation between men that assumes, in their eyes, the fantastic form of a relation between things. . . . . This I call the *fetishism* which attaches itself to the products of labour, so soon as they are produced as commodities, and which is, therefore, inseparable from the production of commodities. I/1/31

5 *Dual Value Form*

This division of a product into a useful thing and a value becomes practically important only when exchange has acquired such an extension that useful articles are produced for the purpose of being exchanged, and their character as values has therefore to be taken into account, beforehand, during production. I/1/32

6 *The Commodity Mode and its Mystery*

The categories of bourgeois economy consist of such like forms. They are forms of thought expressing with social validity the conditions and relations of a definite, historically determined mode of production, viz: the production of commodities. The whole mystery of commodities, all magic and necromancy that surrounds the products of labour as long as they take the form of commodities, vanishes, therefore, as soon as we come to other forms of production. I/1/33

7 *European Middle Ages: Relations of Production*

Here, instead of the independent man, we find everyone dependent – serfs and lords, vassals and suzerain, laymen and clergy. Personal dependence here characterizes the social relations of production just as much as it does the other spheres of life organised on the basis of that production. But for the very reason that personal dependence forms the groundwork of society, there is no necessity for labour and its products to assume a fantastic form different from their reality. They take the shape, in the transactions of society, of services in kind and payments in kind. Here the particular and natural form of labour, and not, as in a society based on production of commodities, its general abstract form, is the immediate social form of labour. Compulsory labour is just as properly measured by time as commodity-producing labour; but every serf knows that what he expends in the service of his lord is a definite quantity of his own personal labour power. I/1/34

8 *Mode of Production*

The mode of production in which the product takes the form of a commodity, or is produced directly for exchange, is the most general and most embryonic form of bourgeois production. I/1/37

9 *Surplus Value*

The exact form of this process is therefore $M - C - M'$ where $M' = M + \Delta M$ = the original sum advanced, plus an increment. This increment or excess over the original value I call *surplus value*. The value originally advanced, therefore, not only remains intact while in circulation, but adds to itself a surplus value or expands itself. It is this movement that converts it into capital. I/4/71

10 *Exchange*

With reference, therefore, to use-value, there is good ground for saying that "exchange is transaction at which both sides gain." It is otherwise with exchange value. I/5/74 (Marx is quoting Destutt de Tracy).

11 *Exchange begets no value*

Turn and twist then as we may, the fact remains unaltered. If equivalents are exchanged, no surplus value results, and if non-equivalents are exchanged, still no surplus value. Circulation, or the exchange of commodities begets no value. I/5/77

12 *Crisis*

No one can sell unless someone else purchases. But no one is forthwith bound to purchase because he has just sold. . . . If the interval in time between the two complementary phases of the complete metamorphosis of a commodity becomes too great, if the split between the sale and the purchase becomes too pronounced, the intimate connection between them, their oneness, asserts itself by producing a crisis. I/3/52

13 *Source of surplus value*

The change of value that occurs in the case of money intended to be converted into capital cannot take place in the money itself, since, in its function of means of purchase and of payment, it does no more than realize the price of the commodity it buys or pays for; and, as hard cash, it is value petrified, never varying. Just as little can it originate in the second act of circulation, the resale of the commodity, which does no more than transform the article from its bodily form back again into its money form. The change must, therefore, take place in the commodity bought by the first act, M − C, but not in its value, for equivalents are exchanged and the commodity is paid for at its full value. We are, therefore, forced to the conclusion that the change originates in the use-value, as such, of the commodity, i.e. in its consumption. In order to be able to extract value from the consumption of a commodity, our friend, moneybags, must be so lucky as to find, within the sphere of circulation, in the market, a commodity whose use-value possesses the peculiar property of being a source of value, whose actual consumption, therefore, is itself an embodiment of labour, and, consequently, a creation of value. The possessor of money does find on the market such a special commodity in capacity for labour or labour power. I/3/79

14 *Labour Power*

By *labour power* or *capacity for labour* is to be understood the aggregate of those mental and physical capabilities existing in a human being which he exercises whenever he produces a use-value of any description. I/6/79

15 *Sale of Labour Power*

.... {L}abour power can appear upon the market as a commodity only if, and in so far as, its possessor, the individual whose labour power it is, offers it for sale, or sells it, as a commodity. In order that he may be able to do this, he must have it at his disposal, must be the untramelled owner of his capacity for labour, i.e. of his person. He and the owner of money meet in the market and deal with each other as on the basis of equal rights, with this difference alone, that one is buyer, the other seller; both therefore, equal in the eyes of the law. The continuance of this relation demands that the owner of the labour power should sell it only for a definite period, for if he were to sell it rump and stump, once for all, he would be selling himself, converting himself from a free man into a slave, from an owner of a commodity into a commodity. I/6/79

16 *Free Labour*

For the conversion of his money into capital, therefore, the owner of money must meet in the market with the free labourer, free in the double sense; that as a free man he can dispose of his labour power as his own commodity, and that, on the other hand, he has no other commodity for sale, is short of everything necessary for the realization of his labour power. I/6/80

17 *Historical Basis of the Category of Free Labourer*

One thing, however, is clear – Nature does not produce on the one side owners of money, or commodities, and on the other men possessing nothing but their own labour power. This relation has no natural basis, neither is its social basis one that is common to all historical periods. It is clearly the result of a past historical development, the product of many economic revolutions, of the extinction of a whole series of older forms of social production.

So, too, the economic categories, already discussed by us, bear the stamp of history. Definite historical conditions are necessary, that a product may become a commodity. I/6/80

18 *Historical Conditions for the Existence of Capital*

It is otherwise with capital. The historical conditions of its existence are
by no means given with the mere circulation of money and
commodities. It can spring into life only when the owner of the means
of production and subsistence meets in the market with the free
labourer selling his labour power. I/6/81

19 *Value of Labour Power*

The value of labour power is determined as in the case of every other
commodity by the labour time necessary for the production, and
consequently also the reproduction, of this special article. So far as it has
value, it represents no more than a definite quantity of the average
labour of society incorporated in it. Labour power exists only as a
capacity, or power of the living individual. Its production consequently
presupposes his existence. I/6/81

20 *Consumption of Labour Power is Production of Surplus Value*

We now know how the value paid by the purchaser to the possessor of
this peculiar commodity, labour power is determined. The use value
which the former gets in exchange manifests itself only in the actual
usufruct, in the consumption of the labour power. The money owner
buys everything necessary for this purpose, such as raw material, in the
market, and pays for it at its full value. The consumption of labour
power is at one and the same time the production of commodities and of
surplus value. The consumption of labour power is completed, as in the
case of every other commodity, outside the limits of the market or of the
sphere of circulation. I/6/83

21 *The Sphere of Exchange*

This sphere that we are deserting, within whose boundaries the sale and
purchase of labour power goes on, is in fact a very Eden of the innate
rights of man. There alone rule freedom, equality, property and
Bentham. Freedom, because both buyer and seller of a commodity, say
of labour power, are constrained only by their own free will. They
contract as free agents, and the agreement they come to is both the form
in which they give legal expression to their common will. Equality,
because each enters into relation with the other, as with a simple owner
of commodities and they exchange equivalent for equivalent. Property,
because each disposes only of what is his own. And Bentham, because

each looks only to himself. The only force that brings them together and puts them in relation with each other is the selfishness, the gain and the private interest of each. I/6/83–84

22 *Why Labour Power is a Source of Surplus Value*

The value of a day's labour power amounts to 3 shillings, because on our assumption half a day's labour is embodied in that quantity of labour power, i.e. because the means of subsistence that are daily required for the production of labour power cost half a day's labour. But the past labour that it can call into action, the daily cost of maintaining it and its daily expenditure in work are two totally different things. The former determines the exchange value of the labour power, the latter is its use-value. The fact that half a day's labour is necessary to keep the labourer alive during 24 hours does not in any way prevent him from working a whole day. Therefore the value of labour power and the value which that labour power creates in the labour process are two entirely different magnitudes; and this difference between the two values was what the capitalist had in view when he was purchasing the labour power. The useful qualities that labour power possesses and by virtue of which it makes yarn or boots were to him nothing more than a *conditio sine qua non*; for in order to create value labour must be expended in a useful manner. What really influenced him was the specific use value which this commodity possesses of being *a source not only of value but of more value than it has itself.* This is the special service that the capitalist expects from labour power, and in this transaction he acts in accordance with the "eternal laws" of the exchange of commodities. The seller of labour power, like the seller of any other commodity, realizes its exchange value and parts with its use value. He cannot take the one without giving the other. I/7/93

23 *Surplus Labour in Different Modes of Production*

The essential difference between the various economic forms of society, between, for instance, a society based on slave labour and one based on wage labour, lies only in the mode in which this surplus labour is in each case extracted from the actual producer, the labourer. I/9/105

24 *Limits to Surplus Labour in Non-Capitalist Forms*

It is, however, clear that in any given economic formation of society, where not the exchange value but the use-value of the product predominates, surplus labour will be limited by a given set of wants which may be greater or less, and that here no boundless thirst for surplus labour arises from the nature of the production itself. I/10/113

25 *Length of the Working Day is Determined by Class Struggle*

We see, then, that apart from extremely elastic bounds, the nature of the exchange of commodities itself imposes no limit to the working day, no limit to surplus labour. The capitalist maintains his rights as a purchaser when he tries to make the working day as long as possible, and to make, whenever possible, two working days out of one. On the other hand, the peculiar nature of the commodity sold implies a limit to its consumption by the purchaser, and the labourer maintains his right as a seller when he wishes to reduce the working day to one of definite normal duration. There is here, therefore, an antinomy, right against right, both equally bearing the seal of the law of exchanges. Between equal right, force decides. Hence is it that, in the history of capitalist production, the determination of what is a working day presents itself as the result of a struggle, a struggle between collective capital, i.e. the class of capitalists, and collective labour, i.e. the working class. I/10/113

26 *Slave Labour in Capitalist Mode of Production* (Negro labour in the Southern USA)

But as soon as people, whose production still moves within the lower forms of slave-labour, corvée-labour, etc., are drawn into the whirlpool of an international market dominated by the capitalist mode of production, the sale of their products for export becoming their principal interest, the civilised horrors of overwork are grafted on the barbaric horrors of slavery, serfdom, etc. Hence, the negro labour in the southern states of the American Union preserved something of a patriarchal character, so long as production was chiefly directed to immediate local consumption. But in proportion, as the export of cotton became of vital interest to these states, the overworking of the negro and sometimes the using up of his life in seven years of labour became a factor in a calculated and calculating system. It was no longer a question of obtaining from him a certain quantity of useful products. It was now a question of production of surplus labour itself. I/10/114

27 *The Struggle for the Normal Working Day*

The changes in the material mode of production, and the corresponding changes in the social relations of the producers, gave rise first to an extravagance beyond all bounds, and then, in opposition to this, called forth a control on the part of the society which legally limits, regulates and makes uniform the working day and its pauses. I/10/144

The creation of a normal working day is, therefore, the product of a protracted civil war, more or less dissembled, between the capitalist class and the working class. I/10/145

28 *Productivity of Labour and Relative Surplus Value*

In order to effect a fall in the value of labour power, the increase in the productiveness of labour must seize upon those branches of industry whose products determine the value of labour power, and consequently, either belong to the class of customary means of subsistence or are capable of supplying the place of these means. But the value of a commodity is determined not only by the quantity of labour which the labourer directly bestows upon that commodity, but also by the labour contained in the means of production.. . . Hence, a fall in the value of labour power is also brought about by an increase in the productiveness of labour, and by a corresponding cheapening of commodities in those industries which supply the instruments of labour and the raw material that form the material elements of constant capital required for producing the necessaries of life. I/12/153–154

The value of commodities is in inverse ratio to the productiveness of labour. And so, too, is the value of labour power, because it depends on the values of commodities. Relative surplus value is, on the contrary, directly proportional to that productiveness. I/12/155–156.

Hence there is immanent in capital an inclination and constant tendency to heighten the productiveness of labour in order to cheapen commodities, and by such cheapening to cheapen the labourer himself. I/12/156

29 *Co-operation Among Labourers in the Capitalist Mode*

.... {W}age labourers cannot co-operate unless they are employed simultaneously by the same capital, the same capitalist and unless, therefore, their labour powers are bought simultaneously by him. I/13/160

The work of directing, superintending and adjusting becomes one of the functions of capital from the moment that the labour under the control of capital becomes co-operative. Once a function of capital, it acquires special characteristics.

The directing motive, the end and aim of capitalist production, is to extract the greatest amount of surplus value and, consequently, to exploit labour power to the greatest possible extent. As the number of the co-operating labourers increases, so, too, does their resistance to the domination of capital and with it the necessity for capital to overcome this resistance by counter-pressure. The control exercised by the capitalist is not only a special function, due to the nature of the social labour process, and peculiar to that process, but it is, at the same time, a function of the exploitation of a social labour process and is consequently rooted in the unavoidable antagonism between the exploiter and the living and labouring raw material he exploits. I/13/161

30 *Functions of the Capitalist*

When comparing the mode of production of isolated peasants and artisans with production by slave labour, the political economist counts this labour of superintendence among the *faux frais* of production. But, when considering the capitalist mode of production, he, on the contrary, treats the work of control made necessary by the co-operative character of the labour process as identical with the different work of control, necessitated by the capitalist character of that process and the antagonism of interest between capitalist character of that process and the antagonism of interest between capitalist and labourer. It is not because he is a leader of industry that a man is a capitalist; on the contrary, he is a leader of industry because he is a capitalist. The leadership of industry is an attribute of capital, just as in feudal times the functions of general and judge were attributes of landed property. I/13/162

31 *Political Economy as Influenced by Manufacture*

Political economy, which as an independent science first sprang into being during the period of manufacture, views the social division of labour only from the standpoint of manufacture and sees in it only the means of producing more commodities with a given quantity of labour, and, consequently, of cheapening commodities and hurrying on the accumulation of capital. In most striking contrast with the accentuation of quantity and exchange value is the attitude of the writers of classical antiquity, who hold exclusively by quality and use-value. I/14/178

32 *Productive Labour as a Social Relation*

Hence the notion of a productive labourer implies not merely a relation between work and useful effect, between labourer and product of labour, but also a specific social relation of production, a relation that has sprung up historically and stamps the labourer as the direct means of creating surplus value. To be a productive labourer is, therefore, not a piece of luck but a misfortune. I/16/251

33 *Determinants of Productiveness of Labour*

Apart from the degree of development, greater or less, in the form of social production, the productiveness of labour is fettered by physical conditions. These are all referable to the constitution of man himself (race, etc.) and to surrounding nature. The external physical conditions fall into two great economic classes: (1) natural wealth in the means of subsistence i.e. a fruitful soil, waters teeming with fish, etc. and (2), natural wealth in the instruments of labour, such as waterfalls, navigable rivers, wood, metal, coal, etc. I/16/253

34 *Changes in the Value of Labour Power*

The value of labour power is determined by the value of a given quantity of necessaries. It is the value and not the mass of these necessaries that varies with the productiveness of labour. It is, however, possible that, owing to an increase of productiveness, both the labourer and the capitalist may simultaneously be able to appropriate a greater quantity of these necessaries without any change in the price of labour power or in surplus value. . . Although labour power would be unchanged in price, it would be above its value. If, however, the price of labour has fallen, not to {1s 6d}, the lowest point consistent with its new value, but to {2s 10d or 2s 6d}, still this lower price would represent an increased mass of necessaries. In this way it is possible, with an increasing productiveness of labour, for the price of labour power to keep on falling and yet this fall to be accompanied by a constant growth in the mass of the labourer's means of subsistence. I/17/258

35 *Determinants of Surplus Value and Price of Labour Power*

I assume: (1) that commodities are sold at their value; (2) that the price of labour power rises occasionally above its value, but never sinks below it.

On this assumption, we have seen that the relative magnitudes of surplus value and of price of labour power are determined by three circumstances (1) the length of the working day, or the extensive magnitude of labour; (2) the normal intensity of labour, its intensive magnitude, whereby a given quantity of labour is expended in a given time; (3) the productiveness of labour, whereby the same quantum of labour yields, in a given time, a greater or less quantum of product, dependent on the degree of development in the conditions of production.

. . . .

On these assumptions the value of labour power and the magnitude of

surplus value are determined by three laws.
(1) A working day of given length always creates the same amount of value, no matter how the productiveness of labour and, with it, the mass of the product, and the price of each single commodity produced, may vary.
(2) Surplus value and the value of labour power vary in opposite directions. A variation in the productiveness of labour, its increase or dimunition, causes a variation in the opposite direction in the value of labour power, and in the same direction in surplus value.
(3) Increase or diminution in surplus value is always consequent on, and never the cause of, the corresponding dimunution or increase in the value of labour power. I/17/256–257

36 *The Value of Labour and the Value of Labour Power*

That which comes directly face to face with the possessor of money on the market is in fact not labour, but the labourer. What the latter sells is his labour power. As soon as his labour actually begins it has already ceased to belong to him; it can therefore no longer be sold by him. Labour is the substance and the immanent measure of value, *but has itself no value.*

In the expression "value of labour", the idea of value is not only completely obliterated, but actually reversed. It is an expression as imaginary as the value of the earth. These imaginary expressions arise, however, from the relations of production themselves. They are categories for the phenominal forms of essential relations. That in their appearance things often represent themselves in inverted form is pretty well known in every science except political economy. I/19/265

37 *The value of Labour as Seen by Economists*

What economists call *value of labour* is in fact the value of labour power as it exists in the personality of the labourer, which is different from its function, labour, as a machine is from the work it performs. Occupied with the difference between the market price of labour and its so-called value, with the relation of this value to the rate of profit, and to the values of the commodities produced by means of labour, etc., they never discovered that the course of the analysis had led not only from the market prices of labour to its presumed value, but had led to the resolution of this value of labour itself into the value of labour power. Classical economy never arrived at a consciousness of the results of its own analysis; it accepted uncritically the categories "value of labour", "natural price of labour", etc., as final and as adequate expressions for the value relation under consideration and was thus led, as will be seen later, into inextricable confusion and contradiction, while it offered to the vulgar economists a secure basis of operations for their shallowness, which on principle worships appearances only. I/19/265–266

38 *The Value of Labour is Greater than the Value of Labour Power*

As the value of labour is only an irrational expression for the value of labour power, it follows, of course, that the value of labour must always be less than the value it produces, for the capitalist always makes labour power work longer than is necessary for the reproduction of its own value... Thus we have a result absurd at first sight – that labour which creates a value of 6s. possesses a value of 3s. I/19/266

39 *The Wage Form*

The wage form thus extinguishes every trace of the division of the working day into necessary labour and surplus labour into paid and unpaid labour. All labour appears as paid labour. In the corvée, the labour of the worker for himself, and his compulsory labour for his lord, differ in space and time in the clearest possible way. In slave labour, even that part of the working day in which the slave is only replacing the value of his own means of existence, in which, therefore, in fact, he works for himself alone, appears as labour for his master. All the slave's labour appears as unpaid labour. In wage labour, on the contrary, even surplus labour, or unpaid labour, appears as paid. There the property relation conceals the labour of the slave for himself; here the money relation conceals the unrequited labour of the wage labourer.

Hence we may understand the decisive importance of the transformation of value and price of labour power into the form of wages, or into the value and price of labour itself. This phenominal form, which makes the actual relation invisible and, indeed, shows the direct opposite of that relation, forms the basis of all the juridical notions of both labourer and capitalist, of all the mystifications of the capitalistic mode of production, of all its illusions as to liberty, of all the apologetic shifts of the vulgar economists. I/19/266

40 *The Capitalist and the Value of Labour*

He {the capitalist} wishes to receive as much labour as possible for as little money as possible. Practically, therefore, the only thing that interests him is the difference between the price of labour power and the value which its function creates. But, then, he tries to buy all commodities as cheaply as possible and always accounts for his profit by simple cheating, by buying under and selling over the value. Hence, he never comes to see that, if such a thing as the value of labour really existed and he really paid this value, no capital would exist; his money would not be turned into capital. I/19/267

41 *The Wage Form and the Value Substance*

For the rest, in respect to the phenominal form, "value and price of labour", or "wages", as contrasted with the essential relation manifested therein (viz. the value and price of labour power), the same difference holds that in respect to all phenomena and their hidden substrata. The former appears directly and spontaneously as current modes of thought; the latter must first be discovered by science. Classical political economy nearly touches the true relation of things without, however, consciously formulating it. This it cannot, so long as it sticks in its bourgeois skin. I/19/267

42 *Division of Surplus Value*

The capitalist who produces surplus value – i.e. who extracts unpaid labour directly from the labourers, and fixes it in commodities – is, indeed, the first appropriator, but by no means the ultimate owner, of this surplus value. He has to share it with capitalists, with landowners, etc., who fulfil other functions in the complex of social production. Surplus value, therefore, splits up into various parts. Its fragments fall to various categories of persons and take various forms, independent the one of the other, such as profit, interest, merchants' profit, rent, etc. I/Introduction to Ch. 23/279.

43 *Converting Money into Capital*

We saw, in Chapter IV, that in order to convert money into capital something more is required than the production and circulation of commodities. We saw that, on the one side, the possessor of value or money, on the other, the possessor of the value of creating substance; on the one side, the possessor of the means of production and subsistence, on the other, the possessor of nothing but labour power, must confront one another as buyer and seller. The separation of labour from its product, of subjective labour power from the objective conditions of labour, was therefore the real foundation in fact and the starting point of capitalist production. I/23/282.

44 *Creation of Capital and Perpetuation of the Labourer*

But that which at first was but a starting point becomes, by the mere continuity of the process, by simple reproduction, the peculiar result, constantly renewed and perpetuated, of capitalist production. On the one hand, the process of production incessantly converts material wealth into capital, into means of creating more wealth and means of enjoyment for the capitalist. On the other hand, the labourer, on quitting the process, is what he was on entering it, a source of wealth, but devoid of all means of making that wealth his own. Since, before entering the process, his own labour has already been alienated from himself by the sale of his labour power, has been appropriated by the capitalist and incorporated with capital, it must, during the process, be realised in a product that does not belong to him. Since the process of production is also the process by which the capitalist consumes labour power, the product of the labourer is incessantly converted, not only into commodities, but into capital, into value that sucks up the value-creating power, into means of subsistence that buy the person of the labourer, into means of production that command the producers. The labourer, therefore, constantly produces material, objective wealth, but in the form of capital of an alien power that dominates and exploits him; and the capitalist as constantly produces labour power, but in the form of a subjective source of wealth, separated from the objects in and by which it can alone be realised; in short he produces the labourer, but as a wage labourer. This incessant reproduction, this perpetuation of the labourer, is the *sine qua non* of capitalist production. I/23/282

45 *The Capitalist and Accumulation of Capital*

But, so far as he {the capitalist } is personified capital, it is not values in use and the enjoyment of them, but exchange value and its augmentation, that spur him into action. Fanatically bent on making value expand itself, he ruthlessly forces the human race to produce for production's sake; he thus forces the development of the productive powers of society and creates those material conditions which alone can form the real basis of a higher form of society, a society in which the full and free development of every individual forms the ruling principle. Only as personified capital is the capitalist respectable. As such, he shares with the miser the passion for wealth as wealth. But that which in the miser is a mere idiosyncrasy is in the capitalist the effect of the social mechanism of which he is but one of the wheels. Moreover, the development of capitalist production makes it constantly necessary to keep increasing the amount of capital laid out in a given industrial undertaking, and competition makes the immanent laws of capitalist production to be felt by each individual capitalist as external coercive laws. It compels him to keep constantly extending his capital, in order to preserve it, but extend it he cannot except by means of progressive accumulation. I/24/292–293

46 *Rising Labour Productivity and Rising Real Wage*

But, hand-in-hand with the increasing productivity of labour goes, as we have seen, the cheapening of the labourer, therefore a higher rate of surplus value, even when the real wages are rising. The latter never rise proportionally to the productive power of labour. I/24/299

47 *Improvement in Machinery*, etc. ('Embodied' and 'Disembodied' Technical Change)

The development of the productive power of labour reacts also on the original capital already engaged in the process of production. A part of the functioning constant capital consists of instruments of labour, such as machinery, etc; which are not consumed and therefore not reproduced or replaced by new ones of the same kind until after long periods of time. But every year a part of these instruments of labour perishes or reaches the limit of its productive function. It reaches, therefore, in that year, the time for its periodical reproduction, for its replacement by new ones of the same kind. If the productiveness of labour has, during the using up of these instruments of labour, increased (and it develops continually with the uninterrupted advance of science and technology), more efficient and (considering their increased efficiency) cheaper machines, tools, apparatus, etc. replace the old. The old capital is reproduced in a more productive form, apart from the constant detail improvements in the instruments of labour already in use. The other part of the constant capital, raw material and auxiliary substances, is constantly reproduced in less than a year; these produced by agriculture, for the most part, annually. Every introduction of improved methods, therefore, works almost simultaneously on the new capital and on that already in action. . . . Of course, this development of productive power is accompanied by a partial depreciation of functioning capital so far as this depreciation makes itself acutely felt in competition, the burden falls on the labourer, in the increased exploitation of whom the capitalist looks for his indemnification. I/24/299.

48 *Rising Real Wages and Accumulation*

Wages, as we have seen, by their very nature, always imply the performance of a certain quantity of unpaid labour on the part of the labourer. Altogether, irrespective of the case of a rise in wages with a falling price of labour, etc., such an increase only means at best a quantitative diminution of the unpaid labour that the worker has to supply. The diminution can never reach the point at which it would threaten the system itself. Apart from violent conflicts as to the rate of wages (and Adam Smith has already shown that in such a conflict, taken on the whole, the master is always master), a rise in the price of labour resulting from accumulation of capital implies the following alternative: either the price of labour keeps on rising, because its rise does not interfere with the progress of accumulation... In this case it is evident that a dimunition in the unpaid labour in no way interferes with the extension of the domain of capital. Or, on the other hand, accumulation slackens in consequence of the rise in the price of labour, because the stimulus of gain is blunted. The rate of accumulation lessens; but with lessening, the primary cause of that lessening vanishes, i.e., the disproportion between capital and exploitable lower power. The mechanism of the process of capitalist production removes the very obstacle that it temporarily creates. The price of labour falls again to a level corresponding with the needs of the self expansion of capital, whether the level be below, the same as, or above the one which was normal before the rise of wages took place. I/25/306

49 *Accumulation and Crises*

To put it mathematically, the rate of accumulation is the independent, not the dependent, variable; the rate of wages the dependent, not the independent, variable. Thus, when the industrial cycle is in the phase of crisis, a general fall in the price of commodities is expressed as a rise in the value of money and in the phase of prosperity, a general rise in the price of commodities, as a fall in the value of money. The so-called currency school concludes from this that with high prices too little, with low prices too much money is in circultion. Their ignorance and complete misunderstanding of facts are worthily paralleled by the economists, who interpret the above phenomena of accumulation by saying that there are now too few, not too many, wage labourers. I/25/307

50 *Movement of Wages and the Industrial Cycle*

Taking them as a whole, the general movement of wages are exclusively regulated by the expansion and contraction of the industrial reserve army, and these again correspond to the periodic changes of the industrial cycle. They are, therefore, not determined by the variations of the absolute number of the working population, but by the varying proportions in which the working class is divided into active and reserve army, by the increase or diminution in the relative amount of the surplus population, by the extent to which it is now absorbed, now set free. I/25/315

51 *Primitive Accumulation*

We have seen how money is changed into capital; how, through capital, surplus value is made and from surplus value more capital. But the accumulation of capital presupposes surplus value, surplus value presupposes capitalistic production; capitalistic production presupposes the pre-existence of considerable masses of capital and of labour power in the hands of producers of commodities. The whole movement, therefore, seems to turn in a vicious circle, out of which we can only get by supposing a primitive accumulation. (The "previous accumulation" of Adam Smith) preceding capitalistic accumulation; an accumulation not the result of the capitalist mode of production, but its starting point. I/26/354.

52 *The Methods of Primitive Accumulation*

In the tender annals of political economy, the idyllic reigns from time immemorial. Right and "labour" were from all time the sole means of enrichment, the present year, of course, always excepted. As a matter of fact, the methods of primitive accumulation are anything but idyllic.

53 *The Process of Primitive Accumulation*

The process, therefore, that clears the way for the capitalist system can be none other than the process which takes away from the labourer the possession of his means of production, a process that transforms, on the one hand, the social means of subsistence and of production into capital, on the other, the immediate producers into wage labourers. The so-called primitive accumulation, therefore, is nothing else than the historical process of divorcing the producer from the means of production. I/26/354–355

54 *The Role of Force in Primitive Accumulation and in Capitalism*

The dull compulsion of economic relations compels the subjection of the labourer to the capitalist. Direct force, outside economic conditions, is of course still used, but only exceptionally. In the ordinary run of things, the labourer can be left to the "natural laws of production", i.e. to his dependence on capital, a dependence springing from, and guaranteed in perpetuity by, the conditions of production themselves. It is otherwise during the historic genesis of capitalist production. The bourgeoisie, at its rise, wants and uses the power of the state to "regulate" wages, i.e. to force them within the limits suitable for surplus value making, to lengthen the working day and to keep the labourer himself in the normal degree of dependence. This is an essential element of the so-called primitive accumulation. I/28/366

55 *Force*

Force is the midwife of every old society pregnant with a new one. It is itself an economic power. I/31/372

56 *Money and Money Capital*

Capital in the form of money-capital is in a state in which it can perform the functions of money, in the present case the functions of a universal means of purchase and universal means of payment. ... This capacity is not due to the fact that money capital is capital but that it is money.

On the other hand capital-value in the form of money cannot perform any other functions but those of money. What turns the money functions into functions of capital is the definite role they play in the movement of capital, and therefore also this inter-relation of the stage in which these functions are performed with the other stages of the circuit of capital. Take, for instance, the case with which we are here dealing. Money is here converted into commodities, the combination of which represents the bodily form of productive capital, and this form already contains latently, potentially, the result of the process of capitalist production. II/1/26

57 *M – L: Capital in the Purchase of Labour Power*

M – L is the characteristic moment in the transformation of money-capital into productive capital, because it is the essential condition for the real transformation of value advanced in the form of money into capital, into a value producing surplus value. II/1/27

58 *M – L: Hallmark of the Money System*

M – L is regarded as the characteristic feature, the hallmark of the so-called money system, because labour there appears as the commodity of its owner, and money therefore as the buyer – hence on account of the money-relation (i.e. the sale and purchase of human activity). II/1/28.

59 *Labour Power as a Commodity*

Once labour-power has come into the market as the commodity of its owner and its sale takes the form of payment for labour, assumes the shape of wages, its purchase and sale is no more startling than the purchase and sale of any other commodity. The characteristic thing is not that the commodity labour-power is purchasable but that labour-power appears as a commodity. II/1/28

60 *M – L: The Exchange and the Class-Relation*

True, in the act M – L the owner of money and the owner of labour-power enter only into the relation of buyer and seller, confront one another only as money-owner and commodity-owner. In this respect they enter merely into a money relation. Yet at the same time the buyer appears also from the outset in the capacity of an owner of means of production, which are the material conditions for the productive expenditure of labour-power by its owner. In other words, these means of production are in opposition to the owner of the labour-power, being property of another. On the other hand the seller of labour faces its buyer as labour-power of another which must be made to do his bidding, must be integrated into his capital, in order that it may really become productive capital. The class relation between capitalist and wage-labourer therefore exists, is presupposed from the moment that the two face each other in act M – L (L – M on the part of the labourer). It is a purchase and sale, a money-relation, but a purchase and sale in which the buyer is assumed to be a capitalist and the seller a wage-labourer. And this relation arises out of the fact that the conditions required for the realization of labour-power, viz., means of subsistence and means of production, are separated from the owner of labour-power, being the property of another. II/1/29.

61 *Capital as a Relation*

The capital-relation during the process of production arises only because it is inherent in the act of circulation, in the different fundamental economic conditions in which the buyer and seller confront each other in their class relation. It is not money which by its nature creates this relation; it is rather the existence of this relation which permits of the transformation of a mere money-function into a capital-function. II/1/30.

62 *M – L: The Historical Conditions*

In order that the sale of one's own labour-power (in the form of the sale of one's own labour or in the form of wages) may constitute not an isolated phenomenon but a socially decisive premise for the production of commodities, in order that money-capital may therefore perform, on a social scale, the above-discussed function $M - C < \dfrac{L}{MP}$ historical processes are assumed by which the original connection of the means of production with labour-power was dissolved – processes in consequence of which the mass of the people, the labourers, have as non-owners, come face to face with the non-labourers as the owners of these means of production. II/1/31

63 *The Production Function is Ahistorical*

Whatever the social form of production, labourers and means of production always remain factors of it. . . . For production to go on at all they must unite. The specific manner in which this union is accomplished distinguishes the different economic epochs of the structure of society from one another. II/1/34

64 *The Different Nature of Means of Production and Labour-Power*

The means of production and labour-power, in so far as they are forms of existence of advanced capital-value, are distinguished by the different roles assumed by them during the process of production in the creation of value, hence also of surplus value, into constant and variable capital. Being different components of productive capital they are furthermore distinguished by the fact that the means of production in the possession of the capitalist remains his capital even outside of the process of production, while labour-power becomes the form of existence of an individual capital only within this process. Whereas labour-power is a commodity only in the hands of its seller, the wage-labourer, it becomes capital only in the hands of its buyer, the capitalist who acquires the temporary use of it.

65 *Interruptions in the Circuit of Capital: Hoard, Idle Capacity, Excess Supply*

Capital describes its circuit normally only so long as its various phases pass uninterruptedly into one another. If capital stops short in its first phase M – C, money capital assumes the rigid form of a hoard; if it stops short in the phase of production, the means of production lie without functioning on the one side, while labour-power remains unemployed on the other; and if capital is stopped short in its last phase C′ – M′, piles of unsold commodities accumulate and clog the flow of circulation. II/1/48

66 *Commodity-Output and Services*

In the general formula the product of P is regarded as a material thing different from the elements of the productive capital, as an object existing apart from the process of production and having a use-form different from that of elements of production. This is always the case when the result of the productive process assumes the form of a thing even when a part of the product re-enters the resumed production as one of its elements . . . . But there are certain independent branches of industry in which the product of the productive process is not a new material product, is not a commodity. Among these only the communications industry, whether engaged in transportation proper, of goods and passengers, or in the mere transmission of communications, letters, telegrams, etc, is economically important. II/1/51–52.

67 *The Process as Seen by Vulgar Economy*

And so we have premised simple reproduction, i.e. that m – c separates entirely from M – C. Since both circulations, c – m – c as well as C – M – C, belong in the circulation of commodities, so far as their general form is concerned (and for this reason do not show any value differences in their extremes); it is easy to conceive the process of capitalist production, after the manner of vulgar economy, as a mere production of commodities, of use-values designed for consumption of some sort, which the capitalist produces for no other purpose than that of getting in their place commodities with different use-values, or of exchanging them for such, as vulgar economy erroneously states. II/2/68

68 *Ever Changing Values*

In order that the circuit may be completed normally, C′ must be sold at its value and its entirety. Furthermore, C – M – C includes not merely replacement of one commodity by another, but replacement with value-relations remaining the same. We assume that this takes place here. As a matter of fact, however, the values of the means of production vary. It is precisely capitalist production to which continuous change of value-relations is peculiar, if only because of the ever changing productivity of labour that characterizes this mode of production. II/2/72

69 *Continuous Expansion of Capital*

The entire character of capitalist production is determined by the self-expansion of the advanced capital-value, that is to say, in the first instance by the production of as much surplus-value as possible; in the second place, however, (see Vol. I Ch. 24) by the production of capital, hence, by the transformation of surplus-value into capital. Accumulation, or production on an extended scale, which appears as a means of constantly more expanded production of surplus-value – hence for enrichment of the capitalist, as his personal aim – and is comprised in the general tendency of capitalist production, becomes, later, however, as was shown in Book I, by virtue of its development a necessity for every individual capitalist. The constant augmentation of his capital becomes a condition of its preservation. II/2/78–79

70 *The Circuit of Productive Capital and Political Economy*

The general form of the movement P . . . P is the form of reproduction and, unlike M . . . M', does not indicate the self-expansion of value as the object of the process. This form makes it therefore so much easier for classical Political Economy to ignore the definite capitalistic form of the process of production and to depict production as such as the purpose of this process; namely that as much as possible must be produced and as cheaply as possible, and that the product must be exchanged for the greatest variety of other products, partly for the renewal of production (M − C), partly for consumption (m − c). It is then possible to overlook the peculiarities of money and money-capital, for M and m appear here merely as transient media of circulation. The entire process seems simple and natural, i.e., possesses the naturalness of a shallow rationalism. II/3/92

71 *Why the Circuit of Commodity Capital Appears as the General Form*

But just because the circuit C' . . . C' presupposes within its sphere the existence of other industrial capital in the form of C (equal to L + MP) – and MP comprises diverse other capitals in our case, for instance machinery, coal, oil, etc. – it clamours to be considered not only as the *general* form of the circuit, i.e. not only as a social form in which every single industrial capital (except when first invested) can be

studied, hence not merely as a form of movement common to all individual industrial capitals, but simultaneously also as a form of movement of the sum of the individual capitals, consequently of the aggregate capital of the capitalist class, a movement in which that of each
individual industrial capital appears as only a partial movement which
intermingles with the other movements and is necessitated by them.
II/3/96–97

72 *The Circuit of Commodity Capital as a One-Sided Conception*

In Formula III {C′ − C′} commodities in the market are the continuous
premise of the process of production and reproduction. Hence, if attention is fixed exclusively on this formula all elements of the process of
production seem to originate in commodity circulation and to consist
only of commodities. This one-sided conception overlooks those elements of the process of production which are independent of the
commodity-elements. II/3/98–99

73 *Commodity Circuit and Quesnay*

C′ − C′ is the groundwork for Quesnay's *Tableau Economique* and it
shows great and true discretion on his part that in contrast to M . . .
M′ (the isolatedly and rigidly retained form of the mercantile system)
he selected this form and not P . . . P. II/3/99

74 *Capital as a Dynamic Process*

Capital, as self-expanding value embraces not only class relations, a society of a definite character resting on the existence of labour in the
form of wage-labour. It is a movement, a circuit-describing process
going through various stages, which itself comprises three different
forms of the circuit-describing process. Therefore, it can be understood
only as motion, not as a thing at rest. II/4/105.

75 *Individual Capital and Revolutions in Value*

The movements of capital appear as the action of some individual
industrial capitalist who performs the functions of a buyer of commodities and labour, a seller of commodities, and an owner of productive capital, who therefore promotes the circuit by his activity. If social
capital experiences a revolution in value the more does the automatic
movement of the now independent value operate with the elemental
force of a natural process against the foresight and calculation of the
individual capitalist, the more does the course of normal production

become subservient to abnormal speculation and the greater is the danger that threatens the existence of the individual capitals. These periodical revolutions in value therefore corroborate what they are supposed to refute, namely, that value as capital acquires independent existence, which it maintains and accentuates through its movement. II/4/105–106

76 *Industrial Capitalism and Other Modes of Production in the World Market*

Within its process of circulation, in which industrial capital functions either as money or as commodities, the circuit of industrial capital, whether as money-capital or as commodity-capital, crosses the commodity circulation of the most diverse modes of social production, so far as they produce commodities. No matter whether commodities are the output of production based on slavery of peasants (Chinese, Indian ryots), of communes (Dutch East Indies), of state enterprises (such as existed in former epochs of Russian history on the basis of serfdom) or of half-savage hunting tribes, etc. – as commodities and money they come face to face with the money and commodities in which the industrial capital presents itself and enter as much into its circuit as into that of surplus-value borne in the commodity-capital, provided the surplus-value is spent as revenue, hence they enter into both branches of circulation of commodity-capital. The character of the process of production from which they originate is immaterial. They function as commodities in the market, and as commodities they enter into the circuit of industrial capital as well as into the circulation of the surplus-value incorporated in it. It is therefore the universal character of the origin of the commodities, the existence of the market as world market, which distinguishes the process of circulation of industrial capital. II/4/109–110.

77 *Profits as Apparent Result of Time of Circulation*

A capital's time of circulation therefore limits, generally speaking, its time of production and hence its process of generating surplus value. And it limits this process in proportion to its own duration. This duration may considerably increase or decrease and hence may restrict capital's time of production in a widely varying degree. But Political Economy sees only what is *apparent*, namely the effect of the time of circulation on capital's process of the creation of surplus-value in general. It takes this negative effect for a positive one, because its consequences are positive. It clings the more tightly to this appearance since it seems to furnish proof that capital possesses a mystic source of self-expansion independent of its process of production and hence of the exploitation of labour, a spring which flows to it from the spheres of circulation. II/5/125

Cost-Price, Profits and Surplus Value: Things as they appear to the Capitalist

78 *The Category of Cost-Price*

The category of cost-price, on the other hand, has nothing to do with the formation of commodity-value or with the proces of self-explanation of capital . . . . The investigation will show, however, that in capitalist economics the cost-price assumes the false appearance of a category of value production itself. III/1/28

79 *Surplus Value as a Product of all Capital, Labour as well as the Stock of Fixed Capital*

We have also seen earlier that though s, the surplus value, springs merely from a change in the value of the variable capital v. and is, therefore, originally but an increment of variable capital, after the process of production is over, it nevertheless also forms an increment of c + v, the expended total capital. The formula c + (v + s), which indicates that s is produced through the conversion of a definite capital value v advanced for labour power into a fluctuating magnitude, i.e. of a constant magnitude into a variable one, may also be represented as (c + v) + s. However, surplus value forms an increment not only of the portion of the advanced capital which goes into the self-expansion process, but also of the portion which does not go into it. In other words, it is an accretion not only to the consumed capital made good out of the cost-price of the commodity, but to all the capital invested in production. Before the production process we had a capital valued at 1680, namely 1,200 of fixed capital invested in means of production, only 20 of which go into the value of the commodity for wear and tear, plus 480 of circulating capital in materials of production and wages. After the production process we have 1,180 as the constituent element of the value of the productive capital plus a commodity capital of 600. By adding these two sums of value we find that the capitalist now has a value of 1,780. After deducting his advanced total capital of 1,680 there remains a value increment of 100. The 100 of surplus value thus form as much an increment in relation to the invested 1,680 as to its fraction of 500 expanded during production.

It is now clear to the capitalist that the increment of value springs from the productive processes undertaken with the capital, that it therefore springs from the capital itself, because it is there after the production process, while it is not there before it. As for the capital consumed in production, the surplus-value seems to spring equally from all its different elements of value consisting of means of production and labour. For all these elements contribute equally to the formation of the cost-price. III/1/34–35

Note Marx is assuming here a 100% rate of surplus-value.

80 *How Surplus Value Appears as Profit on Capital*

In its assumed capacity of offspring of the aggregate advanced capital, surplus-value takes the converted form of *profit*. Hence a certain value is capital when it is invested with a view to producing profit, or, there is profit because a certain value was employed as capital. Suppose profit is p. Then the formula $C = c + v + s = k + s$ turns into the formula $C = k + p$, or the value of a commodity = cost price + profit.

The profit, such as it is represented here, is thus the same as surplus-value, only in a mystified form that is none the less a necessary outgrowth of the capitalist mode of production ... Because at one pole the price of labour-power assumes the transmuted form of wages, surplus-value appears at the opposite pole in the transmuted form of profit. III/1/36

81 *Cost-Price as a Measure of Value*

One minimal limit of the selling price of a commodity is its cost-price. If it is sold under its cost-price the expected constituent elements of productive capital cannot be fully replaced out of the selling price. If this process continues, the value of the advanced capital disappears. From this point of view alone, the capitalist is inclined to regard the cost-price as the true *inner* value of the commodity, because it is the price required for the bare conservation of his capital. But there is also this, that the cost-price of a commodity is the purchase price paid by the capitalist himself for its production, therefore, the purchase price determined by the production process itself. For this reason, the excess-value or the surplus-value realized in the sale of a commodity appears to the capitalist as an excess of its selling price over its value, instead of an excess of its value over its cost-price, so that accordingly the surplus-value incorporated in a commodity is not realized through its sale but springs out of the sale itself. III/1/37–38

82 *The Transformation of Surplus-Value into Profit*

The transformation of surplus-value into profit must be deduced from
the transformation of the rate of surplus value into the rate of profit,
not vice versa. And in fact it was rate of profit which was the historical
point of departure. Surplus-value and rate of surplus-value are, relatively, the invisible and unknown essence that wants investigating, while
rate of profit and therefore the appearance of surplus-value in the form
of profit are revealed on the surface of the phenomenon. III/2/42–43

The way in which surplus-value is transformed into the form of profit
by way of the rate of profit is, however, a further development of the
inversion of subject and object that takes place already in the process
of production. III/2/45

83 *The Composition of Capital: Technical and Value Ratios*

By composition of capital we mean, as stated in Book I, the proportion
of its active and passive components, i.e. of variable and constant capital. Two proportions enter into consideration under this heading. They
are not equally important, although they may produce similar effects
under certain circumstances.

The first proportion rests on a technical basis and must be regarded as
given at a certain stage of development of the productive forces. A
definite quantity of labour power represented by a definite number of
labourers is required to produce a definite quantity of products, say, in
one day, and – what is self-evident – thereby to consume productively,
i.e. to set in motion, a definite quantity of means of production,
machinery, raw materials, etc. A definite quantity of labourers
corresponds to a definite quantity of means of production, and hence a
definite quantity of living labour to a definite quantity of labour
materialized in means of production. This proportion differs greatly in
different spheres of production, and frequently, even in different
branches of one and the same industry, although it may by coincidence
be entirely or approximately the same in entirely separate lines of
industry. This proportion forms the technical composition of capital and
is the real basis of its organic composition.

However, it is also possible that this first proportion may be the same
in different lines of industry provided that variable-capital is merely an
index of labour-power and constant capital merely an index of the mass
of means of production set in motion by this labour-power. For
instance, certain work in copper and iron may require the same ratio of

labour power to mass of means of production. But since copper is more expensive than iron, the value-relation between variable and constant capital is different in each case, and hence also the value composition of the two total capitals. III/8/143

84 *Divergence Between Surplus-Value and Profit*

It is then only an accident if the surplus-value, and thus the profit, actually produced in any particular sphere of production, coincides with the profit contained in the selling price of a commodity. As a rule, surplus-value and profit and not their rates alone are then different magnitudes. At a given degree of exploitation, the mass of surplus-value produced in a particular sphere of production is then more important for the aggregate profit of social capital, and thus for the capitalist class in general, than for the individual capitalist in any specific branch of production. It is of importance for the latter only in so far as the quantity of surplus-value produced in his branch helps to regulate the average profit. But this is a process which occurs behind his back, one he does not see, or understand, and which indeed does not interest him. The actual difference of magnitude between profit and surplus-value – not merely between the rate of profit and the rate of surplus value – in the various spheres of production now completely conceals the true nature and origin of profit not only from the capitalist, who has a special interest in deceiving himself on this score, but also from the labourer. The transformation of values into prices of production serves to obscure the basis for determining value itself. III/9/165–166

85 *The Mystification of the Commodity Form*

'When we speak of the commodity as a materialisation of labour – in the sense of its exchange value – this itself is only an imaginary, that is to say, a purely social mode of existence, which has nothing to do with its corporeal reality; it is conceived as a definite quantity of social labour or of money . . . (The mystification here arises from the fact that a social relation appears in the form of a thing)'. (TSV/1/4/171–172)

86 *Productive and Unproductive Labour*

'These definitions (of productive and unproductive labour) are therefore not derived from the material characteristics of labour (neither from the nature of its product nor from the particular character of the labour as concrete labour), but from the definite social form, the social relations of production, within which the labour is realised'. (TSV/1/4/157)

87 'The use-value of the commodity in which the labour of a productive worker is embodied may be of the most futile kind. The material
characteristics are in no way linked with its nature which on the contrary is only the expression of a definite social relation of production. It
is a definition of labour which is derived not from its content or its
result, but form its particular social form'. (TSV/1/4/158)

88 'The same labour can be productive when I buy it as a capitalist, as
a producer, in order to create more value, and unproductive when I
buy it as a consumer a spender of revenue, in order to consume its
use-value, no matter whether this use-value perishes with the activity of
the labour-power itself or materialises and fixes itself in an object'.
(TSV/1/4/165)

89 'Only this definite *relation* to labour transforms money or commodities into capital, and that labour is *productive labour* which
through its relations to the conditions of production – to which corresponds a definite conduct in the actual process of production – tranforms
money or commodities into capital; that is to say, which maintains and
increases the value of materialised labour rendered independent in relation to labour power. Productive labour is only a concise term for the
whole relationship and the form and manner in which labour-power
figures in the capitalist production process'. (TSV/1/Add 12/396)

Productivity of Labour Appears as Productivity of Capital

90 Since living labour – through the exchange between capital and
labourer – is incorporated into capital, and appears as an activity
belonging to capital from the moment that the labour-process begins,
all the productive powers of social labour appear as the productive
powers of capital, just as the general social form of labour appears in
money as the property of a thing ... Here we have once more, the
perversion of the relationship which we have already, in dealing with
money, called fetishism. (TSV/1/Add. 120389)
(Marx referring in his last sentence to A Contribution to the Critique
of Political Economy)

91 *Value and Price of Prodution*

'Since the price of production may differ from the value of a commodity, it follows that the cost-price of a commodity containing the price of
production of another commodity may also stand above or below that
portion of its total value derived from the value of the means of production consumed by it. It is necessary to remember this modified sig-

nificance of the cost-price, and to bear in mind that there is always the posibility of an error if the cost price of a commodity in any particular sphere is identified with the value of the means of production consumed by it. Our present analysis does not necessitate a closer examination of this point'. (Capital/III/IX/164–165)

NOTES

CHAPTER I

[1]See Aubrey Jones (1973). If Samuelson's classic *Principles* can be said to be mainly in the Whig tradition, the recent book by Joan Robinson and John Eatwell (1973) definitely belongs to the other tradition.

[2]We may note also Marx's fluctuating reputation as a mathematician or a mathematical economist. Engels called him a 'thorough mathematician' and Kautsky said he was a 'poor calculator'. Bortkiewicz is contemptuous of Marx's alleged mathematical ability. (See, for reference to Engels, Kautsky in Bortkiewicz, (1907) especially p. 55 and footnote 130). Recently Morishima has claimed that Marx used his stock of mathematical knowledge efficiently and posed new problems in mathematics – see his bibliography for reference to Marx's mathematical manuscript. Also L. Smolinski (1973) Morishima (1974).

CHAPTER II

[1]For the most recent and rigourous exposition of this view see Arrow and Hahn (1972).

[2]This is a very sketchy summary of the classical view. For further information see Blaug (1958), (1968), Dobb (1973), Meek (1973).

[3]The problem of an invariant measure of value is discussed in Sraffa (1960) and Dobb (1973). For Marx's view on Adam Smith's value theory, see TSV Part 3, p. 71.

[4]For a bibliography see Samuelson (1971).

[5]The reference here is to Joan Robinson (1933). By the definition of exploitation adopted there, labour as well as capital i.e. any 'factor of production' can be exploited. For an econometric application of this idea, see Murray Brown (1966). Where there are imperfections in the labour market such as racial discrimination. Marxian economicst employ the notion of 'super-exploitation'. See Donald J. Harris (1972) and a critique of his view in Barrera (1976).

[6]In Part VIII of *Capital*, Vol. I, Marx discusses the case of the USA and the low degree of exploitation there as a result of the availability of free land.

[7]The State often acts to speed up the process of emergence of free labour. Thus in Central Africa, the mines could not recruit local tribal population as the natives did not wish to leave their land. A head-tax payable in money was imposed to force these people to seek money income which they could do best by some employment in mines.

[8]This is a much debated issue. What I have given is a sketch of Marx's argument. In recent years, this view of the enclosure movement has been challenged by historians. On the historical circumstances leading to the formation of the proletariat in England and the role of the Enclosure movement, see Chambers (1953). A major omission in Marx's scheme is any mention of the formation of an agrarian labouring class. Marx more or less ignores the problem of agrarian class relations. It was left to Kautsky and Lenin in many of his pamphlets, but especially in his *Development of Capitalism in Russia*, to take up the problem. The challenge posed by Chambers can be answered in terms of a Kautsky–Lenin agrarian class structure model, but this has never been satisfactorily done. See for a recent discussion of Chambers' view however Lazonick (1974). See also John Foster (1974) for a rich account of the emergence of an industrial proletariat in eighteenth-century England and the dynamics of class consciousness.

[9]It has been left to historians to bring out the particular circumstances underlying a general pattern. A particularly interesting example is Isaac Deutscher's discussion (1970) of the changing class character of the Russian labour force after the Civil War and the importance it had in weakening the revolutionary tradition of the Russian proletariat. For the English case see Hobsbawm (1957). Jan Breman has studied how the economic position of peasant labour in Western India, traditionally permanently in debt to the landlord/employer worsened with economic growth and legislative reform. J. Breman (1974).

[10]The ambiguities of the definition of the bourgeoisie has led to many problems for revolutionary governments. See, for example, Chapter 3 on 'Class and Party' in Carr (1970). Also see for a recent discussion of the thorny problem of class Ralph Miliband (1977), Chapter V.

[11]This is no more than an outline of the standard Marxian position. Barrington More (1971) has illustrated the thesis with examples from many countries. See also Perry Anderson (1974) for a full and complex study in the best Marxian tradition.

[12]The three pamphlets by Marx on France listed in the bibliography illustrate the full richness of a many class model in Marx's scheme.

[13]See Godelier's article Structure and Contradiction in Capital in Miliband and Saville (1967).

[14]See Nicolaus (1968). Both Nicolaus and Godelier's article referred to above have been reprinted in Blackburn (1972). The nature of Soviet society as well as that of other communist countries is now receiving some attention from a Marxist point of view. We do not deal with this issues here in any detail. Bettelheim has over the many years discussed this issue (see the books cited in the bibliography). He has so far not paid much attention to the status of wage labour in his discussions. Also see Miliband (1977).

CHAPTER IV

[1]See for extensive discussion of Productive/Unproductive labour *TSV* Part I, Chapter IV and especially Addendum 12. The various individual cases of doctors, school teachers, actors, of self-employed artisans are dealt with in these two places. See especially on self-employed (pp. 407–40) and on productivity on transport (pp. 412–413).

[2]Marx does not make the physical output Q explicit in his diagrams of circuits of capital, though he does mention the different physical form of output and inputs. I have added Q to draw more sharply the distinction between the physical, the value and the money (price) measures. Its usefulness will become apparent later.

CHAPTER V

[1]See Leontieff (1966), and Sraffa (1961). von Neumann's model is cited in Samuelson (1971) and in Morishima (1973). In Desai (1974) I erroneously identified the $C' - \acute{C}'$ circuit as Leontieff's Input-Output tables.

CHAPTER VI

[1]The process of Marx's thinking is seen in detail in *TSV* Part I, Chapter II, especially section 10. Marx breaks through to the national income notion in terms of inter-industrial transactions at the end of Section 10. *TSV* comes from the notebooks written during 1861–63, that is, before Marx started writing *Capital*. Simple and expanded reproduction are described in detail in *Capital* Vol. II, Part III, and in a sketchy form in *Capital* Vol. 1, Part VIII.

[2]In this respect, in Desai (1974), I said erroneously that there were only three transactions. Transactions were also not separated properly on that occasion.

CHAPTER VII

[1]*Capital* Vol. I, Chapter XVII, p. 486.
[2]This is from *Capital*, Vol. I, Chapter XVIII, 'Various Forms of the Rate of Surplus Value'.
[3]See above, p. 000.
[4]'The working day is thus not a constant but a variable quantity'. (I/X/p. 223).
[5]Morishima, *Marx's Economics*.

CHAPTER VIII

[1]See Sweezy (1948) for Bohm–Bawerk.
[2]Wicksteed's article 'Das Kapital: A Criticism', along with Shaw's comment and Wicksteed's rejoinder, are published in Wicksteed (1944), pp. 705–733. For the importance of Wicksteed's criticism, see the essay on Victorian critics of Marx in Hobsbawm (1957).
[3]Hyndman's polemical answer under the title 'The Final Futility of Final Utility' was in Hyndman (1896).
[4]These two articles are:
Values and Prices in the Marxian System originally published in Archiv fur Socialwissenschaft und Sozialpolitik Vol. XXII and XXIII (1906–07) and translated in English by J. Kahane and published in A. Peacock (Ed.) International Economic Papers No. 2. On the correction of Marx's Fundamental Theoretical Construction in the Third Volume of Capital published originally in Jahrbuche Nationalokonomic and Statistik (1907) and translated in English and published as an appendix by Sweezy in Sweezy P. M. (Ed.) Karl Marx and the close of His System (London, Augustus Kelley 1948).
[5]Samuelson (1971).
[6]See also Steedman (1977).
[7]Steedman (1975), (1976), Wolfstetter (1976), Morishima (1976).

CHAPTER IX

[1]This discussion is based, on Capital, Vol. III. See also Sweezy (1968) for a comprehensive account of the Marx and Bortkiewicz solutions. Meek (1973) summarises the Winternitz solution and compares it with that of Bortkiewicz. Our notation is slightly different from that of Sweezy.
[2]Okishio N. (1974) mentions two possible interpretations of P_i as

money and value sum and expresses his preference for a value
interpretation.

Shaikh A. (1978) views them as quasi-monetary magnitudes
where money sums are deflated by the (labour) value of
money – number of aggregate social labour hours than one unit
of money will buy. The paradox of unequal prices at the beginning and end of the process remains. He offers a solution to the
paradox identical to Okishio and Morishima (1974). This is as a
first-step of an iteration, of an 'ergodic (Markov Chain) process'
as Morishima proves. We discuss this below.

[3]This interpretation, which is favourable to Marx, can be given some
support from the relevant chapter of Capital {91}.

CHAPTER XI

[1]Dimitriev, *Economic Essays*. This was published in Russian in 1904
but did not become available generally till 1960s. As a result of efforts
by Alfred Zauberman and Alec Nove, a copy was obtained from the
USSR and translated into French. In the 1970s an English translation
edited by Mario Nuti was published. See Samuelson's review in *JEL* as
well as Nuti's introduction for details.

[2]The interaction of theory and the tools available for confirming or
refuting them has been highlighted in Imre Lakatos' 'Methodology of
Scientific Research Programs'. It is not unknown in natural science for
a theory to be eclipsed until the appropriate tools for its rehabilitation
become available. Such tools become available independently of the
theory in question. Such is clearly the case here. See Lakatos in
Lakatos and Musgrave.

[3]All quotations in this chapter are from Bortkiewicz's (1906–07) article
unless otherwise indicated. Only the page number will henceforth be
cited. The notation used differs in many cases from that of Bortkiewicz
to maintain consistency with other chapters.

[4]Readers familiar with Jorgenson's work on econometrics of investment
behaviour will recognize this formula. See Jorgenson (1962).

[5]At this stage in his discussion, Borkiewicz remarks, 'The above algebraic solution of the price problem has been taken, in its essentials from
a work by W. K. Dimitrieff'. He adds in a footnote, 'Since the author
employs algebraic and geometrical means of exposition and of demonstration, it is hardly surprising that his publication (apparently a first
work) has received very little notice (I mean of course from Russians)
although it bears evidence of an exceptional theoretical talent and presents something really new' (p. 22 and footnote 31).

[6]In *A Contribution to the Critique of Political Economy* and in the first few chapters of *Capital* Vol. I, Marx develops the notion of money as a general expression of exchange value of social labour. See also Anwar Shaikh, op. cit., who uses this concept in his discussion of the Transformation problem.

[7]This is not just a debating point. It has bearing on the problem of the role of arms industry or luxury products in capitalist economies. See also Okishio (1974) for a discussion.

CHAPTER XV

[1]Luxemburg (1951) pp. 133–134
[2]Rosa Luxemburg quotes Marx extensively on this point in her book.

CHAPTER XVIII

[1]Morishima has introduced such an assumption in the SER. He does not deal with monetary complications but adds that $a_{it} = a_i = \bar{a}$. Thus both Department capitalists save (and accumulate) at a constant rate. He then is able to show that the SER will exhibit cycles of increasing severity.

CHAPTER XIX

[1]Gillman's measure of the organic composition of capital (g) is C/V rather than $C/C + V$ as we have defined it.

(1) Includes factories and land and neighbourhood industries up to 1899 in cols. 1a–1c.
(2) Excludes the items mentioned in (1) above from now on.
(3) Includes establishments having products valued at $500 or more as hitherto. Subsequent to 1914, only such establishments were included in the census as had products valued at $5000 or more. The effect, as in the preceding case, was to lift the organic composition of capital somewhat.

The first four entries in Tables 3a–3c are for 1880, 1890, 1900 and 1912 rather than 1879, 1889, 1899 and 1914.

CHAPTER XX

[1]This is not to say that trade unions did not exist in nineteenth century but that their emergence as an important and recognized party in the wage bargain is a post – 1914 phenomenon. Similarly, it is not usually appreciated that universal adult suffrage is an achievement of the twentieth century since the abolition of property qualification, of sex discrimination and of racial discrimination in voting rights (for example in the USA) are very recent accomplishments.

[2]This is not to say that we cannot understand precapitalist societies or post-capitalist societies such as the Soviet Union, China or Cuba from a Marxian perspective. Of the many attempts to do this, I shall cite but one. See M. Ellman (1975). He has used Marxian schemes imaginatively to analyse the source of surplus value to finance Soviet First Five Year Plan.

[3]While the theory-data transition has to be done in all subjects, Marxists discussing these problems have usually made a muddle of it. Marx himself did not keep different levels of abstraction separate. One person to emphasize these separate levels and to attempt to keep them separate is the Japanese scholar Prof. Uno, whose work is relatively little known. See, however, T. Sekine Uno-Riron (1975).

An English translation of Prof. Uno's major work is to be published quite soon by Harvester Press.

[4]Some of what follows on Marx, Hegel and the state is a potted version of Joseph O'Malley's excellent introduction to Marx's *Critique of Hegel's Philosophy of Right* (1970). The interpretation of Adam Smith's work is, however, my own.

[5]Milliband (1976) among others.

[6]See the work of Palloix (1977) for use of the three circuits of capital framework.

BIBLIOGRAPHY

Anderson, P. (1974) Lineages of the Absolutist State (New Left Books, London)

Anderson, P. (1974) From Antiquity to Feudalism (New Left Books, London)

Arrow, K. J. and F. Hahn (1972) General Competitive Analysis (Oliver and Boyd, London)

Baran, P. A. and P. Sweezy (1966) Monopoly Capital (Monthly Review Press, New York)

Barrera, M. (1976) Colonial Labour and Theories of Inequality: The case of International Harvester, *Review of Radical Political Economy*, Vol. 8, No. 2.

Baumol, W. J. (1974) The Transformation of Values: What Marx 'Really' Meant (An Interpretation) *Journal of Economic Literature* March, Vol. XII, No. 1.

Bettelheim C. (1976) Economic Calculation and Forms of Property (Routledge and Kegan Paul, London)

Bettelheim C. (1975) The Transition to Socialist Economy (Hassocks)

Blaug, M. (1958) Ricardian Economics (Yale University Press, New Haven)

Blaug, M. (1968) Economic Theory in Retrospect, 2nd Edition, (Heinemann, London) Bohm-Bawerk: See Sweezy (1948)

Bortkiewicz, L. (1907) Value and Price in the Marxian System, in A. Peacock (Ed.) International Economic Papers No. 2.

Bortkiewicz, L. (1906–7) On the correction of Marx's Fundamental Theoretical Construction in the Third Volume of Capital, in Sweezy (1948)

Breman, J. (1974) Patronage and Exploitation: Changing Agrarian Relations in South Gujarat, India (University of California Press, Berkeley, Calif.)

Brown, M. (1966) A Measure of the change in Relative Exploitation of Capital and Labour, Review of Economics and Statistics, May.

Carr, E. H. (1970) Socialism in one country 1924–26, Vol. I, (Penguin, London)

Chambers, J. D. (1953) Enclosures and Labour Supply in the Industrial Revolution: *Economic History Review*, Vol. V.

Desai, M. (1974) Marxian Economic Theory (Gray Mills: Blackwell, Oxford)

Desai, M. (1975) Beyond Bortkiewicz: A Complete Solution to the Transformation Problem (Unpublished, London School of Economics)

Desai, M. (1977) Balanced and Unbalanced Growth in Marx's Model of Extended Reproduction (ANEC, Institut des Sciences Economiques, UCL, Louvain-La Neuve)

Desai, M. (1978) Values and Prices, The Transformation Problem: A Revised Version of Chapters 8 to 12 of Desai (1974) in Itoh, Sakurai and Yamaguchi

Desai, M. and P. Skott (1978) Balanced and Unbalanced Growth in Marx's Model of Extended Reproduction (Unpublished, London School of Economics)

Deutscher, I. (1970) The Prophet Unarmed (OUP, Oxford)

Dimitriev, V. K. (1975) Economic Essays Ed. by M. Nuti (CUP, Cambridge)

Dobb, M. H. (1973) Theories of Value and Distribution (CUP, Cambridge)

Domar, E. (1957) A Soviet Model of Growth in Essays in the Theory of Economic Growth (OUP, Oxford)

Ellman, M. (1973) Planning Problems in the USSR (CUP, Cambridge)

Ellman, M. (1975) Did the Agricultural Surplus Provide the Resources for the Increase in Investment in the USSR During the First Five Year Plan: *Economic Journal*, December.

Foster, J. (1974) Class Struggle and the Industrial Revolution (Heinemann, London)

Gillman, J. (1957) The Falling Rate of Profit: Marx's Law and Its Significance to the Twentieth Century Capitalism (Dobson, London)

Godelier, M. (1967) Structure and Contradiction in Capital in R. Miliband and J. Saville: The Socialist Register (Merlin Press, London)

Gough, I. (1975) State Expenditure in Advance Capitalism *New Left Review*, July–August.

Harris, D. J. (1972) The Black Ghetto as 'Internal Colony': A Theoretical Critique and Alternative Formulation, *Review of Black Political Economy*, Summer

Hobsbawm, E. (1957) Labouring Men (Weidenfeld and Nicolson, London)

Hyndman H. M. (1896) The Economics of Socialism (London)

Itoh, M. (1976) A Study of Marx's Theory of Value, *Science and Society*, Fall.

Itoh, M. (1978) The Formation of Marx's Theory of Crisis, *Science and Society,* Summer

Itoh, M. T. Sakurai, S. Yamaguchi (Ed.) (1978) The Debates on the Transformation Problem (in Japanese) (Tokyo)

Jones, A. (1973) The New Inflation (Penguin, London)

Lakatos I. and A. Musgrave (Eds.) (1970) Criticism and the Growth of Knowledge (CUP, Cambridge)

Lazonick, W. (1974) Karl Marx and Enclosures in England, *Review of Radical Political Economy*, Vol. 6, No. 2.

Lenin, V. I. (1956) The Development of Capitalism in Russia (Foreign Language Publishing House, Moscow)

Leontieff, W. W. (1966) Input-Output Economics (OUP, Oxford)

Luxemburg, R. (1951) The Accumulation of Capital (Routledge and Kegan Paul, London)

Mandel, E. (1975) Late Capitalism (New Left Books, London)

Marx, K. (1934) The Class Struggle in France (Lawrence and Wishart)

Marx, K. (1968) Civil War in France in Marx and Engels (1968)

Marx, K. (1968) Eighteenth Brumaire of Louis Bonaparte in Marx and Engels (1968)

Marx, K. (1968) Wages, Price and Profit in Marx and Engels (1968)

Marx, K. (1973) Grundrisse (Penguin, London)

Marx, K. and F. Engels (1968) Selected Work (Lawrence and Wishart)

Meek, R. (1973) Studies in the Labour Theory of Value (Lawrence and Wishart, London)

Miliband, R. (1977) Marxism and Politics (OUP, Oxford)

Moore, B. (1971) The Social Origins of Dictatorship and Democracy (Penguin, London)

Morishima, M. (1973) Marx's Economics (CUP, Cambridge)

Morishima, M. (1974) Marx's Economics in the Light of Modern Economic Theory *Econometrica*, Vol. 42, No. 4.

Morishima, M. (1974) The Fundamental Marxian Theorem: A Reply to Samuelson *Journal of Economic Literature*, March, Vol. XII, No. 1.

Morishima, M. (1976) Positive Profits with Negative Surplus Value – A Comment *Economic Journal*, September.

Morishima, M. and G. Catephores (1978) Value, Exploitation and Growth (McGraw Hill, London).

O'Connor, James (1973) The Fiscal Crisis of the State (St. Martin's Press, New York)

Okishio, N. (1974) Value and Production Price *Kobe University Economic Review, 20*

O'Malley, J. (1970) (Ed.) Karl Marx's Critique of Hegel's Philosophy of Right (CUP, Cambridge)

Palloix, C. (1977) The Self-Expansion of Capital on a World Scale, *Review of Radical Political Economy*, Vol. 9, No. 2.

Robinson, J. (1933) Economics of Imperfect Competition (Macmillan, London)

Robinson, J. (1942) An Essay on Marxian Economics (Macmillan, London)

Samuelson, (1957) Wages and Prices: A Modern Dissection of Marxian Economic Models, *American Economic Review*, December

Samuelson, (1971) Understanding the Marxian Notion of Exploitation: A Summary of the so-called Transformation Problem between Marxian Values and Competitive Prices *Journal of Economic Literature*, Vol. IX, No. 2.

Samuelson, (1974) Insight and Detour in the Theory of Exploitation: A Reply to Baumol, *Journal of Economic Literature*, March, Vol. XII, No. 1.

Sekine, T. (1975) Uno-Riron: A Japanese Contribution to Marxian Political Economy, *Journal of Economic Literature*, September Vol XIII, No. 3.

Shaikh, A. (1978) Marx's Theory of Value and Transformation in J. Schwartz (Ed.) The Subtle Anatomy of Capitalism (California, 1978).

Shaikh, A. (1978a) National Income Accounts and Marxian Categories (Unpublished, New School for Social Research, New York).

Smolinski, L. (1973) Karl Marx and Mathematical Economics Journal of Political Economy, Sept–Oct.

Solow, R. M. (1971) Discussion on The State of Economics, *American Economic Review*, May, pp. 63–68.

Sraffa, P. (1960) The Production of Commodities by Means of Commodities (Cambridge University Press, London)

Steedman, I. (1975) Positive Profits with Negative Surplus Value, *Economic Journal* March.

Steedman, I. (1976a) Positive Profits with Negative Surplus Value: A Reply, *Economic Journal*, September

Steedman, I. (1976b) Positive Profits with Negative Surplus Value, A Reply to Wolfstetter, *Economic Journal*, December.

Steedman, I. (1978) Marx after Sraffa (New Left Books, London).

Sweezy, P. M. (1948) Karl Marx and the Close of his System (Augustus Kelley, London)

Sweezy, P. M. (1968) The Theory of Capitalist Development (Monthly Review Press, New York)

Walker, A. (1971) Karl Marx, the Declining Rate of Profit and British Political Economy, *Economica*, Vol. 38 152.

Wicksteed, P. H. (1944) The Commonsense of Political Economy (Routledge and Kegan Paul, London)

Wolfstetter, E. (1973) Surplus Labour, Synchronised Labour Costs and Marx's Labour Theory of Value, *Economic Journal*, September

Wolfstetter, E. (1976) Positive Profits with Negative Surplus Value: A Comment *Economic Journal*, December.

INDEX

Index 259

accumulation, expectations and,
179–87; Marx's theory of, 102,
161–71, 175; Rosa
Luxembourg on, 154–60
agriculture, 26–7
alienation, of worker from his
labour, 31
American Civil War, 15
armaments, output, 158–60

balanced growth, and market
clearance, 178; in planned
economy, 173; and rate of
accumulation, 167, 168, 175
Baumol, W. J., 60
Bernstein, E., 200
Bohm-Bawerk, E., 57, 58, 59, 68,
81, 93, 94, 188, 200
Bortkiewicz, 58–9, 60, 61, 72, 94,
120, 144; Basic Ricardian
Theorem, 116, 117; price
equations, 85–90; Ricardo,
90–93; transformation
procedure (fixed capital case),
81–93, (simple case), 73–80;
value equations, 83–5
Bretton Woods System, 207

calculus, neoclassical, 86
Capital (Marx), 4, 8, 41, 47, 48;
notion of national income, 152;
on price and value, 50, 68, 94;
rate of exploitation, 51;
revolution in value, 147;
turnover of capital, 123
capital, circuits of, 32–8, 179;
commodity circuit, 28, 29, 32ff;
constant, 40–42, 51, 52, 59, 85,
86; heterogeneity of, 29; money
circuit, 28, 29, 32ff; organic
composition of, 51, 52, 65, 66;
productive circuit, 32ff;
turnover of, 41; valuation of,
11; variable, 85, 86

capital goods, and joint
production, 122, 123, 126; in
price equation, 85–6
capital goods industry, productive
assumption, 104
capitalism, and accumulation, 180,
181, 183, 184; and commodity
fetishism, 16, 17, 20;
competitive, 204; consumption
demand, 184; contemporary,
199, 200; contradictions of,
156; creation of exchange
values, 27
civil society, separation from
political society, 201, 202, 203
class monopoly, of means of
production, 14
class relation, in buying labour
power, 30, 31, 58
class struggle, 22, 80, 147; and
economic relationships of
exchange, 7; and rate of
exploitation, 142, 144
classical economics, 6, 7; and
value theory, 9–11
commodity, and exploitation, 35;
notion of, 27, 34; cf. product,
19; value of, 136; value ratio
between, 84
Commodity Capital Circuit, 95,
130; and accumulation, 161,180
commodity exchange, 157
commodity fetishism, 16, 17, 61
commodity market, 16, 20, 34
competition, and rate of profit, 67
competitive sector, O'Connor on,
208, 209, 210
consumer goods, and joint
production, 123, 126
consumption, 37
consumption demand, capitalist,
184, 185
*Contribution to the Critique of
Political Economy, A* (Marx), 4